The Secret Keepers

An Inspiring Story of Betrayal, Survival, and Hope

Best wishes ~
margi

D1571915

Heidi Tucker

ISBN 978-0-9966146-2-7
Published by Redstone Media 2020
Order your copy at RedstoneMedia.org

Inside Book Layout – Dennis Powers
Cover Illustration - Cindy Briggs
Cover Design - Dylan Tucker

DEDICATION

To all the survivors.
May you find peace and hope.

"Courage does not always roar.
Sometimes courage is the quiet voice
at the end of the day
saying *I will try again tomorrow*."

- Mary Anne Radmacher

TABLE OF CONTENTS

PART FOUR
ABUSED CHILDREN SPEAK A LANGUAGE
YOU CAN'T LEARN

PART FIVE
YOU CAN'T FIND PEACE UNTIL YOU
FIND ALL THE PIECES

PART SIX
THERE IS NO GREATER AGONY
THAN BEARING AN UNTOLD STORY INSIDE YOU

PREFACE

As an author, I am asked on a regular basis to help people share their stories. I'm a strong believer that a good story can not only teach an important principle but can make us feel it. As I listen and learn, I often make a few notes that I add to an ongoing list of future book ideas.

Among those many requests, one phone call got my immediate attention.

Margi had read both my previous books, *Finding Hope in the Journey* and *Servie's Song*. She complimented me on my writing and said she loved my messages of hope before telling me she had a story too.

"Tell me about yourself," I said. I relaxed in a comfortable chair, ready to listen.

Within five minutes I was up scrambling for a paper and pen. For the next hour I listened as Margi spoke honestly about where she had been and who she was becoming as a result of childhood abuse and trauma. She introduced me to the term DID, or Dissociative Identity Disorder—what used to be called Multiple Personality Disorder. Margi is a multiple.

"Who am I speaking with?" I asked. I wondered which part of Margi might be talking.

"It's just me," she answered. Months later I learned "Just Me" is a strong part capable of helping Margi under stressful conditions—like talking about childhood trauma to someone she'd never met before.

Why would I be interested in writing about such a dark subject? If that's all there was to it, I wouldn't. But what I heard on the other end of that hour-long phone call was a woman who was the very definition of hope. *That* got my attention.

Margi embodied gifts of courage, faith, and gratitude. She seemed to have this amazing ability to endure to the end of something that is beyond our imagination. That hour spent with her was both incredibly inspiring and heartbreaking. I definitely wanted to continue our conversation, and we agreed to meet in person a few months later when I planned to travel to her state for some book and speaking events.

"I imagine there are lots of other people with great stories," she said.

"Yes, Margi, there are, but they don't have *your* story," I replied.

I hung up the phone and tears filled my eyes. Thoughts of *I need to write this story* argued fiercely with *This is too big—too difficult*. But I recognized the prompting and felt a strong push to learn this woman's story.

Learn is exactly what I did for the next two years. I spent hundreds of hours with Margi as well as with her family members, friends, and therapists. When I wasn't interviewing people or reviewing my transcripts, I was reading every book, article, and website recommended to me.

At first Margi was guarded, but soon we developed a loving friendship and trust. Once that happened, there were parts of Margi that felt comfortable enough to come forward and share some details. I understood that her beautiful parts were there to tell the story. They deserve to be heard.

Most of the conversational quotes and thoughts from Margi and others in her story come directly from interviews in which I was told about the events. As an author, I have taken literary license in creating the scenes in which the events took place, but I made a conscious effort to maintain authenticity by using the exact words told to me. They tell the real story.

There was a time in Margi's life when she was lost. She felt invisible because no one listened to her. At those times when she felt truly lost, Margi says she would have benefited from a book like this—something to help her realize she was not alone. Now her words have the potential to lift others. It has given purpose to her pain. Margi told me that it is her goal to touch just one soul. What quiet humility. I believe there are thousands who will be changed forever by her words.

Something Margi and I share is the desire to make a difference. Together we hope her story will educate and inspire those who are familiar with trauma, as well as those who simply want to learn and grow from this story.

During one day of interviews, Margi was struggling. She apologized for not feeling as cheerful and optimistic as usual. She poured her heart out in true honesty.

"I'm having trouble finding hope today," Margi confessed.

I respect Margi for her honesty and humility. It's one of many things I love about her. After a moment of silence, I shared my own thoughts.

"Hope is not only for the strong and the mighty and the powerful," I replied. "That's not what hope is about. You can still be at the bottom of your barrel, crumpled on the floor, but if there's just one glimmer of hope, then you've got it."

"There *is* a glimmer," Margi whispered. "That's what I want people to know."

"Yes, Margi," I promised. "They'll read your story and know."

PART ONE

HURT PEOPLE HURT PEOPLE.

Chapter 1

Margi sat quietly in the driver's seat. A rapid heartbeat pounded in her chest. Was it hers? She didn't know who or what she was anymore. It was time for this terrifying fear to end.

The words were clear. *No one can help me. I'm going to be like this forever. I have to die.*

There were no tears. Just a desperate, empty pain of hopelessness. Margi grabbed the key in the ignition. She looked back, a quick double-check. The garage door was closed, and the lights were off.

This will be a good way to go, she thought. *I'll just go to sleep.*

Margi twisted the key, and the engine roared to life. She heard the words. *Everyone will be better off if I'm gone, and because I'm not real, they won't even miss me. In fact, I never existed. I might not even be able to die, because I'm not human.*

It would be easy to say it had been an exceptionally bad day. But that wasn't entirely true. They were all bad days. Every single one. At least the ones she could remember.

There was a common thread in all those days: fear. Gut-wrenching, horrifying fear. The kind of fear not seen, heard, or felt by anybody . . . other than her. Every time she mentioned it to someone, there was that *look.* An expression that told Margi she was crazy. Every time it happened, Margi quickly changed the subject. Brushed it off as a bad day or a bad dream. Margi quickly learned to keep everything to herself. Not to let anybody in. They might see that her world was different.

By now, Margi believed that *look* and knew everybody else was right. She must be crazy.

Crazy was making its appearance in all forms and places. *Crazy* was unpredictable. But most of all, *crazy* generated fear.

In *crazy*, time and space rarely matched. Margi didn't know where she was. *Who* she was. The time of day came and went without any warning. Time was lost. As a child, she was playing with dolls one moment and then suddenly gone to another place—another dimension—for hours. As an adult, she was taking a can of vegetables off the grocery store shelf then suddenly not remembering where she was or why she was there. Some days Margi didn't recognize her body. Didn't know her voice. It was a world where reality could be snatched away in an instant.

In *crazy*, even her home was not safe from the jaws of this thief that ripped apart her reality. There were triggers everywhere. A song, a television program, a strangely familiar sight or sound. Nothing was real. The walls changed in size and shape and then began to shrink and close in. It was suffocating. It was claustrophobic. And it was terrifying.

Margi was mortified by her own behavior. She always second-guessed herself in adult conversations with friends in her neighborhood or with co-workers at the office. She wanted to be strong and intelligent, but she often heard words come out of her mouth that sounded ridiculous. Child-like. It was embarrassing. *What is wrong with you? Why would you say that? People are going to see how stupid you are. They are going to see what you really are: crazy.*

Suddenly Margi was back in the present. The clock on the dashboard showed it was close to midnight. For fifteen minutes she had been sitting in the front seat of the car and remembering all the reasons why this needed to end. The car engine hummed, and the smell of exhaust was thick. *Why is this taking so long?*

Days were bad, but nights brought on a whole new level of fear. Things always took a turn for the worse after nine p.m. Each day Margi watched the clock and dreaded the moment the hour hand reached up to the nine. Inching toward terror. That hour ushered in a range of fear and horror that was both physical and emotional. The nightmares were vivid, increasingly graphic, and somehow real. And they were getting worse. Peace did not exist at night. And tonight had been no different.

Earlier when she climbed into bed, Margi had prayed the familiar prayer. *Please, God, just make me die.* Now she looked down at the rise and fall of her chest and thought, *Just make it stop. Make my heart stop. Something . . . just make me die.*

Margi looked at the clock. Twenty minutes. *I really want to die. I can't take another step. I can't go back into my house. I can't live another day.*

Suddenly something shifted. Within all the darkness, Margi felt a quiet, soft beam of light. She felt present and keenly aware that she wasn't alone in her grief. New words seemed to find their way through the dark abyss into her broken soul. The words were full of love. *You don't want to do this. You don't want your children to come out and find you.*

A tear rolled down Margi's cheek as she felt the words. *The children.* Why was she thinking of them now? She didn't want anyone to love her. She just wanted to die. She didn't want anyone to mourn. Margi just wanted to disappear.

She felt the words again, words that seemed surrounded by light. *You don't want to do this.* Through all the other thoughts and pieces that were fighting to take control, the words stood out. Some small part of her recognized them as truth.

The tears were flowing freely now. Hot, angry tears of fear and despair and all the unfairness of life blended with cold, sad tears of empathy for her children. Those beautiful children were gifts from God. She couldn't do this to them. They would never understand. They would never forget.

Margi lowered her head as a quiet sob escaped her lips. She reached up, turned the key, and pulled it out of the ignition. Margi paused, then opened the door. Looking at her legs, she willed them to slide over and step out of the car. She was so very, very tired. She looked at the door to the house and somehow found a small slice of strength that enabled her to walk toward it. Margi clung to the sliver of light in the dark garage and embraced it as her feet shuffled over the threshold and into the house.

She would need to face it all again tomorrow. The darkness would return. The fear. The fractured reality.

But tonight, *crazy* did not win.

Chapter 2

The two elementary school teachers stood together on the field. It was a bright, sunny day, and recess was a celebration. Children climbed on the monkey bars and pumped their legs to swoop higher and higher in the swings. Boys chased each other and played army games while girls turned cartwheels and giggled at the silliness of the boys' imaginary battles. The year was drawing to a close, and the sights and sounds on the field indicated that kindergarten had been eagerly embraced by all the children. Well, all the children but one.

Margi had found her usual isolated spot under a tree. Her brown, chin-length hair blew gently in the afternoon breeze. She wrapped her arms around her knees and hugged them close to her chest. Quietly she watched the other children play.

"I'm so worried about Margi," Miss Simon said. "I don't think I've ever seen her smile. She's not engaged in anything we do in the classroom, and her reading skills are way below average. Most children love reading time, but Margi seems to disappear. I just don't know how to reach her."

"Have you pulled her aside and tried to talk to her?" Mrs. Robinson asked. "Maybe she needs more individual attention. Some extra time away from the other kids."

"Oh, believe me I've tried. It doesn't help that she's missed sixty days of school this year. I've repeatedly tried to get a response from her parents, but they never return my calls. Have you noticed the dark circles under her eyes? Maybe she's not well."

Both the teachers looked at Margi, still sitting alone under the tree. "There are just a few more weeks of school left this year," Miss Simon said. "I'm going to keep trying, of course, but maybe the best I can do is document her scholastic and behavioral issues for next year's teacher. And I'll bring attention to the absences."

Mrs. Robinson put her arm around her friend and gave her a quick squeeze. "You've done your best. Maybe next year will be better for Margi."

. . .

Margi sat in her assigned seat at the front of the classroom, where Miss Simon had moved her. It was terribly uncomfortable. She really wanted to sit in the back next to the door in case she needed to escape. Now all the students were behind her, and that made her uneasy. *What are they doing? Are they looking at me?*

Margi tried to pretend she belonged here, but she knew that was a lie. Everyone else looked so normal. Laughing and playing. Talking to the teacher. She couldn't even do that. She wasn't like the other kids. She was different, and she knew it.

Storytime was the worst part of school. Miss Simon explained to the class that books were wonderful because they created a new place the children could visit in their imagination. She said they were filled with new adventures, surprises, and characters that came to life! Margi tried hard not to listen as the teacher read a story describing the thrills and wonders of children discovering new and unpredictable events in a faraway land. Instead of listening, she studied the wood on the desk in front of her. She noticed the lines in the grain and the pattern created by the shadows—anything to distract herself. The thought of leaving her mind to go into a story was terrifying. Margi knew she might never come back, and she simply couldn't take that chance. *I might get stuck in the story.*

Some days Margi could just stay quiet. Keep to herself. Pretend to be a good student and hope that nobody noticed her. But other days were dark and frightening. On those days, she couldn't find *real*. On days like that, Margi looked down at her body, at the green dress that covered it up. *Whose body is this? Why am I in this room?* On those days, the walls suddenly began to move, creeping closer and closer toward her desk. She struggled to breathe. *I can't get air.*

On those days, she told the teacher she needed to go to the nurse—that she didn't feel good.

The nurse never helped, but at least Margi got out of the classroom. Going to see the nurse gave her a reason to run through the door and leave that scary classroom behind.

It was a desperate chance to go find *real*.

Chapter 3

Margi stared at her feet. After each long day at school, they took her back to the place she knew as home. Margi didn't want to be in school, but she dreaded going home even more. That day, as on all other days, she crawled through the hole in the playground fence that surrounded the school and found her way through the neighborhood streets.

The neighborhood where Margi lived was a middle-class area where well-kept homes were surrounded by green lawns out front and where verdant trees lined the streets. Flowers spilled from pots on porches and filled manicured gardens. The happy sound of children's voices could be heard throughout the block.

Margi's feet took her to the front of her house. She stopped on the front sidewalk and looked up at its threatening shape. The front entrance of the red brick structure was wide; cracked, cement stairs led up to a black front door flanked by white, wood-trimmed windows on each side. The roof over the entrance was framed and supported by two gray beams. To Margi, it looked like a wide, angry mouth. Smaller gray windows wrapped in cement snaked along the ground, letting minimal light into the basement.

Margi looked back at her feet and watched as they led her up the front steps to the gaping entrance. She lowered her head and twisted the knob. One step inside, she could already hear her mother's familiar, shrill voice.

"I married a dentist, yet you never provide. My friends are all rich. They all drive nice cars. I'm so embarrassed! We *rent* this house because we can't even afford to buy a home. What a disgrace!"

Margi watched her father slink across the room and quickly slip down the stairs to the basement. It was his hideaway and his playground. A place to escape the wrath of his wife.

Margi's mother continued to scream. Although she could no longer see her husband, she made sure he could hear every word until she was finished.

"You're good for nothing! You hear me? Worthless! How long do I have to keep this charade up?" she screamed.

It was the unspoken rule of the house. Don't cross Mother, or her wrath will crash down on you. Her mercurial nature was sharp and intense. Margi had no idea what had set her mother off that day. Maybe her father forgot something or said something upsetting. Anything that might place blame on her mother or even the slightest negative reference to her mother would do it.

Margi looked down at her body and felt the urge to run. The familiar sensation returned—an immediate response to her mother's yelling. The sensory result was always the same whether her mother was screaming at her father or hollering at the cat.

Margi felt naked from the waist down.

Her hands grabbed at the hem of her dress. Some part of her knew she was still wearing the dress she'd worn to school. But another part of her mind betrayed the reality of the skirt's hem in her hands. The two opposite sensations fought for control.

Margi hurried down the hall to her bedroom, away from the sound of her mother's voice. Away from the strange response of her body. And away from a frightening reality that someone else might see her nakedness.

. . .

Margi walked behind her mother, who was tossing items from the grocery store shelves into the basket. A safe distance was best. Margi was embarrassed by her mother's behavior—flirting with the man stocking the shelves, smiling with her bright-red lips, and carrying on with the boys bagging the items. Margi just wanted to get away.

Occasionally men appeared at the house. It didn't matter the time of day. Her mother was happiest at times like those, when all the attention was centered on her. At those times it looked as though she was throwing a party for herself, and she was definitely the life of the party. Sometimes the men looked familiar—like the man from the grocery store—but often Margi didn't recognize them.

Margi wasn't the only one embarrassed by her mother. Her two older sisters—Janet, fourteen, and Barbara, almost eighteen—did their best to separate themselves from anything that went on at home. Their friends' parents described Mother as *scandalous* and didn't allow them to come to the house.

Mother strutted around in such small shorts that Margi wondered why she never bought any that fit. Jewelry glistened on chains around Mother's neck, and a lacy bra completed the outfit. Her sandy brown hair framed her delicate features, and her long, slim legs made her look years younger than her age. Bright-red lips framed her flirtatious conversation and suggestive smiles. Light-blue eyes danced with excitement when the attention was focused on her, but those same eyes narrowed and shot daggers at anyone who dared to condescend or steal the limelight.

Margi noticed the eyes of her sisters' boyfriends when they stopped by the house. Their eyes looked at her mother. After lowering, those eyes looked again.

Margi couldn't understand why all these men wanted to be in her house. Didn't they understand that Mother was easily upset? What if they said the wrong thing? *What if Mother gets angry?*

Margi just kept her head down when strange men came to visit. She watched her sisters run out the front door to a different life and wished she could go with them. Her sisters looked happy. Their friends looked happy. *How does that feel?* Margi just felt invisible. How she wished she could wake up to a new life. A life outside this house.

This dark, scary house.

. . .

"Hurry up, Margi! Hurry up—we have to go!"

Margi jumped at the command. Her stomach twisted into a knot, and she felt her heart race as she ran to her closet to fetch some shoes. *Where are we going?* She didn't dare ask the question out loud. Mother didn't like questions.

Trips in the car were a required adventure. Margi never knew where the road would lead. At least the sun was up, and it was daylight. Night trips were the ones that frightened Margi the most—trips to homes she didn't know and people she didn't recognize. Her parents put her in the back seat and told her to be quiet. No questions were allowed. Margi could always sense when something scary was going to happen. When Margi woke up the next morning in her bedroom, she had mere snapshots and glimpses of the night before, but she never forgot the *feeling* she experienced on the way over.

Margi looked out the car window and noticed neighbors out in their front yards watering flowers, checking mailboxes, and walking their dogs. Perhaps it would be okay. She took a deep breath.

Sitting up straight in the back seat, Margi peered ahead. Things were looking familiar. The houses—the trees. The car rounded the corner, and her grandmother's house appeared. Margi breathed a sigh of relief.

Nana sometimes watched Margi when her mother had places to go where a little girl wasn't welcome. Mother pulled the car into the driveway, and Margi climbed out. She looked up at the house. It was dark and old. Tiny windows allowed very little light into the main living area. The garage entrance was covered by two large, wooden doors with metal handles. The opening of those doors revealed the inside of the garage, which was dark and musty and filled with old trunks that sat on high, dusty shelves laced with spider webs. The garage ran the entire length of the house, and deep at the end of the dark garage was an old door that allowed a separate direct access to bedrooms in the basement.

This house scared her because it had a basement, but she loved her grandmother. Margi liked to visit, too; Nana's husband had died many years before, and Margi was certain Nana must be sad and lonely.

Mother hauled Margi up the walkway to the front door. Pulling a key out of her purse, she unlocked the door. Nana was sitting in her wheelchair watching television. Her gray shirt matched the surroundings. She quickly turned off the television and smiled at Margi.

"Margi, it's nice to see you, my dear," Nana said. "Maybe we can draw some pictures together."

Margi met her gaze then sat on the couch next to Nana's wheelchair. Drawing pictures sounded okay. She would stay close and not leave Nana's side. A bad car accident years ago had left Nana unable to walk, so she moved from room to room on the main floor in her wheelchair or with crutches. Margi felt safe being with Nana because they never went down to the basement. Nana couldn't get down the stairs.

"You know I'm worried about this one," Nana said, nodding her head toward Margi and talking like Margi wasn't even there. "She never smiles. And I swear she's not all there. It's like she goes into a trance and just stares. You can't talk to her—she just won't answer. Something is not quite right, and I can't put my finger on it."

"She's fine," Mother quipped. She quickly checked her lipstick in the mirror on the wall next to the front door and smiled at her own reflection. "I'll be back in a few hours to pick her up. All my friends are waiting for me."

Mother swung her purse on her shoulder and turned to open the front door. She left without glancing back.

Margi's grandmother ran her crooked fingers through her gray hair then quietly tapped her fingers on the side of her wrinkled face. She looked over at her granddaughter and must have noticed the dark circles under her eyes.

"Are you tired, Margi?" she asked.

Margi shook her head. She always felt tired, but no sense telling anyone about it. Margi looked around the room. Nobody else was there. They would be safe up here in the family room. Maybe she would draw a dog . . . or a butterfly.

"Be a dear and go get the paper and crayons out of the cabinet in the kitchen," Nana said. "Let's sit together at this table and see what we can create today."

Margi walked swiftly through the family room into the kitchen, where a small brown cabinet held the supplies. She grabbed a handful of paper and the box of brightly colored crayons. As she turned to hurry back to Nana, she caught sight of the top of the stairs that led down to the basement. The staircase was directly accessible both from an outside door in the backyard and from a small entrance off the side of the kitchen.

Margi took a few tentative steps toward the staircase and peeked around the corner. She stood and stared at the basement door, which was shut at the bottom of the stairs. It was strangely familiar. Had she been through that door before? Certainly not with Nana, but maybe with her mother? Maybe with Daddy? Margi's eyes widened at the fear she felt slowly creeping up the stairs toward her. She didn't remember what was behind that door, but she recognized the *feeling* that it wasn't good. Basements were never good. She stood frozen in fear.

"Margi, did you find them?" Nana asked.

Margi jumped at the sound of Nana's voice and muffled a quiet gasp. Clutching the supplies to her chest, she hurried out of the kitchen to where Nana was waiting in the family room.

Margi held out the supplies, and Nana thanked her for being such a good helper. Today Margi would draw happy things. Things that were safe and peaceful. Bright, colorful things that lived in the light.

Not the dark, scary things that happen in basements.

Chapter 4

Margi's father reached for the bottle of nitroglycerine in the front pocket of his brown slacks. He clutched his chest, then swallowed the pill with a good stiff drink from the cabinet in the kitchen. He knew the alcohol would numb his anxiety while he waited for the medicine to provide relief, but in the meantime, he needed to lie down and rest. And he knew just the place.

Five-year-old Margi was playing with dolls on her bedroom floor when he entered the room. Beads of sweat erupted on his flushed face as he tiptoed over to Margi's bed. It was his refuge. His wife would soon find him and demand that he go to the hospital, but he was not going to go. He wanted to be here—in his place of comfort. Margi's bed.

Every night at nine he started the routine. He took Margi by the hand into the bathroom and filled the tub with warm water. He washed and dried her then dressed her in a nightie. She was his favorite, and he would climb into her bed and show her just how much he loved her each night until slumber came.

Margi's bed was both a paradise and an escape. It provided pleasure and a place of destination in his mind. But it also allowed his senses to leave the world's pressures and recall events that pulled him into darkness.

Margi's father lost his twin brother at the age of seven due to complications from a tonsillectomy. Both boys went into the hospital for the routine surgery, and the brother died while under anesthesia. He never woke up. The family was devastated. They were wealthy and prestigious and led busy lives in the medical community, but they also traveled the country helping out and volunteering to make a difference.

Despite their devotion to medical events, they never fully emotionally healed from the tragedy. Margi's father took the death of his twin especially hard. His own mother was often heard telling others her boy had never been the same since his brother died. As families often do following a tragedy, they ultimately found the strength to move forward.

In college, Margi's father found a wife that was a perfect fit—one who lived for wealth, social ranking, and all the celebrations that came with success. He followed his own father into the medical field by studying biochemistry and microbiology with the ultimate goal of building a career in dentistry. Two daughters provided a nice start on the blueprint for a family. Life looked promising.

But life didn't follow perfectly laid plans. Margi's father was called to serve for two years in the Korean War as a dentist, where he served the United Nations troops. War brought its own level of darkness, inflicting death, illness, and incredible hardship on the people of Korea and the soldiers serving there. For Margi's father, alcohol, drugs, and prostitution became the crutches that helped him tolerate separation from everyone and everything he knew.

Some of the things he saw in Korea should never be seen by anyone. People were treated as objects—nothing more than numbers in a sea of statistics. When he returned to the states, he never spoke of the war to his family. But he couldn't leave it completely behind—his connection to drugs was strong and consuming. After returning home, he continued his military service in the National Guard reserves.

While he served for two years in Korea, his wife saved enough money to get them out of debt. That allowed them to purchase an office where he could set up a new dental practice. He poured his efforts into starting a career and hoped the alcohol would numb everything else—just as it had in Korea.

His two daughters were now entering their teen years, finding their own way and starting to forge their own paths. They seemed to notice a change in their father—a despondence, a sense that his mind was elsewhere. Shortly after his return, a final daughter completed the family. They named her Marjorie.

He tried to embrace the illusion of "the dentist with the beautiful life," but eventually the façade became too difficult to live. Drugs and alcohol took him to secret places away from the office. Sometimes he really did intend to go to the office, but a force stronger than the disgust in his wife's face caused the car to detour for the day. The dental staff was left confused and apologizing to their patients for his unexpected absences. Eventually he lost patients due to too many canceled appointments and no-shows.

His wife openly expressed her disappointment on a daily basis. She was, of course, the reason he needed to be successful. She had an image to build.

"How will I ever have money like my friends?" she bellowed. "I have important events on my calendar every day, yet you can't even find your way to the office? You are truly useless."

Eventually they lost the office space because of delinquent payments. He was not entirely surprised; in fact, he almost expected it. His heart had never been engaged in his practice. It had always felt like only half a commitment, and even that was mainly for his wife.

He brought one of the dental chairs home and put it in the basement to make his wife think he would bring in income by seeing patients in their home. He convinced her that their friends would trust him and book appointments. In the meantime, he looked for another way to make some money. Money would keep his wife quiet.

Ultimately, he accepted a job as a microbiologist with the state health department. His work in microbiology was exceptional, and he had a reputation for being the best in the state. The job didn't pay much, but the recognition and continued friendships he enjoyed at the Officers Club gave him purpose and a passion that consumed his senses. The power behind the position made him feel important. Important, controlling, and manly.

. . .

· Margi followed her father through the front doors of Fort Douglas. As an officer, Margi's father had access to the buildings and surrounding property. A swimming pool was located in the back. Margi's father greeted several people then motioned for Margi to follow. Margi walked briskly to keep pace with her father and kept her head down as she walked behind him.

Margi didn't like meeting new people. She didn't like the way they looked at her. It made her feel uneasy in a way she couldn't describe. At the same time, she felt a little proud that her father wanted her to come with him. It must mean that he loved her. Maybe he wanted to show his friends what made him happy. He always told her when they were alone together that she was here to make him happy.

Margi could hear the echoed sounds of voices down the hallway and knew where they were headed—the bathroom. She took a seat to wait while her father changed into a bathing suit. Daddy always took her into the bathroom with him at home when he had to change or use the toilet. She simply sat on the edge of the tub and waited. But this was a public place. She looked down at the ground and kept her eyes lowered until he emerged.

"Come along, Margi. I want you to watch me swim."

Margi sat in a chair at the edge of the pool. She watched as her father's hands pulled at the water to glide effortlessly on the surface to the other side. He was handsome, lean, and athletic, with a striking combination of dark hair and blue eyes.

Daddy had never taught Margi how to swim. But that was okay with her. She had a strange fear of water. The pool looked plenty safe, but the water in her nightmares was dark and frightening. Hands pulled her underneath the surface and left her gasping for air when she woke in the middle of the night.

Daddy also loved the water behind their house where a little river ran through the bottom of a secluded gully. Daddy often took Margi down to the river, telling her it was a place they could be alone. A place they could show their love and enjoy each other.

Water skeeters danced along the surface in the summer, skating and twirling as if they didn't have a care in the world. They were not afraid; every day in their world seemed like a brave new dance.

Sometimes Daddy carved little boats out of wood. Margi watched as the little boats tossed and turned in the ripples of the water. She stared in wonder at their amazing ability to float. Margi preferred to watch from the river's edge, but Daddy often coaxed her into the water. He promised to hold tight, but she could feel hands pulling at her legs and body. The hands clenched and jerked from behind as she gasped in pain and fear.

Water simply could not be trusted.

. . .

Margi quietly slipped out of bed. After the nighttime routine with Daddy, he had stumbled into his own bedroom to sleep. It was very late. Margi peered out through the white curtains at her bedroom window. It was so dark she couldn't see the moon or the stars. The dark, black sky defined the feeling in her heart. She knew nightmares would follow when the pillow cradled her head.

I must change my pajamas. I need new, clean pajamas that don't make me feel icky. Clean pajamas that won't give me bad dreams.

Margi found a clean nightie in her dresser. She pulled it over her head then climbed into bed. Her fingers grasped the edge of the blanket and pulled it up under her chin. She rolled over onto her side, closed her legs together tightly, and brought her knees up to her chest. She would lay very still. Maybe no one would notice her. Not even the monsters in her dreams.

Margi closed her eyes tight to shut out the world. She would not let anybody see the hurt. Not a trace.

Except for the single burning tear that rolled down her cheek.

. . .

Margi's eyes blinked at the glimmer of sunlight trying to find its way through her bedroom curtains. She felt the warm glow of the sun pierce the darkness, announcing that a new day had begun. But it wasn't the light that woke her from sleep. It was a sound—the squeaking sound of an old antique chair that belonged to her father.

Margi squinted through heavy lids to see Daddy staring at her face. He often pulled his chair beside her bed so he could sit and watch her. This morning he laced up his shoes before heading out the door to work. The chair squeaked as it fought against his weight.

Margi suddenly sat upright. Daddy's face had a distant expression—one she couldn't understand but that she had seen before.

"Please don't ever grow up," he said softly. "Don't ever grow up. You make me happy just like this."

He reached over and squeezed her leg that was tucked under the blankets. Margi saw his eyes darken for a moment, then move back to her face. He stood up to leave.

"Bye, Daddy," Margi whispered.

He quietly turned and left without saying anything in response.

Margi considered her part in this family. Her mother always seemed annoyed, and Margi tried hard to stay away from her. When she was around her mother, Margi felt defective and unlikable. But Daddy was different. She felt like a necessary part of his world—almost like he couldn't function unless she was around. She had a role to play in the family—a dance she had to do with each parent. A dance unique to each parent's needs.

A dance that was breaking Margi's soul.

Chapter 5

Margi was in her bedroom when she heard her father's voice.

"Margi, it's starting. Come sit with me," he yelled.

As she walked down the hall, she heard the familiar theme song. *Bonanza* was on television tonight. Daddy loved watching old Westerns, and this was his favorite. Margi walked over to the couch where her father was sitting and quickly sat down beside him. He looked over at her and patted his lap.

"This is your seat, Margi. Right here on my lap."

Margi obediently climbed onto his lap. He always wanted her there when he watched television. Daddy told her it was more comfortable that way. She shifted slightly on his lap to get comfortable, then looked up at the screen. She liked watching the horses. Maybe she would live on a farm one day and have some horses and other animals. She would be kind and gentle and make sure all the animals were loved and cared for.

The front door opened. In came Margi's sister Janet with her best friend, Ruth Ann, and a boy who had been hanging around a lot lately. When the group of teenagers entered the room, they were having a lively conversation about favorite songs on the radio. They looked over and saw Margi on her father's lap.

"Hi, Dad," said Janet. "We just stopped by to grab a snack. We're starved!"

Daddy quickly lifted Margi off his lap and placed her on the couch. He stood and made his way to the basement stairs. He didn't seem to like people much—especially teenagers. He didn't spend much time with his teenage daughters, so it made sense that he didn't want to invest any time getting to know their friends. The basement was his respite.

Janet rolled her eyes before saying, "Hi Margi. These are my friends."

Margi waved a hand to indicate that she had heard her sister. She quietly wandered back down the hall toward her bedroom.

. . .

"That is the saddest girl I have ever seen," Ruth Ann said to Janet, indicating both curiosity and concern. "She just has this blank look on her face. The only time I ever see her, she's sitting on your dad's lap. Does she just stay in her room all the time?"

"Yeah, she's like the invisible sister. She stays out of sight most of the time and just does her own thing, I guess," explained Janet. "I've tried to bring her to little parties with me, but she'll never go. It's like she's afraid of people."

Ruth Ann put her hands on her hips. "What can we do to make her happy?"

"Nothing. Nothing makes her happy," replied Janet.

"Well, can I read her a book or something? I feel really bad for her."

"No. Nothing will help her." It was a discouraging predicament for Janet. Her little sister was painfully shy and scared of everything. Mother was never around. Dad was always hiding out in the basement. And, well, she had her own life to live. Life was depressing in this house, and she did her best to avoid being at home.

Shaking off her reflections, she said, "Come on, you guys. Let's head over to the high school. Maybe we can catch the second half of the game."

. . .

"Wake up, Margi! There's no time to sleep in today. We're going to church."

Margi rolled over to see her mother standing in the doorway to her bedroom.

"Put on that pretty little blue dress. It'll brighten up your eyes. Now hurry up," demanded Mother.

Margi heard her mother's high heels clicking down the hallway. Church was another showcase for Mother. She put on her nicest dress and marched whatever family members she could summon to the church building. Their attendance at church was spotty, but Mother made sure everyone noticed them when they did go.

The practice of religion at home was superficial at best. Prayers were occasionally said over food at the dinner table, but usually only when guests were there; Mother wanted extended family and friends to witness their devotion. Margi watched and listened as family members prayed. She wondered about this God they called *Heavenly Father*. He seemed safe and good.

After listening to speakers in the main chapel, Margi was escorted to another room where the children met. After singing songs, they separated into classes to participate in activities and learn more about Jesus. Margi sat in a classroom with other seven-year-olds.

Margi liked the way she felt when she was at church. She looked at the pictures of Jesus on the walls. Margi wanted to know all about Him and to understand His part in her life. *Does He know me? Can He see me?*

During class time, the teacher told stories about Jesus. The teacher's soft, kind eyes glistened as she told the children about Jesus loving and blessing the children when He lived on earth. They learned that He wanted to hear from them now, and the best way to talk to Jesus was through prayer. She explained that His love was real, and He wanted to help them find joy.

Margi listened intently as something stirred within her soul. It confirmed what her heart was feeling. She felt a sense of comfort and peace—a sense of belonging to something bigger and better than her frightening world.

Margi thought only an adult or an important person at church could pray, but now she considered the idea that she could pray by herself. If the teacher was right, Margi not only had permission, but was encouraged to talk to Jesus. She sat in her chair and considered this new notion. So often she felt alone and invisible. Maybe Jesus could be her friend.

. . .

Margi heard the slam of the back door and the roar of the car engine. She walked over to her bedroom window and peered out in time to see Mother backing the car down the driveway. Mother was probably off to another bridge club meeting. It was all she could talk about—all her rich friends who came and who was the best bridge player that week. Margi didn't understand the game; she just knew that it meant Mother was away from home.

"Margi, come with me."

Margi jumped at the sound of her daddy's voice. He stood in the doorway of her bedroom. He must have also been watching her mother's car drive away.

"I want to show you something in the basement," he said.

Margi didn't like the basement. It was creepy, and she was sure images from her nightmares lived down there. As she walked by her bed, she reached up and grabbed her favorite stuffed monkey, Mugs, from the pillow; she wrapped her arms tightly around the monkey's waist.

She followed her father down the stairs into the basement. It was a dark, depressing space which had never been finished. Small, dirty windows allowed little light from outside. Gray cement shelves and old cupboards were covered in dust. An old gingerbread house from years before sat on one shelf covered in webs. Margi's mother never came down, but it was her father's destination of choice.

Daddy loved trains, and he had set up a little village of houses and trees along a circular track in the very back part of the basement. Just the flick of a switch sent the train moving along the tracks, circling around and through the various scenes along the railway. He wanted Margi to love them too.

"Look! It's a new red caboose," Daddy said. "And here are some new people who will live in this village. I've set them up here by this building to watch the train as it goes by."

Daddy's eyes were wide and childlike as he played with his trains and the little figurine people that were part of this town. He spent hours in the basement watching his engine pull the cars through the imaginary world he had created. Mother would have been angry if she knew they were down here. Margi had heard her yell at Daddy for spending money on ridiculous playthings and wasting money that could better be used. Margi wondered if Mother knew about the new caboose.

Margi watched as the train went around and around. Life was so predictable in this imaginary village. Nothing changed except for the train schedule—but even that was simply decided by a switch.

Margi saw her father watching her eyes as she followed the train. He seemed to like the fact that she admired what he loved. Like father, like daughter.

"Margi you look tired. Come and sit in my chair. I have something to help you."

Margi looked across the room at the gray dental chair in the opposite darkened corner of the basement. Her arms tightened around Mugs. She hated that chair. Margi watched as her father reached and took a little cup from the small cabinet next to the chair.

"Sit down and drink this, Margi," he ordered.

Margi walked slowly over to the chair and climbed up into the seat. Her father handed her the drink and watched as she swallowed the contents of the cup. He put the cup away and then placed a hand on her leg.

"You'll feel better soon," he soothed. "Just give it a minute."

Margi looked down at her monkey. She just wanted to go back upstairs and play with Mugs, or maybe get her Barbie dolls out of the closet and change their clothes. Margi looked down at Mugs and noticed the monkey's quiet smile. How she loved Mugs.

Suddenly there were spiders. Margi looked down at her body; it was limp and lifeless. She tried to yell out for help, but the screams only resonated inside her head. Nothing in her real world would respond. A sucking sensation pulled her from reality into a black, terrifying world that she had never seen before.

Eventually, Margi found the ability to escape. Blinded by unknown figures and darkness, she somehow crawled up the stairs and out of the basement. Mugs was still by her side. *Where's my bed? I just need to find my bed!* Her eyes focused on the hallway and recognized it as a path to her bedroom. If she could just get to her bed, everything would be okay.

She scrambled down the hall and climbed up into bed. She closed her eyes tightly. *This must be one of those really bad dreams.* She opened her eyes to see spiders along her walls and witches in her room. Quickly she pulled the blankets up over her head. Margi curled up and closed her eyes again. *Why can't I wake up? Why can't I leave this nightmare?*

Margi's hands lowered the blanket from the top of her head to her chin. She slowly opened her eyes just enough to peek over the edge of the pink flannel. The darkness was filled with spiders, and grotesque creatures lunged at her bedside. Her mind felt detached from her body.

Oh, please wake up. Somebody help me. I can't get back!

Margi pulled the blanket back over her head and hugged Mugs tightly. Her screams for help echoed in her head. Could anybody hear her? Margi was inside her bedroom in a single-family house, and she was alone.

Tears continued to wet her cheeks as she endured her dark world. At that moment, Margi had no way of knowing this would be a world she would later visit over and over. A violent force of angry fingers pulled her inward to a mad world beyond anything she had ever felt. In the depths of anguish, Margi curled into a ball and found the courage to ask a desperate question. Her lips trembled as words from her soul pled for relief.

Jesus, are you there?

Chapter 6

The snow was deep, and the cruel, icy fingers of the wind found their way into the collar of Margi's coat. The first week of January signaled the time to flock back to school to begin the second half of the scholastic year, and Margi shuddered from the chill as she carefully made her way along the snow-covered sidewalks.

The seating chart had been changed for the new semester, and Margi found herself seated in the second row of desks next to a girl she recognized named Kathy. The second-grade teacher welcomed the students back and asked them to partner up with the student next to them for a teamwork assignment. They were to learn about each other's families and share their favorite memories from the holiday week.

Kathy turned to Margi.

"You first," she stated. "Tell me about your family."

Margi felt her throat close. Margi just wanted to be like everybody else—to blend in and be happy—but she knew she was different. She decided to create a story about her family that would divert attention away from her real home. Her real parents.

"My dad is a movie star," Margi said. She imagined the main detective on the show *Hawaii Five-O*. He was handsome, and she decided he would make a good father image. "But he's really mean. He beats me and does other bad things to me."

Kathy's eyes widened at the revelation. "You mean like spanking you?"

Margi cringed at the word *spanking*. It was such a dirty word. Something about the image tore at her stomach and twisted it into a vicious, tight knot. She couldn't even say the word.

"I—I don't know," Margi stuttered. "You know—like hitting me with belts and things."

Kathy's eyes widened and her mouth dropped open. She stared at Margi and said nothing more. Kathy turned her chair away from Margi.

Margi shook her head. *Why did I tell such a crazy story? I should have stayed quiet.* But lately she found thoughts and words coming out of her mouth as though someone else was speaking. It was becoming a pattern, and she couldn't control herself. It was confusing, embarrassing, and frightening.

Time was also baffling. Sometimes she was at home in the backyard while the sun was shining brightly, and she closed her eyes. When she opened her eyes again, it was dark. Or one minute she was building a puzzle, and the next she was somewhere else. It made her question everything.

Margi figured the same thing happened to a lot of people. Sometimes she heard one of her parents say, "I don't know where the time went" or "Is it really that late?" or "Where on earth did the day go?" But part of her believed that it happened more often to her than to others.

There were nights when her parents took her places. She rode in the back seat of the car late at night but suddenly woke up in her bedroom at sunrise. She couldn't clearly account for the time in between, but there were glimpses of fear and pain in her dreams. She also remembered spinning sensations. The chanting of evil people in hooded capes consumed her nightmares.

God was not good in her dreams. Sometimes she remembered vague references to a laughing God who could not help her. He was a very different God from the one she learned about at church. Were there two Gods?

Maybe God didn't give me a good mind. That was it—her mind must be broken, and all the broken pieces made no sense. She had never seen anything like the evil people from her dreams on television, but they were very real to her. They even felt familiar. She often asked her parents if she was hypnotized. *Hypnotized.* Margi knew she had heard that word before. She wasn't sure exactly what it meant, but she felt certain it had something to do with an eerie space and frightening visions. And because her reality seemed distorted, it was an honest question. But instead of getting an answer, Margi was either ignored or scolded for asking too many questions.

At home, when she felt herself being pulled out of reality by images and sounds in her mind, the impulse was to run outside. She wanted to run away from herself and her collapsing house. She knew an episode was starting when walls started to shrink and warp. Voices lowered. Familiar people transformed into people she didn't recognize—or sometimes into horrific images.

During those confusing times, Margi found that sitting on the back porch with her pet dog or cat helped her find a comforting sense of *real*. Her dog seemed to understand as she stroked the hair on his back and hugged his head. As he licked her face and wagged his tail, Margi was able to focus on staying present. Margi also held her cat snuggled against her. The sound of the purring was soothing. She loved her animals, and they rescued her.

Margi decided that her broken mind required her to try harder. Be stronger. She must learn to keep secrets and find a way to carry on conversations that wouldn't attract more attention to herself. Margi felt the need to save her daddy. She wanted to protect both her parents and didn't want any trouble. Whenever there was trouble, people saw her as the problem. Besides, she didn't trust her own mind and the senseless, fractured pieces of her life.

If others saw her brokenness, they might take her away. The *others* were both the bad people in the world as well as the horrible monsters from her dreams. Both were equally terrifying.

In her twisted view of life, secrets were Margi's only safety.

. . .

29

Margi rummaged through her mother's sewing drawer, looking for the pins. *They must be in here somewhere.* She finally found the small red pincushion next to the scissors. She carefully pulled a pin out of the cushion, closed the drawer, and walked back to her bedroom. *This will do.*

Margi opened her closet, where she kept the dolls she had been given over the years. She loved her dolls and played with them often. Some of her favorites were from Nana. Margi dressed each doll in layers of clothes and sometimes also wrapped each one in blankets so nobody could touch it. Margi always made sure everything was covered.

She arranged the dolls in a row and quickly undressed each doll. As she pulled down the pants or lifted the dress, she noticed the many pin holes in their bottoms. It was time again for them to receive a poke.

Margi didn't understand what it meant; she just knew that's what happens. Dolls get pins stuck in their bottoms. After she finished sticking the pin in each doll, she made sure all the clothing snugly covered every part of the doll. She wrapped the dolls up tightly and carefully placed them in a row in the closet.

Somehow it seemed the only way to keep them safe.

Chapter 7

It was a cold, blustery day; leaves on the neighborhood trees were long gone, leaving just brown branches that seemed to scratch the gray sky. Winter days in Utah signaled the onset of skiing, building snowmen, and having snowball fights. But those were things other people did, and Margi heard other kids at school talk about them. Her family was different. There was no such fun for them.

It was the weekend, and Mother had places to go, so she drove up the long driveway to Nana's house with Margi in the back seat. Maybe it was the cold weather or all the holiday fuss from the past few weeks, but Nana said she wasn't feeling well. Even so, Nana told Mother that everything would be okay; she and Margi would just have a quiet day together. With that, Mother turned on her heel and left as swiftly as she had arrived.

Nana asked Margi to bring her the sweater from the chair in the bedroom. Margi found the black sweater draped over the arm of the chair in the corner and carried it back toward the family room. Coming around the corner, Margi stopped immediately.

Nana was on the floor; her body writhed and twisted, and her eyes were rolled back. Margi stared at her grandmother. *Is this real? Am I having a bad dream?*

"Nana!" she cried out. "Nana, I'm scared!"

Nana didn't respond. Margi took a deep breath and gathered the courage to approach her. Margi touched her softly on the arm, but Nana continued to move with rapid, jerking movements.

"Nana, please stop," begged Margi. "Please . . ."

Margi ran across the room, climbed under a table, and pulled her knees up tightly against her chest. She would hold herself that way until somebody came to help. Nana always said that they were a team. Margi tried hard not to cry because she didn't want to scare Nana.

Two hours later, Margi's aunt walked into the house and found Nana on the floor. Margi was still curled up under the table across from Nana. Nana was rushed to the hospital, where she was diagnosed with high blood pressure and failing organs. Nana was in critical condition.

. . .

It was difficult to attend school and go about her other daily activities when Margi's real worries were centered on Nana. Children were not allowed to visit at the hospital, so Margi just waited and wondered in her bedroom.

Days later, Mother and Father called Margi into the kitchen; they told her Nana had died at the hospital. Margi listened in disbelief as her worst fears were confirmed. Nana had lost the fight, and the family began preparations for a funeral. Margi could see that everybody was sad. She felt the sadness too, but she also felt the paralyzing fear of being deserted.

Margi ran into her bedroom and shut the door—somehow closing herself in her room might separate her from the devastating news. She felt utterly alone. Margi had always felt different, separated from everyone around her, and she felt completely abandoned without Nana. Nana's love had been the last hope in Margi's sad life.

Margi crawled into the corner of her closet, pulled her knees up to her chest, and wrapped both arms around them. She lowered her head and let her tears quietly fall. She wept for Nana, and she wept for a future without love, friendship, or security.

It had been a hard year. One by one, those around her had deserted Margi. Both sisters had left home that year without ever developing much of a relationship with Margi.

Her oldest sister, Barbara, set out to find her own path. Her sights were always set far away from home. Her mind was focused on success, and she consistently set and achieved goals. Because money was tight at home, Barbara worked part-time to buy clothing and the other things teenage girls desire. She grew weary of her father's constant request to borrow money; though he always promised to pay her back, the money was never returned. Barbara left to forge her own path of wealth and prestige and to distance herself from her beggared father and critical mother.

Margi's other sister, Janet, fell into the wrong crowd in junior high and found herself pregnant at fourteen, but miscarried the baby. Once again pregnant at seventeen, she left to find her own support outside of her parents' home. Janet's mother had made it clear that no money would come from them to support the baby. Janet felt bad for her quiet little sister, but she didn't have the means or the maturity to care for Margi. Besides, she had bigger problems to tackle in her own life.

So, the tears Margi shed for Nana were really shed for everyone who had left. Her sisters moved away, and now Nana was gone forever. In church, people talked about eternal families—that we would see our loved ones again in heaven. She hoped with all her heart that was true.

But for now, Margi was the only one left in her strange and scary world. *Who am I?* With that came an even darker thought: *What am I?* She wasn't sure she knew.

Margi would need to figure it out alone.

. . .

Margi's finger started at the top and ran down the alphabetical index along the side of the spiral address book Mother kept in the kitchen drawer. Mother was at bridge club, and Father was at the Officers Club at the military base, so Margi was home alone. She had waited for this private moment.

Margi wanted to reach out to her sister Janet. Maybe she could answer some questions, perhaps even help. Margi knew better than to reach out to Barbara. Her oldest sister had rarely taken an interest in anything to do with Margi. But Janet had been more involved in Margi's life when she lived at home.

Janet would surely be listed in Mother's address book. Margi opened the page under the tab labeled *J* and found Janet's name along with her phone number. Margi picked up the telephone that was hanging on the kitchen wall and dialed the number.

"Hello." Margi recognized Janet's voice.

"Umm . . ." replied Margi, pausing to gather up courage. "It's Margi."

"Oh. Hi, Margi. How are you? Anything wrong?"

"Well . . . I, uh . . . am having these feelings, and I'm afraid, and . . . well . . . I wanted to talk to you about it. Maybe you could help me?"

Margi could hear Janet take a deep breath and blow it out with what sounded like impatience.

"Margi, I love you, but I can't help you. You've got to stop calling me."

Janet's words were followed by a heavy silence on the line. Margi's fingers began to twirl the telephone cord as she felt hot tears fill her eyes. She bit the corner of her lip to keep it from quivering.

"Okay," whispered Margi. She tried to say good-bye, but her throat closed so tightly that she couldn't make a sound. She put the receiver back onto the base of the phone.

Margi closed the phone book and returned it to the kitchen drawer. Her feet felt heavy as she walked down the hall to her bedroom. Message received. She would not call her sister again.

. . .

It had been a long, terrifying night. The dreams were increasing in frequency and horror. Blurred images of frightening people and things Margi couldn't make sense of filled her mind. What she did know was the way she felt in the morning. The combination of flashing visions from bad dreams and unknown voices in her mind was a mentally exhausting way to greet a new day, so bad nights turned into long, hard days.

Had they been dreams? Who did the voices belong to? Sometimes Margi wasn't sure if she was asleep or awake. She was always so tired; it felt like she didn't sleep all night. While she couldn't recall details, there seemed no question that the monsters who crawled up the basement stairs during the night were somehow real.

It was Saturday morning, and that meant Margi didn't have to get ready for school. It also meant that her parents were probably somewhere in the house. Her stomach was in knots from thinking about last night. She had mentioned her "feelings" a few times to both Mother and Father, but they seemed indifferent. *Maybe I can help them understand. Calling Janet again is out of the question.*

Margi tiptoed down the hallway and peeked around the corner into the kitchen. Her father was sitting in a chair at the kitchen table reading a newspaper. She approached the side of the chair so he could see her out of the corner of his eye.

"Daddy, I'm having my feelings again," she said quietly.

Margi's father slowly lowered the newspaper and looked at his daughter. "Stop saying that," he responded gruffly.

"But Daddy, I'm so scared. I don't understand why this is happening."

This time the newspaper came down with an abrupt jerk as her father shouted, "Go away, Margi. Just go away!"

Margi quickly left the kitchen, embarrassed at the outburst. *Why won't anybody help me?* She moved quietly down the hallway toward her parents' bedroom. Maybe Mother was there.

When she entered the room, Margi saw her mother moving some things around in her closet. Margi climbed up on her mother's bed and looked out the window. Her sense of reality was slipping. She could feel her mind distorting things both outside and inside the room. *What if my mind takes me someplace else and I can't get back?* Margi took a deep breath and found the courage to speak.

"Mom, something's wrong . . ." she started.

Before she could finish, her mother whirled around to face her. "I've told you before—don't talk to me in the morning!" she growled.

35

"But I'm having these feelings," Margi said. Though she felt like crying, she would never allow herself to cry in front of Mother. There was already enough emotion in the room.

"You're having feelings?" her mother snarled.

Margi looked down at the floor. She was to blame for her mother's anger. Margi felt a combination of shame along with a desperate cry for help.

Mother turned and stomped into her bathroom. She opened the medicine cabinet and pulled out a bottle of paregoric. Margi's father registered for the liquid opium at the pharmacy to make sure they had it in their home for regular use. Mother poured some of the liquid into a cup on the counter and handed it to Margi.

"Here. Drink it up. It'll make those feelings go away," she demanded.

Margi looked into her mother's eyes. They meant business, but Margi didn't want any medicine. It didn't seem to fix anything—just created chaos in her mind. But refusing the paregoric would ignite Mother's wrath, so she obediently grabbed the cup and drank the awful solution. The taste was sharp and bitter.

"Now go get back in bed, Margi, and don't speak of these feelings again."

Margi stepped out of her parents' bedroom and leaned against the wall in the hallway. *Just get through today. Tomorrow is going to be the same, but just focus on today.* Margi knew something was terribly wrong and there were no answers—today. She would have to survive one day at a time.

Margi walked into her bedroom and found Mugs on the edge of her bed. She gently lifted the stuffed monkey, placed him under the blanket in her arms, and curled up tight. The manifestation was painfully clear. As the youngest of three children living in a house with two parents, Margi should have been surrounded by love. But she finally understood something about herself: she was alone.

She had been abandoned.

And she didn't matter.

Chapter 8

"Let's go faster. Faster!" shouted Margi. "Follow me!"

The wind pulled at Margi's long brown hair as she galloped through the open field on her imaginary horse. The green grass of summer tickled her ankles as her feet pranced to a happy beat.

"Come on, Jennifer! Try to catch me," Margi said with a grin. "See if your horse can catch mine!"

Margi turned to see her niece Jennifer pick up the pace. Playing and laughing and enjoying the sunshine together for the weekend, both shared an intense love for horses and spent hours dreaming of the day when both of them might own a real horse. For now, imagination would supply the horse and the story.

Jennifer was Barbara's oldest daughter. Technically, Margi was Jennifer's aunt, but they were only five years apart and had a fun relationship as friends. When Jennifer came over for family dinners or other events, the girls found themselves listening to Beatles albums on the record player, brushing each other's hair, or racing fanciful horses through open areas in the neighborhood.

As a middle-schooler, Margi loved the distraction that Jennifer provided. Jennifer was beautiful, adventurous, and silly. Margi finally understood what having a friend felt like when she was with Jennifer. Jennifer was happy and carefree—two things Margi seldom felt. She loved her little niece and secretly wished she could be just like her.

The admiration was mutual. Jennifer adored her aunt Margi, looked up to her, and somehow felt a connection deeper than the amount of time they actually spent together. Jennifer believed they would be best friends forever.

When Jennifer was around, Margi felt a great release—an interruption to dark events and routines that had been taking place in Margi's life for as long as she could remember. Jennifer's countenance gave Margi a glimmer of hope. Perhaps there was a better future somehow. Maybe there could be joy. Perhaps there was promise.

For Margi, Jennifer was a light.

. . .

The children in junior high were on the edge of their seats as they gathered in the auditorium for a school-wide assembly. The girls clustered to share secrets and swap notes written to best friends, while the boys poked each other and wrestled when the teachers weren't looking. Everyone was excited to be out of the classroom and to hear the guest speaker.

Margi sat next to some girls from her class. She noticed the other girls' dresses and wished hers were pretty like theirs. The girls giggled and began to braid each other's hair. The principal stood at the front and spoke sternly into the microphone.

"All right, boys and girls. Time to quiet down. We need to be on our best behavior today," she demanded.

The children quickly stopped the chatter and pulled their attention to the front.

"I would like to introduce our very special speaker today. His name is Revell. He is a performer who is an illusionist and a hypnotist. I think this will be very entertaining. Let's give him a warm welcome."

The children erupted in applause—all except Margi. She sat frozen in fear. Her eyes scanned the faces of the girls next to her. They were excited and happy to learn about hypnotism. *Don't they know?*

Revell stepped to the microphone and began his introduction. Margi could feel panic gripping her senses. She needed to bolt before it was too late.

Margi ran to the back of the large room; finding the exit door, she ran toward it as though something were chasing her. She grabbed the door handle and launched through the doorway into the hallway on the other side. After taking a few quick strides, she slid down onto the floor with her back against the wall. Reaching up, she squeezed the sides of her head.

It's too late. His words are already in my mind. Frightened, Margi sensed herself being pulled away. She felt disconnected to herself and to the school.

Margi heard laughter coming from the assembly room. *Why is everyone else happy?*

What is wrong with me? Margi sat and tried to stay present. She opened her eyes and focused on the school windows. The trees outside. She would not let this man take over her mind. *I might never find my way back.* She heard the laughter again.

The hypnotist's demonstration was filled with intrigue, silliness, and amazement for hundreds of children.

Except for one girl sitting in the hallway.

. . .

Margi didn't want to go to the hospital. Hospitals were places to treat sick people, and she was sure that involved pain or death. At first, she decided to refuse to go, but then she thought better of it. Better to keep her head down and stay silent.

At the facility, Margi sat quietly in the chair and folded her arms. A woman with blonde hair told her to take a seat. She looked up occasionally to watch the other girls. They looked about her age—that awkward age of twelve when girls weren't little children anymore but were not yet teenagers. Who were they? There was an uneasy tension in the air as the girls glanced at each other and fidgeted. *Why am I here with these other girls?*

Margi noticed a sign on the wall: *Welcome to the Neuropsychiatric Children's Clinic.* The smaller plaque next to it said only one word—*Office.* A picture on the wall of a man in a gray suit was labeled *Dr. Bowen.*

Margi thought about what had happened before she was led to the waiting area. The blonde-haired woman had taken her to a room where she was given multiple Rorschach Inkblot tests by Dr. Bowen. One by one, Margi was shown a maze of black dots and asked what she saw in them. Someone then recorded her perceptions. Margi didn't like the tests; they were frightening, and she worried they would suck her into some other dimension.

During the testing, the woman spoke to Margi as if she knew her from previous visits. The woman referred to past feelings and procedures discussed in earlier appointments, but Margi had only vague recollections of coming to the hospital before. She wondered why other girls at school never talked about coming here. One thing was certain—Margi hated it here.

Margi was abruptly brought back to the present when the woman said, "I have an announcement to make." All the girls sat up in their chairs to hear the message from the smiling woman.

"We're going to meet next week," she stated, "and you're all going to graduate from the program on Wednesday!"

Am I cured? Am I going to get better? Margi couldn't quite understand what was happening, but it did sound positive.

"Everyone except Margi," continued the woman. "Margi will never get better."

Heavy silence fell over the room. Margi felt everyone looking at her, and she lowered her eyes in embarrassment. She desperately tried to pull details to the forefront. *What program? Why am I here?* So many questions raced through her mind, but she was sure of only one answer.

She was a failure.

. . .

Mother pulled into the driveway at home and came to an abrupt stop. She jerked the gear into park, shook her head, then turned around to face Margi in the back seat of the car. Her red lips were drawn and angry.

"I can't afford this, Margi. You're costing me too much money."

"I . . . I don't understand," Margi stammered. "I don't need to go to the doctor. I'm fine." It was a lie, and Margi knew it.

"For heaven's sake, Margi, you're *not* fine. Just do what the doctor says."

Margi felt bad that she cost her parents money. She didn't want to be a burden and had never asked to go to the hospital. It occurred to Margi that her mother just wanted her to be someone else's problem.

Margi stiffened as she made a promise to herself. There would be no more discussions about "feelings" with her mother—or with anybody else. Perhaps that was part of the reason Mother felt the need to take her to the hospital. Margi understood now that if she mentioned anything at all about not feeling well, it would land her in the hospital. Who knew what the doctors there might do? They had access to all kinds of drugs. She didn't trust the drugs or the people administering them.

Nobody can fix me.

I am a freak.

Chapter 9

The air was cool and crisp, and fall leaves signaled the start of high school and a new season of life. A girl in her high school class had invited Margi to hang out at the park. It seemed like a cool group of kids, and Margi just wanted to fit in. Feel comfortable.

She thought this group would be different from others she had met. Earlier in the week, Margi sat by another group of girls in the cafeteria. They were smart, and they talked about high school clubs, favorite teachers, and future college plans. They even dreamed of and looked forward to beautiful weddings and children in their happily-ever-after. *Why would I want that?* Margi made a conscious effort to separate herself from girls she had nothing in common with.

Margi saw the group of teens in the corner of the park area. Zipping her sweatshirt up tightly, she summoned enough courage to approach. This was a much better place to be on a Friday night than at some dumb high-school football game. The bright lights and crowds of students cheering in the bleachers was a bit too much. This was more her scene.

"Hey, glad you came!" said a girl who had invited her.

Margi took a breath and found enough voice to respond.

"Hi, I'm Margi," she said timidly.

"Come on over! Jimmy managed to sneak some beer out of his uncle's house. I'll get you one if you want," said the friend.

"I'm okay right now," replied Margi. "Maybe later."

As the evening wore on, Margi knew she had found her people. Their expectations about school and life were low, and the future was anybody's guess. Goals were simple and focused on the next weekend. It felt like a space where she could be accepted for who or what she was.

And it was a path that would lead Margi away from her dark house.

. . .

"Just do it, Margi."

Her friend's parents were out of town and they had the house to themselves. Margi held the marijuana joint in her fingers. She didn't have a desire to drink or do drugs. Though drinking and experimenting with drugs appealed to all the others, deep down in her gut Margi felt it was wrong. It scared her a little—but why shouldn't she try? Nobody in her life cared what she did. Nobody would ever ask her about it. Margi wanted to belong—to anything.

"It's natural from a plant, Margi," they chided. "It's not going to kill you."

Margi took a long, slow drag. Maybe her friends were right. She sat back and started to enjoy their company.

Suddenly Margi's mind began to betray her. She saw distorted images in the room, and people's voices sounded distant, nothing more than echoes. It was immediately familiar. *I've had this before. This is what they did to me in my childhood many, many times!*

Margi closed her eyes tightly and curled up on the sofa. What had seemed nothing more than a way to fit in was instead becoming a horrible experience. Frightening images and distorted perceptions played in her mind. She fought the nightmarish images, but the fear that she was going to die or get stuck in this twisted dimension took control.

Margi tossed and turned on the couch then sat up quickly. One of the guys looked over and smiled.

"Bad trip, huh?" he said.

"Yeah – I didn't expect this."

"Well, Joe got that stash of pot from a special friend. It was laced with PCP. Maybe you and PCP don't have a good relationship."

Margi recognized the link. There absolutely *was* a relationship, one that was somehow connected to her childhood. Eerie memories flashed forward in her mind as she remembered some terrifying nights from her childhood. She knew this feeling. *Why would anyone want to do this for fun?*

Margi's thoughts were fragmented. She couldn't even think a complete sentence. Time was so warped in this dimension.

"Please . . . help me," Margi begged. "I don't feel . . . Drive me?"

"Okay, sure. Where to?"

"My sister . . . Janet . . . house."

Margi grabbed her shoes and headed for the door. She needed to breathe the cool outside air. She climbed into the passenger seat and swiped at a tear. The moon was full and bright, and Margi focused on the brilliant sight. *Heavenly Father, please save me from this night. Save me from this scrambled mind.*

Margi was miraculously able to give directions to her sister's house. She stumbled out of the passenger door and found her way to Janet's front door. It was unlocked. She ran down the hall and climbed into her sister's bed. Margi began to cry and curled up next to Janet.

"Margi, is that you? What's wrong?" Janet asked.

Margi looked up at her older sister but couldn't even speak. The nightmarish images were close. Maybe tonight her life would end.

"Oh, honey—you just need to sleep. You'll be okay in the morning." Janet reached over and pushed the hair off Margi's face. Janet could see her sister was in a bad place tonight. The words could wait until morning. Margi was safe now and they could talk later.

Margi curled onto her side and pulled the blanket up tight around her neck. She fought through the terror and found her faith like she had so many times. She hoped that God could hear her desperate thoughts. She reached out from the darkness toward a light she trusted was real. *Help me wake up different—not in this scary dimension. If you'll give me my mind back, I'll never touch alcohol or drugs. Never, ever again.* It was a solemn promise to God. A promise that Margi would keep and never forget.

Margi's friends could make their own choices. They could experience life through outside substances if that's what they wanted. But she knew this was not for her.

Please God . . . stay with me tonight.

. . .

Leaning against the wall of the room by herself, Margi stood off to the side and watched. It was a youth activity for teens at church, and the girls were laughing together and hurling silly comments at each other. Margi had gone to the activity in hopes of making some new friends. Now she realized the girls there were nice and pretty, but they were different. *I am different.*

Leaving the church activity, Margi headed toward home. She felt an impulse to keep driving past her street and up the hill behind her neighborhood. She turned the car into the gas station at the top of the hill, pulled off to the side by the curb, and put the car in park. The windshield offered a panoramic view. Margi looked down the valley and saw her home nestled in with all the others. *Home?* Considering it as *home* was more than a disconnect. It was a dark, hollow void that made her heart ache and filled her soul with anguish. *Where do I go? Everybody else has family, and they belong to each other.*

Her mind wandered back to the girls at church. They lived such a carefree, happy life. She noticed the way they interacted with their parents. It was so different, so foreign. Margi wanted that, but she didn't even know how to reach it.

The contrast between those families and hers was a sharp one for Margi. There were nights she didn't show up at home and days she never attended school. Her parents never asked. Margi had heard girls at school talk about trouble with parents and punishments for being out too late. Margi wondered what it would be like to have parents who asked about school. Parents who even knew where she was. Parents who cared.

Margi had started calling her mother *Reen*, short for her first name of Reenie. It bothered Margi to call her mother *Mom* because the word suggested a real relationship. It was an attachment that felt foreign.

46

Somehow wrong. Referring to her as *Reen* allowed a safe separation in Margi's mind.

Margi's eyes burned as they filled with tears. The dark sky beyond the gas station lights matched the deep feeling of hopelessness in her world. The bright lights in homes below were a stark contrast to her despondent reality. There was a physical ache in her chest that pulled her lower and deeper than she had ever felt. Life was never going to change. Margi felt different from everyone else. Broken. She wanted to be invisible, yet she desperately needed to be noticed.

Why did God make me this way? Margi's thoughts took a new direction as tears rolled down her cheeks. *Is God even real?*

As the sky darkened, Margi wept. Minutes turned into hours. The despair was thick and gripped its fingers around hopelessness, fear, and dejection. *I am alone. Nobody loves me.* The walls of blackness were closing in and filling the space.

Suddenly, Margi had a quick vision—a scripture one of the girls had read during church:

"… faith is things which are hoped for and not seen; wherefore, dispute not because ye see not, for ye receive no witness until after the trial of your faith."[1]

The light in her heart lasted just a brief moment and left as quickly as it had come, but the walls of blackness had parted for just one tender moment. Though it was fleeting, the feeling was real, and she felt a glimmer of hope. A sense of belonging. A sense of love.

Even though Margi felt like a disappointment to everyone in her life, she wanted God to be pleased with her. Perhaps she could make Him happy. She must find a way in this dark world to shine.

Maybe she would even make Him proud of her one day.

Chapter 10

It was difficult not to be obvious. He was sitting one row over and two seats back in her sophomore English class. He was out of her field of peripheral vision, so Margi would have to turn her head to get a really good look. He would notice her stare.

Mr. Carter introduced himself and began calling names from the class roster. Taking attendance was a real chore the first day of class as teachers tried to match the names with faces. As the roll was called, Margi twisted slightly in her seat, finding an excuse to check a pocket in her backpack so she could turn and catch another glimpse.

He was so incredibly cute—brown hair, a bit on the long side, with sunny blonde highlights and piercing blue eyes. His tan skin indicated he must spend time outdoors. She noticed jeans and loafers with no socks. He was the vision of some dreamy guy she'd expect to be living in a small beach town on the coast.

"Dennis?" said Mr. Carter.

"Here," he replied. The teacher smiled at the response. So did Margi.

On the surface, she didn't recall ever seeing Dennis before, but deep in her soul there was a connection. Margi felt like she knew him.

Margi turned around again, pretending to notice some of the other students in class. But there was only one student in her sights. This time they locked eyes.

Margi whirled around and recognized a flicker of hopefulness. Why was he so familiar? *I'm going to marry him.*

The thought startled Margi. *Why would I think that?* She had never thought about marriage before. Why would she? Why would she want anything even remotely like the example her parents provided? But when she considered Dennis, the thought wasn't frightening or desperate. It simply felt right. And it felt safe.

Margi smiled at such curious thoughts. She fidgeted in her seat and twirled her long brown hair in her fingers, wondering if Dennis was watching her. She hoped so.

Suddenly high school English class wasn't such a bad place after all.

. . .

Dennis's eyes followed Margi as she placed her test on Mr. Carter's desk and returned to her seat. Dennis was glad she didn't seem to notice his attentive gaze, because he was sure he didn't even blink. She was gorgeous.

Margi's long, dark-brown hair cascaded down her back and encircled her tall, slender body. Dennis shook his head as he considered whether he was even in her league. He didn't really know anything about her other than the obvious fact that she was beautiful. He figured she must have fifteen other guys trying to hit on her.

Dennis wasn't much for the social scene at school. He worked hard at part-time jobs and didn't have much time to spend at school after classes—or interest in it, either. Dennis was a hard worker, and that strong quality had him on the path toward his goal of independence. He was determined to make his own way. The relationship with his mother was rocky, and the sooner he could support himself and move out, the better.

The bell rang, and the students gathered their belongings to walk to the next assigned class. Dennis placed the English book into his backpack and was working the zipper up and over the sides when he noticed someone standing close to his desk. He looked up to see Margi.

"How do I know you?" she asked with a smile. "You look familiar."

Dennis chuckled nervously while he tried to find his voice. "I don't think we've ever met." *She's even more gorgeous up close; I would have definitely remembered meeting her before.* His mind raced as he tried to think of the perfect comeback.

"Hmm . . ." Margi responded. "It just kind of feels like I know you from somewhere. Oh, well—see you in class tomorrow."

Dennis watched as Margi walked out the classroom door. He followed the other students out and managed to catch sight of Margi further down the hallway. He committed himself to the idea that he was going to overcome his shyness and get brave enough to ask her out. He promised himself he would find the courage.

It wasn't a question of *if* . . . it was a question of *when*.

· · ·

"Margi, you can tell me anything."

Dennis didn't want to pressure Margi, but she had told him earlier that she wanted to talk. The expression on her face made him think it might be something serious. Worrisome.

The two had been dating for months. Dennis had finally mustered up the courage to ask Margi to a movie over Christmas break. When she accepted his awkward invitation, Dennis felt like he'd won the lottery. After that, they spent every day together.

The two met at Sugar House Park, where they walked for a bit and enjoyed the warm sun; the blanket of snow had melted, and in its place was tender spring grass. Margi motioned to some bleachers under a tree and climbed up to take a seat. Dennis followed and sat close. After six months together, he finally felt brave enough to put his arm around her. It was a simple gesture, but one that signaled a relationship. She was beautiful, and he wanted her to know that he noticed.

"I want to be honest with you, Dennis."

She had his full attention.

"I just want you to know there's something wrong . . . well . . . with me. Sometimes my mind does these things. It's like I'm dreaming, but I'm not. It's almost like there's another reality out there pulling on me."

Margi's voice began to quiver. Dennis could tell this was hard for her to talk about.

"It's okay, Margi," Dennis whispered.

"I don't know what it is, Dennis," Margi cried. "I just know that I've had these strange feelings for as long as I can remember—since I was five years old."

Dennis knew better than to ask if her parents might help, because Margi consistently found any excuse to get out of her house. It was obvious to him that there was no support for Margi at home.

Dennis sat quietly and listened. He had no medical training or understanding of psychology—he was just a kid trying to graduate from high school and earn a decent wage, but he knew he was falling in love with her. This new information made no difference.

"We'll figure this out, Margi. It'll be okay."

Dennis squeezed Margi's arm and pulled her in close. He gazed at her eyes, which seemed to hold a pain he didn't understand. He didn't know how to fix things, but there was one thing he did know.

Dennis wanted to protect and take care of Margi.

PART TWO

PAST IS PRESENT WHEN YOU CARRY IT WITH YOU.

Chapter 11

Margi opened the front door of her house and listened for voices.

"Anybody home?" Margi called out.

There was only silence. Nobody was home. Not that it mattered; she might as well be invisible.

Margi hardly stayed at home anymore. During the last two years of high school, she found reasons to be elsewhere and gratefully accepted invitations from friends. Any couch or floor was a far better place than sleeping in her bedroom. Her home had an eerie sense that magnified Margi's fears. Those fears manifested themselves in both nightmares and episodes of distorted reality. In her mind, it was a house of horrors.

Margi quickly walked down the hall to her bedroom. She threw some clean clothes into a bag and walked toward the kitchen. Maybe there was some fruit she could grab or some bread with which she could make a sandwich. She would see Dennis later, so she'd better make one for him too.

Before twisting the knob of the front door, she paused for a moment. Margi turned around and surveyed the rooms. A wave of conflicting emotions formed a hard lump in her throat.

How she wished this had been a real home. Her parents never asked where she was staying. Nobody ever looked for her. She longed for any conversation to show they cared. It felt as though she didn't exist. This wasn't a home. This was just an old, foreboding house that felt empty and cold.

Margi wondered if she was ever loved as a child. She didn't remember most of her childhood. It was strange hearing friends talk about memories from early years. The bulk of Margi's memories were gone; all that remained were a few frightening flashbacks that filled her nightmares. She wondered why she couldn't remember anything. *If I have no memories, I'm not worth anything. My role and part in this family are irrelevant.* The realization made her feel empty.

Margi pulled the front door shut. She was going to meet Dennis. At least *he* loved her. Margi smiled at the thought that Dennis was waiting for her. What she felt with him was unlike anything she had ever known. For the first time in her life, she mattered. For now, she would leave her broken mind behind in that old, dark house.

Margi couldn't know then that she would have to carry those broken parts with her for a lifetime.

· · ·

"Let's do this, Margi," Dennis said. "We love each other, and that's all that matters. I want to marry you."

Sitting in his car in the driveway of Margi's house, Dennis leaned over and grabbed her hand. He kissed it tenderly then looked into her eyes. He repeatedly told her she was the most beautiful girl he had ever seen—and that he felt like the luckiest guy in the world.

They had spent three years together and felt ready to leave their teenage years behind. Dennis said he was eager to find good work and set his sights on a future. A future with Margi.

"Let's go inside and tell your parents. We'll just tell them that's what we want to do," Dennis urged. "Come on—I'll be right here with you."

Margi looked up at Dennis. She had never belonged to anyone or anything in her entire life. She was certain of her feelings and had given Dennis her whole heart. He made her feel as close to whole as she could ever be. She felt ready to embrace every dimension of living and loving with Dennis. She needed to take this next step and launch herself. Margi felt a quiet voice of courage whisper, *This is love, Margi.* A feeling of peace followed.

Margi thought back to that first day in English class. From the first moment she saw Dennis, she felt a connection. He had looked so familiar. Now she believed that he was a gift. A gift God had given her.

Margi pulled Dennis in and kissed him.

"Okay. I'm ready." Margi took a deep breath. She hoped her mother and father would be happy about the news. Maybe even proud of her.

When Margi and Dennis walked in the front door, her father was sitting in his chair in the family room. He tossed a quick glance in their direction, seeming to discourage them from interrupting his television watching.

"Dad, we have something to tell you. We want to get married."

Margi's father shifted his eyes to look at Margi, then stared ahead at the television screen.

"Go tell your mother, Margi," he replied. "I don't care."

Dennis tightened his grip on Margi's hand as if he was trying to give her courage. Margi pulled on his hand and walked toward the kitchen. She heard the kitchen cupboards slamming and assumed she would find her mother there.

"Reen, we want to get married," Margi uttered. Her voice was timid. Her father had made his feelings clear, but her mother always presented a very different battle. Margi never quite knew how she would react to anything.

Margi's mother turned and looked them both up and down. She placed one hand on her hip. "Well, you can't wear white, because you're not pure. Pick a date and go find a dress that's not white. I'll call a few people."

· · ·

Dennis locked eyes with Margi. He could see the disappointment in her face. No wonder she never wanted to be at home. There was no joy here. No congratulations. In her parents' estimation, Margi was not even worth a conversation. In the face of such a major announcement, there were no questions. Not even a hint of affection.

Dennis had issues with his own mother; she was critical of everything he did. But this was different. There seemed to be a complete disconnect of emotion in this family. His heart ached for Margi, and he longed to deliver her from this setting. Together they would love each other. Together they would build a new start.

And together they would rescue each other.

Chapter 12

Margi sat on the floor of her old bedroom. The simple beige dress she found at the store the week before lay across the foot of her bed. It wasn't white, so it would not upset her mother. Margi ran the brush through her long, brown hair one more time. She had tried unsuccessfully to get her hair to curl; twisting her hair around her fingers with the brush didn't work. She wasn't sure how women got their hair to curl; nobody had ever really taught Margi about those things.

Her wedding day. This was supposed to be the happiest day of Margi's life. She loved Dennis, but this was not how she imagined her day would be. On television, wedding days were filled with family and laughter. Bridesmaids who dressed the bride and made her look beautiful with makeup and jewelry. Decisions about flowers and colors and music coming to life at the anticipated event. Brides who wore beautiful gowns. But here she sat alone in her dark, old bedroom. A living room wedding would soon take place in this house of horrors.

Where are my sisters? Margi had secretly hoped they would arrive early that morning as a surprise. Wake her up and spend the morning making sure their youngest sister looked beautiful on her special day. Instead, Margi felt a deep sadness for happy dreams that never materialized. Her sisters' absence just amplified the depressing mood. Quiet tears rolled down Margi's cheeks. *I shouldn't have expected anything more.*

Margi noticed Mugs sitting on the floor in her closet. He had been a comfort for as long as she could remember, and his stitches were coming loose from so many hugs. Once again, he was a witness to another day of going through the motions, pretending that everything was okay.

This should have been a joyous day. Maybe Mugs understands.

. . .

"I do," Dennis replied.

The beautiful girl in front of him was becoming his wife. Dennis never took his eyes off Margi. Her face was expressionless. Perhaps she was nervous. Soon the formalities of this ceremony would be over, and they could start their lives together. Love and honor. His heart swelled as he promised himself, Margi, and God that he would take care of her.

Dennis's brother held a video camera to record the whole event, and a friend took pictures with his camera. Margi's sisters had arrived just before the vows were spoken and quickly sat on stools to witness the marriage. Those present also included Dennis's parents, a couple of his relatives, and a few close friends that Margi's mother had invited. It was a small, quiet gathering.

. . .

Margi's father dutifully came up the stairs from the basement to hear the wedding vows, then shook hands with Dennis's family and mingled with the other guests. The photographer motioned for newly married Margi to stand with her father for a picture. She looked up at her father's face, hoping to see assurance. Instead, her stomach tightened as she recognized the familiar look in his eyes and remembered his words: *Don't you ever grow up. You make me happy like this. Don't leave me.*

Margi quickly averted her eyes from her father's face toward the camera as she fought the urge to run out of the room. The reflection of some mysterious longing in her father's eyes made her uncomfortable, but she didn't know why.

Margi watched as her father quickly disappeared down the stairs and back to his basement hideaway. Memories with her father were so confusing and erratic. Just looking at his eyes or his mouth immediately triggered ugly feelings that vanished as quickly as they had surfaced. Those ugly feelings intensified in terrifying nightmares of unspeakable events.

Margi blinked hard as she forced her attention away from the basement stairs and her father. Today was her wedding day. She looked for Dennis and caught sight of him across the room, where he was talking to his parents. Margi took a deep breath. She needed to focus on him. Dennis was loving and kind. He would keep her safe.

He would keep her away from this dark, lonely house.

. . .

The apartment was tiny—a modest place with no heat and one twin bed. It was certainly nothing fancy, but it was theirs. Dennis and Margi kept each other warm and celebrated the start to a new season of life.

As Dennis kissed his new wife good-bye and headed for work, Margi considered her place in this new chapter of life. She didn't know how to be a real wife. What did that mean? Margi certainly didn't want to follow any example left by her mother. Maybe she could work; having a job herself would help them financially. She decided to begin looking very soon so she could find a job, earn some money, and eventually buy a car for herself.

For now, Margi would settle in their apartment and start adjusting to their new married life. She reflected on her wedding day and the wide range of feelings she had experienced. Could anyone see her deepest thoughts? There had been a real struggle in her mind that day regarding time and space. Her realities were conflicting, and portions of the day were fuzzy.

Suddenly she remembered the pictures. They might tell the story and clarify some things in her mind. Margi picked up the phone, called her mother, and asked about the wedding video and pictures.

"Well, there are a few problems," Reen said. "They forgot to load film into the video recorder, so there's no video of the ceremony. And we just got the film back this morning from the drugstore on the corner, and all the pictures came out yellow. There are a few that are somewhat usable, but most of them won't work. I'll leave them on the table. See for yourself. I'm late for an appointment."

With that, Margi's mother hung up. There was no greeting, no discussion about new married life, and no interest in any part of her life. *I don't know why I'm surprised.* Margi was annoyed with herself for continuing to hope for something more.

It was a tough first week. Her expectations of new married life were deflated. Somehow, she thought the marriage might repair her mind—close the gaps in different realities and quiet the voices she heard in her head. It didn't. Somehow, her nightmares had found their way into a new bed. *They must be part of me—a piece of my broken mind.* How she hated her mind.

Margi walked over to the window and noticed the healthy, green summer grass. There were little potted flowers outside the doors of some of the apartments. She would get something like that for herself when she earned her first paycheck.

Once again, Margi determined to go through all the motions and pretend she knew how to live this so-called married life. Maybe it would begin to feel true and real over time. She did love Dennis. That was certainly real. But she still couldn't shake the feeling inside that she was alone.

Margi had found Dennis, and she was grateful for him in her life. But Margi was still lost.

Chapter 13

Margi placed her hand on her growing belly and smiled. There it was again: the slightest flutter that Margi recognized as the baby moving inside her body. What a beautiful reminder to start the day.

Thank you, dear God, for this gift.

During moments like this, Margi felt peace. She could hardly believe that God would entrust her with this incredible responsibility. The pregnancy came with an enormous dose of love that filled Margi's entire soul along with a resolute desire to give everything to this future child. Everything she never had.

For the first time in her life, Margi felt whole. There was a focus and an emotional anchor in the pregnancy that kept her present. She had prayed so many times for God to help her feel whole. To find peace in her fragmented world. Here was the unexpected answer. She was determined to make God proud.

The first few years of marriage had been a real adjustment. Margi tried and failed at holding down jobs. She started new jobs with the best intentions, focused hard, and learned the duties required in the position. Those were the good days. Then she would arrive at work and not remember any of the training. There was no continuity. There were dozens of "first days" on the job. It felt like somebody else had been there. Margi tried to fake her way through days like that, something she had practiced throughout her life. She knew her broken mind was at fault. Before the point of total embarrassment, she usually created a far-fetched excuse and quit.

. . .

Dennis continued working hard to provide a solid foundation for their new family. He had worked hard since the age of thirteen, and he believed good things were in his future. As he listened to his wife's excuses about why jobs weren't working out, he began to see a pattern. *Was it related to those "feelings" that she had confessed to having for so long?*

Dennis worried about Margi but felt that doing his part to support and care for her was all he could do.

. . .

Margi looked over at Dennis's face. The final tranquil moments of sleep caressed his features. The sun was barely peeking in the windows, and he would soon leave for work. She reached for his hand and placed it on her belly. Dennis opened one eye and looked at Margi.

"It happened again," she whispered. "Just hold still. I want you to feel it too."

Margi and Dennis nestled together and pondered their future as parents. A new season of life was beginning. Dreams and new wonders were just around the corner. Today was a beautiful start. One quiet morning. One twin bed.

Two sweethearts filled with hope.

. . .

Dennis woke to the sound of Margi's voice. She was sobbing, and her arms and legs were thrashing. It was clearly a nightmare.

"Margi, wake up," he urged. "You're dreaming again."

Margi sat up with a bolt. He looked at her face. He could tell by her eyes that she was terrified.

"Wake up, honey," he continued. "Everything is okay. You're here with me."

Dennis could tell it was another bad one. There were bad dreams, and there were *really bad* dreams. The look in her eyes and the sweat on her forehead spelled the difference.

"Want to tell me about it?"

"No; it was just a crazy dream. Sorry I woke you."

. . .

Margi rolled over, pulled up the sheet, and wiped a tear before Dennis could see that she was crying. It always took a while before the nightmare really ended. Even awake, she still felt the horror from her nightmares. It was difficult to keep the two realities separate from each other.

As Margi approached the due date for their first child, her nightmares had taken a heightened twist. Images were increasingly graphic and real: Dark basements filled with evil. Men and women dressed in black, hooded cloaks who grabbed her and tied her down. Physical and emotional torture. Ceremonies for the purpose of donating reproductive organs to Satan. And ultimately, declarations that she belonged to Satan and, therefore, her children would be his.

I don't know what could have created such horrible dreams. Margi had never watched frightening movies or read anything that could translate to these nightmares. She scolded herself for having such thoughts and blamed them on her broken mind.

Margi pulled the blanket around her mouth to muffle another sob. *Please help me, God. Bless this new baby.* She was alone in this fight. Who could she reach out to for help? Margi couldn't tell her husband that she might be carrying Satan's child. She couldn't even say it out loud. She thought about her obstetrician. He was kind and interested in her health and well-being. But she quickly dismissed any possibility of confiding in him. *I can't tell him or anybody else. They'll lock me away.*

Maybe Reen was right. When Dennis and Margi walked into her parents' house to tell them about her pregnancy, her mother was disappointed. All the reasons why Margi couldn't possibly raise a child flew from her mother's lips like darts. Margi's father said nothing, just stared blankly ahead with no response. Though Margi looked for a hint of approval, his expressionless face said plenty.

Margi opened her eyes and carefully took in all the furniture and décor of her apartment. Being able to see things was key to finding *real*. Margi prayed again to feel whole and present, a desperate prayer she had uttered hundreds of times. She was frightened of fractured glimpses that took her to other dimensions and made her question her own worth and purpose. They were glimpses of events that felt real enough to be a part of her soul.

Glimpses trying to take away her joy.

. . .

Margi sat on the couch cradling her newborn baby. He was beautiful and perfect. Margi felt a new sense of purpose in her life. God had trusted her with a child. She loved her new little boy with a love she had never experienced. It was exhilarating just to watch him sleep.

A quiet strength came with this new role of motherhood. For the first time in her life, Margi felt defined by something good. It offered a promising path, and she felt motivated to rise up and make a difference.

Fleeting images and phrases from her nightmares attempted to steal her happiness, but Margi fought for control. She felt defined by a fierce desire to build her own family with love. This new definition was a stark contrast from nightmares that defined her as evil. Thoughts of passing that evil on to her children were alarming. She watched for signs as she watched her new little boy. *Are you going to float in the air? Is your face going to change into something evil? Are you going to suddenly start speaking?* As Margi poured herself into caring for her baby, those fears were quieted, but they always lurked in the shadows.

The bishop from church came to their apartment to give a blessing to the baby. The words were beautiful and filled Margi's soul with peace and hope for the future. The words spoke about a child growing up to be a happy, healthy adult. Margi's heart burst with joy at the revelation.

From that day on, Margi listened to her heart. She knew that she could love this child and give him a beautiful life. She promised God she would give it her all. Margi knew that God trusted her because He had given her this sweet gift. A gift He knew she needed.

Margi considered the thought that her greatest blessing would one day call her *Mom*.

Chapter 14

"Who wants to go again?" Margi said with a smile.

"I do! I do!" they squealed.

Three little kids all bundled up in snow pants and jackets were jumping up and down, determined to be the next lucky pick for another ride on the sled. The snowstorm had buried the yards and prevented cars from traveling on the streets—perfect for pulling her children on sleds along the snow-packed roads. Margi rotated the sled and positioned it right in front of three rosy-cheeked faces.

"I have an idea. Before we finish for the night, what if all three of you sit close for one final ride together? Adam, you sit first at the back, and then Megan and Emily can sit in front of you. Can you hold on tight to your sisters?"

Adam nodded enthusiastically. Nighttime sled rides were magical. After big storms, the houses and the trees were covered in white. The moon's reflection off the snow provided a natural nightlight for the evening ride. The air was cold and crisp, but there was always hot chocolate afterwards to warm them up.

Dennis's hard work at the theater had given them the opportunity to purchase their own home. They couldn't be happier. It was a start to raising their three adorable children.

Margi chuckled at the sight of three chocolate mustaches at the kitchen table. The mugs heated their little fingers, and the hot chocolate warmed their bellies as they sipped between the floating marshmallows. They giggled and retold silly stories about slipping on snow and how hard it was to chase each other in the frozen powder. Margi knew this was a family tradition they would repeat every winter.

"Okay my little snowflakes—you have school tomorrow. If you hurry and get into your warm pajamas, we'll have time to read bedtime stories."

Little feet raced down the hallway to their bedrooms. Margi loved snuggling with the children as they read stories each night. She had never been read to as a child but wanted that foundation for her own children. It was a tender connection with them she cherished every evening. Margi hoped story time would send them to sleep with sweet, happy dreams. The kind of dreams she never had as a child.

Or any other time.

. . .

Dennis rolled over and looked at the alarm clock. It was seven a.m. He swung his legs over the side of the bed and stood to start the day. The afternoon and evening hours as a projectionist and manager at the local movie theater made for difficult early mornings. The schedule was tough, but it allowed him to make enough money to support his little family. Every night when he came home late from work, he gently kissed each of his children as they slept soundly in their beds. Dennis still felt the need to make up for those evenings away at work, so mornings became a necessary priority.

Dennis walked down the hall and poked his head into the girls' bedroom. Margi was already cheering on their efforts and had their clothes laid out—a cute shirt with pants to match for each of them. Never skirts. Margi always said pants were safer for girls.

. . .

"Megan! Emily! Come on, girls! Let's line up in the bathroom. I'll comb your hair and we'll find a pretty bow for school today," said Margi. She could hear Dennis talking to Adam. It was a team effort to get the kids ready and out the door.

The kids sat around the kitchen table looking polished and ready for the day at school. Margi served some breakfast, and they chatted about upcoming events. Where had the time gone? When they were babies, Margi kissed their little chubby cheeks and told them she loved them a hundred times a day. Now they were growing so fast and already attending elementary school. Margi wanted their school mornings to be bright and cheerful. It was her greatest mission to provide happy mornings before school—nothing like the dismal mornings she remembered as a child during which her mother insisted on silence. She kissed each of the children again on their way out the door.

"I love you, sweetie," she gushed to each child.

Words she never heard growing up.

. . .

Sunday. It was Margi's favorite day of the week. It was the one day when she put cute dresses on her little girls and helped her son look his very best. There was so much to learn at church—for so many reasons.

The speaker at the pulpit spoke about forming a foundation. Margi's thoughts went to her childhood home and upbringing. That was certainly no foundation. The gentleman at the pulpit read a scripture:

> . . . remember, remember that it is upon the rock of our Redeemer, who is Christ, the Son of God, that ye must build your foundation; that when the devil shall send forth his mighty winds, yea, his shafts in the whirlwind, yea, when all his hail and his mighty storm shall beat upon you, it shall have no power over you to drag you down to the gulf of misery and endless wo, because of the rock upon which ye are built, which is a sure foundation, a foundation whereon if men build they cannot fall.[1]

Margi considered the foundation of Christ. It was a sure foundation. Margi's heart burned within her chest. This was the foundation she needed—a stark contrast to the cracked foundation from her childhood.

Margi loved learning more about God. She found great comfort in the stories, scriptures, and principles that were taught, and she hoped her children would grow up to feel the same. Margi believed that a deeper understanding of God would transfer to a deeper relationship with Him. Her prayers were heartfelt, and even when she couldn't immediately see the answers, she believed He heard them.

For a time, Margi and Dennis taught a children's class in Sunday school. She cherished the opportunity to make a difference in the lives of other children. Perhaps she could be a light to help these little ones look for God in their lives. It was a privilege to take what she knew in her heart and testify of that peace to these young, beautiful minds.

Church also filled another need for Margi. It gave her the opportunity to watch other families. She saw mothers interact with their children. She noticed the clothing and all the accessories. The communication and all the interaction that she observed in other families was educational and inspiring. Margi wanted to emulate everything. Families in the congregation became a real-life demonstration of how things could be in a household, something she never experienced or learned in her home while growing up.

Margi could hardly believe how blessed she was to have three treasured children. She worked hard at home to create a positive environment and felt immense gratitude for even the simplest household items. Everything contributed to the nest she called home. Appliances helped her make dinners that nourished her family. She was grateful for furniture, decorations, curtains, and everything else that provided comfort and beauty. When the children were at school, Margi spent hours in her gardens planting flowers along the walkway that welcomed both family and neighbors. Even with hands in the dirt and a smudge on her face, Margi never forgot to thank God for the beauty in her world.

Events such as piano lessons and soccer provided both fun and opportunities for her children to learn. Margi wanted to make sure those things were available for them. But Margi's focus was her home.

She wanted family and friends to enter her home and feel welcome. She wanted a cozy place that was warm and inviting. A place of peace.

And, most certainly, a place of safety.

Chapter 15

"Bring the kids over for dinner," Margi's mother ordered. "I haven't seen them in a while. See you Sunday."

The phone conversation was quick and to the point. Reen never expressed concern or asked how things were going or what might be happening in Margi's life. The purpose of all phone calls from Margi's mother was clear: it was never about a connection but was more of a demand.

Margi's stomach twisted as Dennis turned the corner and drove the last mile up the street to her parents' home. The children were poking at each other in the back seat and telling the latest knock-knock jokes. Margi wished she could feel just a sliver of their delight. It was always both a physical and emotional struggle just to walk into her parents' home. As soon as she walked through the door, a knot formed in Margi's gut that sucked her into a somber place. She had to constantly fight the desire to run out the door and away from the house. Her mind seemed to fracture into fleeting pieces of dark emotions that made it difficult to focus on the present.

But Margi kept going whenever they were invited in the hope that her children might have a better relationship with her parents. They enjoyed seeing their grandparents, and Margi sensed no hesitation on the part of her children. Clearly the flawed relationship with her parents must have been her fault. Margi knew that she should love her parents. Wasn't that expected? The confusion in her mind produced such guilt whenever she was around them.

"Hi, Reen," said Margi.

"There you are! I've been waiting for you." Reen's eyes were focused solely on the kids, and she gave each of them a friendly pat on the head. Reen laughed as she gathered the kids and made an effort to bring excitement to their union. Margi noticed the attention and the gesture and forced a smile in response.

Mother's eyes then left the kid's faces and focused directly on Margi.

"You hate it when I'm happy don't you?" Mother snarled. Her red lips smirked as she spit the accusation at her daughter. Margi hated the familiar expression that her mother had hurled at her many times. She felt shamed because it was partly true, and it hurt because Reen had never seen Margi's pain. Not as a child—and not now.

It was the usual grandparent routine. Margi's mother talked with the kids while finishing dinner. When all the food was ready and the table was set, Reen yelled for Margi's father to come up from the basement. He quietly came up the stairs, ate with the family, then quickly returned to the basement. He didn't seem to be interested in much interaction with the kids. That was okay with Margi; his mere presence at the dinner table made her queasy. She tried not to look too long at his face or mouth as he ate the food. *There's something so repulsive about his mouth.* Margi had to force herself to look away before "those feelings" returned. He was definitely a trigger. *Why do I always have this reaction to him?*

When the meal was over, Dennis and Margi gathered the kids and began to head out the front door.

"Margi, I almost forgot. I want to take the children shopping and buy them cute Easter outfits. Maybe tomorrow. I'll pick them up at your house after school," Reen stated.

"Okay, Reen. Guess I'll see you tomorrow."

Margi looked out the passenger window all the way home, trying to make sense of it all. The physical pat her mother gave each child on the head. The questions about school and friends. Shopping for Easter clothes. It made no sense. *Why didn't she do any of that with me?* Margi was happy that her children were cared about, but it reinforced that something must be wrong with *her*. Where was that attention and charming conversation and concern when she was little?

Like so many other things in Margi's life, it was puzzling.

. . .

I can do this. Please, God, help me stay whole.

Margi gave herself a final pep talk in the parking lot at the school where she came to volunteer in Megan's classroom. She had been there to volunteer a few times, but she always came home feeling discouraged. The other mothers were so confident and smart. Margi desperately wanted to help her children at school and be a part of their experience, but she knew she fell short.

Margi couldn't trust her mind. One minute she was helping a small group of children, and the next she was somewhere else. Occasionally Margi said something that sounded stupid and immature. Even as she heard herself say it, she wondered where it had come from.

Mrs. Johnson noticed Margi as she entered in the back of the classroom. Another parent stood in the back as well. Mrs. Johnson announced the assignment, and the children gathered their notebooks and pencils. The teacher walked toward the parent volunteers and smiled.

"Thank you so much for helping today," she said. "I want the kids to work on their math problems. They need to complete the equations and show all their work. If you could both help these last two tables, that would be great. I'll focus on the tables up front."

Margi's heart sank. Math? She felt ill equipped. It was difficult to stay present just long enough to hear the instructions from Mrs. Johnson. Margi immediately wondered if her expression showed the doubt she was feeling. There had been far too many missed days of math in Margi's early education. She quickly glanced at Megan, who was sitting at her desk. She didn't want to embarrass her daughter. Margi purposely avoided eye contact with the other parent volunteer, forcing a smile and walking over to one of the tables.

"I'm here to help if anybody needs it," she offered.

One little hand went up, and a sweet girl wearing a cute yellow dress looked up at Margi. The curls in the girl's hair were pulled back with a shiny pink headband.

"I don't understand this. Can you help me with the first one?" she asked.

Margi bent down and looked at the paper. Certainly, she could handle elementary school math. All at once Margi's mind took her to her grandmother's basement. *Oh, no—what am I doing here?* It was as clear as if she was standing in the basement. Margi quickly averted her eyes from the paper and scanned the walls of the classroom. *Here I go again. I can't let anybody see this.* Margi focused intently on the posters and the chalkboard. She fought to stay present and not let herself slip away.

"Can you help me?" the little girl asked again.

The boy in the next seat leaned over and pointed to his paper. He muttered something about adding the numbers together and pointed with his pencil. He told her it was easy.

"Okay—now I see. I think I can do it myself," she proudly exclaimed to Margi.

I'm a grownup! Act like one. What is wrong with me?

It was one thing to fight off images within the privacy of her home. It was quite another to fight the ability to stay present in public. Margi wondered what her face looked like when her mind took her to the basement. Surely others noticed. All she wanted to do was help her children and be a part of their schooling—be a good mom. Show them that she loved them and was interested in their lives.

But even that was becoming increasingly more difficult.

. . .

It was Halloween night, and Margi didn't know which was worse: walking with the children down neighborhood streets filled with ghosts, goblins, and witches, or opening her door at home to the costumed ghouls. Margi had hated Halloween for as long as she could remember. She never went trick-or-treating as a child. Her mother tried forcing her to participate with the neighborhood kids, but Margi hid in her bedroom and refused to go outside.

As an adult, Margi embraced the beauty of fall leaves in October and decorated her home with festive, orange pumpkins. It was a good attempt at distracting herself from the wicked side of Halloween. She and Dennis had even hosted a few fun Halloween parties, but Margi always worried about the evil that might join the festivities. She worked hard to separate herself. One Halloween was fine, and another Halloween had the power to take Margi into its world of witches and evil.

Somehow, deep inside, she recognized the darkest side of that holiday.

Chapter 16

"Mommy, I feel weird."

Megan stood next to the bed, shaking Margi's arm and trying to wake her from sleep. It was the middle of the night.

"I have a tummy ache," Megan whimpered.

Margi's heart immediately began pounding. She felt a panic rise in her chest. Margi quickly uttered a whispered prayer as she pulled back the covers to climb out of bed. *God, please don't let me go away. I need to stay whole to help Megan. Help me stay . . .*

There were certain phrases that immediately transported Margi to something really frightening from her childhood. Phrases such as *I feel weird* or *I feel funny* triggered memories of Margi as a child asking for help with her "weird" or "funny" feelings. When her children complained of health issues, Margi felt a conscious switch in her mind. In a split second, she felt childish and frightened and terrified of her own crying child. It was a strange sensation of going back in time. *Here I go—just like I did as a child.* At the same time, Margi also considered the crazed idea that someone had given a drug to her child. *What if they begin to go away like me?* It was a terrifying battle between past and present.

Please, God, help me. Margi battled for control and tenderly escorted her tired daughter into the kitchen. Margi needed to understand her daughter and whispered a barrage of questions.

"Sweetie, tell me why you feel weird. Where does it hurt? How long has your tummy had this feeling?"

Most often, a quick drink of water and a dose of medicine solved the predicament. On those occasions, Margi nudged the child back to bed and tucked the blankets under the child's chin. A kiss on the forehead and an extra hug was needed comfort for the children—and for Mommy. Despite her pounding heart, Margi was able to comfort her children when they needed her most. But it was never easy.

Common colds, flu bugs, and other childhood ailments regularly made the rounds from school classrooms to homes. But in her home, illness became a huge concern for Margi. Since the kids were babies, she had quietly waited and watched for signs. Margi couldn't tell anyone about her worst fears. She knew they were irrational, but they felt so real. She worried that someone had snuck drugs into their food. She feared that evil from her worst nightmares had found its way to her children.

She was terrified that her children would be just like her.

. . .

Adam's eyes were red and tired from another sleepless night. Boys sometimes find themselves embroiled in monster battles and chase scenes in their nightmares. The evidence of another bad night was visible on Adam's face at the breakfast table.

"Another bad dream, Buddy?" asked Dennis. He reached over and ruffled his son's hair. "I remember having a few bad dreams when I was your age too."

Margi's heart sank. *Please don't let him have my nightmares.* Margi poured a glass of milk and placed it in front of her son.

"Mommy, my stuffed coyote was flying around the room last night." Adam's eyes were wide as he shared the details. "I was awake, Mommy, and I saw it."

Margi steadied herself by gripping the counter. *This can't be normal. Something is in this house. Something is causing the coyote to move.*

Adam grabbed the glass and gulped the milk, seeming satisfied that he had reported all the pertinent events.

Margi looked over at Dennis. "Okay, that's really weird," she said to her husband. "Why would he say that?"

Dennis chuckled. "Oh, I don't know, Margi," he answered. "Just a kid having nightmares—that's all. Bad dreams are full of all kinds of impossible things. He's fine."

Margi wasn't convinced. Adam had claimed to be awake. This was the first she had heard about the coyote, but Adam had suffered a pattern of nightmares. When Margi was a child, such things were swept aside, never to be spoken of again. That was not going to be the case in this home. She decided to take Adam to the doctor so she could be sure that nothing serious was wrong.

Later that day, the doctor gave Adam a clean bill of health.

"It's common for children his age to have nightmares, or *night terrors* as we sometimes call them," explained the doctor. "It's nothing to worry too much about. He'll outgrow them."

Margi left the appointment both relieved and distraught. Medically speaking, everything looked okay. She didn't dare tell the doctor what she was really thinking. *The strange pieces of scary things that happened to me as a child are just beginning to happen to my son.* She couldn't say that out loud. Someone might haul her away to a hospital.

Those kinds of thoughts would be hers alone to hide.

. . .

Months went by, and Adam's nightmares became much less frequent, just as the doctor had predicted. The doctor said the nightmares were nothing to worry about. Margi tried to trust his professional opinion and ignore her own private anxiety.

As the kids got older, Margi noticed her own pattern. Days were busy and good. Margi had a mission to raise these little children; it was a reason to be alive. Her babies had filled a place in her heart and soul. For that she would be forever grateful, and she thanked God every morning for the opportunity to be a mother. Margi never imagined she could be so happy.

Nights, however, brought increasing fears to the surface. There was a stronger pull to disconnect. It wasn't a desire to disconnect from the children; instead, it was an odd separation from herself. A sense that she was mentally stepping aside. *What is wrong with me? Why am I not like other people?* Margi tried her best to hide lonely tears and seclude herself in her bedroom as soon as the children were preoccupied with something. Dennis worked late at night, so she battled alone. When the children saw her cry, she brushed it off as a sad moment and promised that everything would be okay.

During her worst nighttime fears, Margi never forgot words given in blessings to her children—promises of healthy, happy futures and the blessed gift of loving parents. God knew Margi was trying her hardest. She hoped He was proud of her efforts. Margi's children were her world. It was a calling and a beautiful responsibility. Margi knew she would love, value, and cherish her children forever.

Even with her broken mind.

Chapter 17

Margi shifted in the uncomfortable chair. The waiting room was decorated with a few green plants, and some colorful pictures hung on white walls. It was clearly an attempt by the hospital to bring some cheer to a place that everyone disliked.

It was her mother's birthday. Margi's parents had gone to a restaurant for dinner to celebrate when her father began having chest pains. Despite her father's protests, Mother had rushed him to the emergency room, and he was admitted to the hospital for further testing.

Earlier that evening, the family had gathered in the waiting room, but they were told that results from the tests would not be available for some time. Margi suggested they all return home to eat their dinner, promising to stay at the hospital and call them with any updates. Margi felt a need to stay close—a strange emotional pull to protect her father and keep him happy. It was an unexplainable calling she had felt for as long as she could remember.

Margi glanced at her watch. It was getting late. Dennis was at home with the children, and by this time, they were certainly all tucked in and sleeping. She smiled at the thought of their sweet faces.

Suddenly Margi jumped at the announcement—something about a code blue blared through the speaker above her head. Within a few seconds, a flurry of doctors and nurses raced through the area. She froze with fear as she watched them run down the hall toward her father's room. She sat on the edge of the chair, stared straight ahead, and waited. She strained to hear anything that might reveal what was happening.

After a short period of time, a pretty nurse walked over to Margi and sat down in the chair next to her. She reached up and put an arm around Margi.

"Margi, is it?" she asked.

"Yes."

"I'm so sorry, dear. Your father died. His heart stopped. We did everything we could to save him."

Margi sat motionless, still staring straight ahead. Once again, she was all alone. How many times had she felt alone, abandoned, and afraid? The irony was not lost on her.

"Are there any other family members here?" asked the nurse.

"No, I sent them all home. I told them nothing was going to happen."

"I'm sorry," continued the nurse. "Would you like to see your father?"

Margi shook her head. The thought of entering the room alone was too much.

"I need to use the phone," replied Margi. "I need to call my family."

The nurse motioned toward a phone on a small desk and stood close to Margi as she walked over and sat down. She called her sister Janet first.

The words tumbled out all at once. "Janet, Daddy just died. It was his heart. I'm here all alone at the hospital."

"Oh, no," cried Janet. "Honey, I'll be there in ten minutes."

Margi placed the phone back on the receiver. She felt a wave of sadness, and her eyes filled with tears. She picked up the phone and called her mother, her sister Barbara, and Dennis.

As Margi hung up the phone following the last call, Janet walked in and wrapped her arms around her younger sister.

"Oh, Margi," Janet sobbed. "I really did love him."

Both of Margi's older sisters had a distant relationship with their father. Over the years, Margi overheard a number of conversations between the two sisters. Barbara confessed on more than one occasion that she had a strained relationship with her father. But Janet often defended his strange disinterest in the family, declaring that he was still their father. Neither of the two girls understood their father's

86

silent demeanor or his emotional disconnect. They brushed it off as his typical odd behavior.

"Margi, we need to go say good-bye," Janet whispered. "Come on—let's go in together."

Janet and Margi held hands as they walked down the hall toward their father's hospital room. Margi paused at the door before glancing into the room, silently praying for courage. A deep sense of fear was creeping into all her senses. Margi could feel part of herself pulling away at the sight of her father in the bed.

Tears streamed down Janet's face as she approached the bed and grabbed her father's hand. She looked over at Margi and motioned for her to stand beside the bed. Margi slowly approached her father. She stopped beside him and lifted her eyes to his motionless face.

Hundreds of emotions grabbed at Margi's soul. They were violent, frightening, and caring all in the same perplexing moment. Margi wanted to turn and run, but she willed her feet to stay planted next to her father. With her heart pounding and with all the strength she could muster from so many conflicting sensations, Margi slowly leaned over and kissed her father on the forehead. A tear rolled down her cheek and fell onto her father's head. She moved her lips toward her father's ear.

"Good-bye, Daddy," she whispered.

. . .

The next morning, Margi drove to her mother's house. Margi wanted to be strong for her mother—help her through this difficult time. Margi pushed open the front door and walked into the family room.

Her father's plaid jacket was still draped on a chair. Margi's stomach dropped; the sight of the jacket startled her. It could have opened a floodgate of tears, but Margi didn't respond. She felt a bit of sadness, but mostly she just felt numb.

Margi's eyes scanned the room as she called out for her mother. She caught sight of her mother's birthday cake still sitting on the kitchen table—a beautifully decorated, untouched cake, a visual reminder that her father had died on her mother's birthday.

"Reen, are you home?" Margi asked.

She heard her mother yell out from the bedroom. Margi walked back and into her mother's room, where she found her mother rummaging through some paperwork.

"Hi, Reen. I just wanted to see how you're doing today. How can I help you?"

"There's so much to do," snarled her mother. "I'm left with a mess of paperwork."

"I'm here to help."

Her mother blew out a huff of disgust. She looked up at Margi, glaring at the intrusion. Reen murmured something under her breath and turned her attention back to the papers in front of her.

Margi had come to the house wanting to serve and comfort her mother. just She shook her head at the ambitious thought. *I thought that helping my mother through this period of mourning might open up a new connection between us. But not today.*

Margi decided she would keep showing up, keep opening her heart and offering comfort. Perhaps it was just going to take time. She would try again tomorrow.

Margi just wanted to matter.

. . .

Margi compared the account numbers again. It was a different account number. Another loan! Margi was going through some earlier bank statements to better understand her father's financial situation when she found records of multiple payments. Her father had taken out many different loans from the bank and had even filed bankruptcy. Margi was shocked. Her parents rented their home; what was the loaned money being used for?

Over the months following her father's death, Margi learned that several acquaintances had loaned money to Margi's father and had never been paid back. It seemed he had borrowed from anybody who would listen and that he had spent every cent. Where did all that money go? Like everything else about her father, it was a mystery.

Margi looked for ways to pull her mother into the family for years following her father's death. But that compassionate gesture was a challenge. Her mother's critical tongue was now lashing out at Margi's children. As the children transitioned from children to teenagers, Reen boldly voiced expectations for each of her grandchildren. If they didn't fit a particular image, she used cutting remarks to let them know. If someone was too fat or not pretty enough, she called it out. The children had heard their grandmother's harsh judgment of others when they were little. Now that they were growing up, that harsh tongue turned on them.

Reen's raised voice and insulting comments continued to trigger Margi. Whether her verbal criticism was aimed at Margi or her children, the trigger was the same. Margi suddenly felt naked from the waist down, especially if Margi's back was to her mother. It was a markedly vulnerable and defenseless reaction, one that Margi had felt for as long as she could remember. It made no sense, but it felt very real. Every time it happened, Margi had to leave the room quickly and force a present reality to the surface to dismiss the sensation. She would not speak of it to anyone. Margi could imagine what they might think of it.

Visits to her parents' home increased in the years after her father's death.

As her mother aged, Margi invited Reen over for Sunday dinners.

When each dinner ended, Margi called out, "Okay, time to take Grandma home. Who's going with me?"

Dennis and the children just assumed it was a package deal; anybody who was able came along for the ride when Margi drove her mother home. What they didn't know was the trepidation in Margi's heart every time her car pulled into the driveway. One step into the house to make sure her mother was safely delivered and settled triggered a warped sense of time and space. Margi felt the sensation of walls shrinking and closing in on her, as if she was too big for the room. Faces were suddenly unfamiliar. She knew the faces yet wondered how she was connected to them. It was all a strange shift in time. At her mother's house, Margi had to focus hard on Dennis or her children to help bring herself back to the present.

Dennis could see the effect that Reen had on Margi and noticed the criticism and the tension that Reen directed at the family. "Why are you spending so much effort on your mother, Margi?" Dennis asked. "She was never there for you. You don't owe her anything."

But Margi felt a compulsion to try to make her mother happy. The bond between them was strained and unusual, compounding the thought that Margi often felt completely removed from her mother. This relationship was completely different from the mother-daughter relationships she heard others talk about at church. Women there talked of mothers teaching daughters how to bake perfect cookies, of families gathering for picnics and scripture study, and of fishing trips to the lake.

One Sunday night at the dinner table, one of the children announced that the neighbors down the street had just welcomed a new baby. Margi chimed in with her own stories of when the children were born. The children had heard these stories many times but never tired of hearing them again. Margi then turned to her mother and asked a pointed question.

"Did you give birth to me? Because I've never heard you talk about it."

"Yeah, I sure did."

"Really?" Margi said. "Because I don't feel that. I feel like I was just made."

"Oh, don't be silly," Reen snapped. "I'm sure of it."

What appeared to be a ludicrous question was heartfelt. Margi felt the weight of her own words even though no one else seemed to understand that she was serious. As absurd as the idea seemed to everyone else at the table, it felt very real to her. *How does any child feel so detached from her own mother?* Margi was sure it was all her fault.

And she would spend her life trying to make up for it.

Chapter 18

It was an incredible break: A friend who worked in television called Dennis and offered him a job at the station. Dennis had dreamed of a career in broadcasting since high school, and this opportunity not only gave him a foot in the door, but a chance to take a new direction. The job offered better income and the potential for career growth, both of which fueled Dennis's strong desire to provide a comfortable living for his wife and children.

Dennis considered the small miracle that launched this new journey. It was no coincidence; Dennis knew God's hand was surely involved. The friend had called him out of the blue knowing that Dennis didn't have much experience. The timing was perfect. He was eager and ready to learn more about the cameras, the writing, and the production value in the television world. Dennis was certain that God knew the desires of his heart.

Stories and events throughout the United States needed to be covered, so some travel was going to be a necessary part of the job. Dennis tried to convince Margi to travel with him to some of the locations.

"Come with me, Margi," Dennis often pleaded. "The station is already covering my hotel expenses. We'll buy you an airplane ticket and travel together. It's just a couple of days."

But Margi always refused, explaining, "I think deep inside I am really adventurous, and I would love to travel and experience all the things that make life fun. I want to go with you, but I just can't. To be in a new place—my mind isn't going to understand. I know it doesn't make sense, but it just doesn't feel safe."

. . .

Margi knew that Dennis couldn't possibly understand—not because of some failing of his, but because there were no words to communicate her irrational fears. It always boiled down to her broken mind. She couldn't trust that it wouldn't take her away to those dark, confusing places when time disappeared. In new surroundings, Margi wouldn't know where to run when time disappeared, and she wouldn't be able to focus on the familiar environment of her own home to bring her back to the present.

Just thinking about the travel opportunity made her heart pound. The dread of leaving her home for any reason was increasing over time, and she recognized the paradox. Margi's home was a place of security and safety, but it was also a prison.

. . .

"Don't worry about it, Margi," Dennis replied. "I'll go on my own. I'll only be gone a few days. There will be more trips. Maybe another time . . ."

Dennis shook his head as he left the room. There was always an excuse. It sounded so absurd to him, but he knew that it was very real for Margi. Dennis kept asking—maybe Margi would eventually find the courage to travel.

Over the years, there would be short work trips to various destinations in Utah. He traveled to the Native American reservation at Christmas bearing gifts for the children. In the beginning, Dennis brought his son, Adam, along, then started bringing the girls as well. He wanted the kids to see his work, but he also wanted them to get a glimpse of poverty on the reservation, a dose of reality he knew would give them a real education and perspective. Stories and events happened in Moab, Bluff, and Monument Valley.

Dennis took advantage of as many opportunities as he could to take his kids with him. Doing so gave Dennis some company on the road and allowed for time with each of the kids. He felt it helped make up for so many nights spent away from home in his previous job at the theater.

Dennis loved his three children. He wasn't a perfect father—there had been no example of that in his childhood home—but time spent with them on trips and the living example of hard work was his way of teaching and loving. They were growing up fast. Time was slipping through his fingers, and Dennis often counted the remaining years they would likely be living under his roof. Time with them was a treasure.

On one trip, the Christmas music pouring out of the car radio was festive and joyful; Dennis and his daughter Emily sang along to the tunes as they drove south toward a large holiday giveaway event he was filming for the television station. These stories always pulled at his heartstrings, and he was excited for Emily to see for herself that there were families who really struggled—especially during the holidays.

Dennis had hoped that Margi would come along on this trip. After all, it was centered around the holidays and Christmas. What could be more positive and happier than that?

But Margi explained that the holidays were troubling, and she would take a rain check.

"Maybe next time," she promised.

.   .   .

Margi hoped there really would be a time that she would feel brave enough to go with Dennis. But she knew it wouldn't happen during the holidays.

Her dread always began in October. Margi knew it was the first of October without ever looking at a calendar; something deep inside confirmed the season had arrived. She remembered hating Halloween as a child; the whole event was frightening, and that eerie feeling was still with her as an adult. Images of witches, black-hooded clothing, and evil still flashed through her mind. Orange and yellow tree branches reached down to cover houses; the sight of the branches draping over the homes made Margi feel trapped in a wicked world where she was unable to go home. During the daytime, the sun headed south, and shadows always seemed to shift. That always signaled that something scary was about to happen. In the evenings, the moon and lights from house windows illuminated the colors and triggered strange flashes of haunting October events.

November was always a great relief, and Margi embraced the opportunity to thank God for all her blessings. She had food on the table every night and a beautiful family gathered close for dinner. She was grateful for Dennis and her three beautiful children, and she considered what her life would be without them. Margi recognized God in all her gratitude. She believed He heard her prayers, and she was thankful for the understanding that she could pray to Him whenever necessary.

Though it was an opportunity to feel such gratitude, the month of November always led to December. Margi couldn't understand her disconnect from everyone else's holiday spirit. She heard the festive music and loved Christmas decorations, trying to focus on the red and green colors and all the glitter and bows that went with the holiday. She understood and believed in the beautiful story of the birth of the Savior. But despite all the decor and the spiritual significance, December always ushered in snowy days. Those were the hardest. For as long as she could remember, snowy days had made her feel cornered, ambushed, and trapped. In December, Margi lost a sense of time more than in any other month.

As an adult, Margi gave the appearance of celebrating all the holiday festivities—but it was a façade. As a child, Margi prayed to die during the Christmas season. During that time, Christmas vacation days as a child meant more time at home. Now, on the inside, the holiday was something very different from what it looked like on the outside.

On the inside, it was a living hell.

Chapter 19

Margi sat quietly in the soft, blue chair. The warm rays of sunshine filtered into the room through the window. *I can do better today.* Margi's scriptures lay open in her lap, and she tried to find strength from her study that morning:

". . . have patience, and bear with those afflictions, with a firm hope that ye shall one day rest from all your afflictions."[1]

Patience. Hope. All your afflictions . . . She wondered if the prophets who wrote those words even partially understood her suffering. Were the promises she was reading about true and applicable for her? Margi hoped so.

Her gaze left the pages in her lap and focused on the world outside her window. The neighbor across the street was mowing his lawn. Two people rode by on their bikes. *They're in the real world, and I'm not. I see the world, but I'm not part of it.*

Margi's disconnect from reality was happening more frequently. The strength of its ability to take her away was alarming. As a child, Margi was sadly familiar with losing herself for periods of time when fears closed in, but she should surely have gotten over this by now. She questioned the time every single day, and the space around her didn't fit with time. *Have I been here too long? Am I in the right time?* Margi doubted there was anybody else in the world who was exactly like her.

It became necessary to look out the window and watch the position of the sun. *Does it match the time?* Margi often doubted what day of the week it was and needed to repeat it to herself over and over throughout the day. *Today is Tuesday . . . today is Tuesday. Is it still the same day?* It felt necessary to confirm her own reality.

Margi's fears made no sense. She had never heard another adult speak of anything that even slightly resembled what went on in her crazy world. Rooms changed size and shape. People did too. Dennis could be walking through a room, and suddenly he became way too small. It was risky to look into her children's eyes too long; doing so caused a gradual change in her perception of their faces and their voices until they became unfamiliar. She recognized them as family, but in her worst moments Margi wasn't even sure how they were connected to her. She was stepping away from one world into another.

Days were filled with anxiety as Margi tried to avoid anything that could be a trigger that took her to another dimension. Unfortunately, everything was a trigger. They were everywhere—unavoidable. Lyrics to songs on the radio. The color of the sky. Certain clothing. The change of seasons. Nothing was safe.

Margi even hated her own body. She felt a separation from herself and longed to be unattached. Her body had betrayed her along with her mind. Any physical ailment like nausea or a headache was enough to make Margi feel more attached to a body that she didn't want and often didn't recognize.

An old friend had recently called and shared her story about a hard childhood with a father who was a frightening drunk. As she listened, Margi tried to understand her friend's struggle. She heard the pained voice, and Margi's heart ached for her friend's trial. She nodded and listened while wishing her own story was something she could share with others. Her trials seemed to come from another place, and she knew nobody could ever understand. *Do you know what it's like to not be in the world with everyone else? Do you know what it's like to have your house shrink every night, holding you prisoner? Some days you don't even know whose body you're in.*

Margi closed the scriptures on her lap and silently prayed that the light and truth found in the pages would sustain her for the day. Margi believed the words in the scriptures and found comfort and promise for the future in them, but she also knew other dark truths that consumed her mind. She knew the dark truth that horrible things happen all the time and they can't be prevented. The dark truth that at any moment, she could be annihilated by one of those horrible things. And the dark truth that if she survived, it would only be to wait for the next horrible thing that would inevitably occur.

Light versus dark. Two truths at war with one another every single day.

. . .

It was the dreaded hour. Margi had felt it approaching—the hour hand creeping forward, ready to announce that it was time to enter a new world. A world of horror. The hands on the clock read nine o'clock.

Margi knew what time it was without even looking at the clock. She *felt* it approaching. This was the hour every night that unseen, eerie forces consumed Margi in her bedroom. She seemed obligated to lie in her bed and somehow blend with a frightened little girl. Margi knew she would have to go live in that little girl's world for the rest of the night. Margi busied herself around the house, finding reasons not to wind down for bedtime, but still it happened every night. All Margi's fears—all the dark, gruesome images—had intensified since the death of her father. *How are the two connected?*

Margi loved her home, which she had created into a beautiful, cozy space. It was a calming environment—all except for her bedroom. When the intensity of her nightmares started increasing, she bought new sheets. She bought new comforters. Perhaps they were giving her the nightmares. She had to find a reason. But there was always the sad realization: *No matter what I do, my bedroom is never going to be my friend.*

Margi tried pretty, new, ruffled pillowcases. Surely they would cradle her head and bring happy thoughts during slumber. But on most mornings, she found the sheets ripped off after a torrid night of violent visions.

Margi wished she didn't have to sleep at all. She never took a nap during the day. Why invite the dreaded dreams to stalk her during the day?

Eventually, Margi tired late each night and surrendered to bedtime. Laying down in her bed at night was the most frightening part of her existence. She immediately felt a floating sensation coupled with fear. Her body was not her own. Someone else seemed to have it, and she didn't know what or who it was. She felt soulless, scared, and alone. Her mind raced with panic. *Where do I have to go tonight? I just want to stay here with my husband and children. Please don't take me away.*

Margi didn't just dream about wicked people raping and torturing and chasing her; those images were visceral. Wildly real. And she was part of them.

In her nightmares, Margi was always taken somewhere. She often found herself in her grandmother's basement. Three evil bedroom doors waited to be opened, and Margi was dragged to the other side. The evil in those rooms consumed her insides. Men and women who initially appeared to be good people turned into frightening monsters trying to have sex with her. So many men manipulated her body, doing awful things to her.

Each time she awakened from a nightmare, Margi could still feel bodies on top of her. Could still see their faces. Could still feel them touching her and still smell their hot breath on her face. The nightmare was over, but the grisly sensations lingered.

Nightmares often took her to other basements where torture consisted of spinning. Spinning dental chairs. Spinning tables. Spinning upside down and hanging, her feet wrapped with rope. All the spinning came with the same sensation—a completely terrifying inability to stop. Men dressed in black stood in circles and watched. These ritual dreams also included blood from tortured animals, triangles and other markings, and people chanting scriptures or other strange phrases.

Margi hated her brain. Why would she dream such vulgar things? She had never seen anything remotely like it on television, and she had never read anything about it. *I must be evil. Why else would my brain conjure up such evil, dark things?* She couldn't tell anybody. If they knew, they would call her crazy.

Increasingly more often, tears stained her pillow; her moans and cries for help were becoming routine. Dennis tried to comfort her, but Margi brushed each one off as just another one of her bad dreams. Sometimes when Dennis leaned over to wake her from a nightmare, Margi didn't even recognize his face. Her broken mind failed to separate the dream from reality.

Sometimes she fell back to sleep only to return to the horror. Sometimes she lay awake until morning, trying to shake the fear and lingering emotions that continued to plague her. And sometimes she fell to her knees, pleading with God and angels to deliver her from this perdition.

Please, God, help me.

PART THREE

BRAVERY IS BEING THE ONLY ONE WHO KNOWS YOU'RE AFRAID.

Chapter 20

"What's wrong, Mom?"

Adam stood at her bedroom door. Margi had consistently tried to hide in her bedroom when things started to unravel, but the kids were getting older, and it was getting more difficult to keep her emotions from them.

"Nothing is wrong, honey." Margi quickly wiped her tears with the back of her hand, trying to hide the evidence. Attempting to divert Adam's attention from her tears, she asked, "Is your homework done?"

"We didn't have any today," Adam stated with a grin.

Margi wondered if she had ever done homework as a child. She couldn't remember doing any, but that might be just another lost detail in the vault of unknown childhood years.

"Well, let's get some dinner going," Margi said. "I'll bet you're hungry."

The children were growing up fast. Middle school opened the door to more friends, more school decisions, and a few trials and problems that come with the preteen years. Margi could feel herself pulling inward. When the children were little, it seemed easy to be a nurturing mom; she loved them, and during those years she felt needed every day. Now that her children were older, Margi felt like she needed to be a grownup. She felt inadequate, uneducated, and lost.

As the children started focusing their attention outside the home, Margi lost her sense of purpose there. A sense of worthlessness combined with increasing fears and nightmares caused Margi to hide in her bedroom increasingly more often. She always had an excuse for the tears, but she tried not to offer much explanation. *I need to keep this to myself. Nobody wants to hear me complain.*

. . .

The children noticed a change in Margi. Adam loved to have friends over to play loud music and watch movies. Margi loved the houseful of people most of the time, but on certain days she sent everybody to the basement, telling them to turn off the music.

Adam noticed that his mom spent more and more time in her bedroom, and he could tell by her eyes that she was crying a lot. She seemed to enjoy his friends and often joined in on their conversations as they joked and laughed about the day's events at school. Then suddenly she disappeared, and he knew she was hiding. Nobody talked about her worries; it seemed some things were better left unsaid.

Megan noticed the crying as well and wondered what she had done to contribute to her mother's sadness. Perhaps she just wasn't good enough. Maybe she was a failure, and her mother knew it. Megan determined that was probably the reason for her mother's tears and why she sometimes isolated herself. When she was little, Megan loved how absorbed her mother was in her life. Now that Megan was a teenager, her mother was physically there but emotionally absent. Megan started looking for attention from her friends at school.

Emily formed close relationships with her teachers. She latched onto female teachers and other mother figures who paid special attention and cared about her. Emily knew her mother loved her, and her mother said it often. But there was something different about the praise and affection her teachers gave Emily. They smiled and listened to her with undivided attention as Emily discussed stories from books or the latest hot musical group. Emily needed "happy," and she found a healthy dose of it with caring teachers.

. . .

On vulnerable days, Margi sometimes hinted to her children that her struggles were real and frightening. She mentioned that nightmares were difficult for her and that her own parents had not been the supportive, loving parents she had hoped for. But she kept the confusing glimpses of ugly scenes from all her family members; nobody wanted to hear those kinds of things. She felt it would just frighten her children and push them away.

Margi knew she had great kids. They were talented and smart, and they all had healthy minds—not her crazy mind. She felt so blessed, but she also knew that her children were struggling. Margi knew she was slipping and was not as emotionally present as a good mother would be. Certainly, God had made a mistake with her, but she would continue to pray for guidance in this new chapter of raising teenagers.

Margi thanked God each day for the honor of raising children— even in her broken state. Those children were her world.

. . .

"See you in a few days," Dennis said, smiling at Margi before walking out the door. He had tried to convince Margi to come with him on this business trip—as he always did—but she offered all the same excuses. Perhaps this was better anyway. They both needed a few days away from each other. A few days to just breathe.

Dennis backed the car out of the driveway. He paused in front of the house with his foot firmly on the brake. Dennis noticed the meticulous work Margi had put into the flowers along the front walkway. There was even a beautiful wreath hanging on the front door. It all gave the appearance of a lovely home filled with joy and happiness, but that perfect picture was deceptive.

Dennis had loved Margi since that day in class when he first laid eyes on her. God knew he loved her now. But their relationship was being tested in ways he didn't understand. There were mixed signals. Margi was pulling away, and his marriage felt emotionless. She didn't know how to communicate what was bothering her, and he didn't know how to fix it. The two of them were roaming around in the same house like roommates.

Dennis took his foot off the brake and eased forward. He would leave his troubles behind. He just needed this time to get away. Clear his head. He looked forward to working and focusing on this new project out of town. It would keep his mind occupied.

. . .

Margi watched through the front window as Dennis's car stopped then pulled away. She felt relief merged with sorrow as he disappeared down the street, and she recognized the conflict of both emotions. How could she tell her husband that sometimes it was hard to really see him? That if she looked too long, her perception of his features changed and appeared familiar, but not in her present reality? At those times, she detached from him and he became a stranger. It made no sense, but it terrified her when it happened. So, she avoided looking too long into his eyes. Margi wondered if he noticed.

Everyone's patience seemed stretched. Margi wanted to be rescued but couldn't communicate what was happening—not if she wanted to appear the least bit sane. She knew Dennis didn't have the tools to fix whatever was happening to her. They were two people loving each other, yet two people not understanding each other.

And two people silently suffering alone.

Chapter 21

Margi, you can do this!

Every morning Margi gave herself a pep talk of sorts, something she needed to force herself out the door and to work. Getting a part-time job had been a big step, but Margi knew it was time to push outside the comfort zone of hiding in her home. She always felt there was a part of her brain that was smart; it just got scrambled by so many distracting thoughts. She was determined to stay focused and succeed at this new job.

Margi had been hired at an oral surgery office to greet customers, handle insurance billing, and answer phones. A team of people staffed the office, and Margi was proud to be part of that team.

That morning, the front door opened, and a patient walked up to the desk. *Please stay whole. Please stay whole.* Margi forced herself to stay present and remember her training. She bravely looked up at the approaching client.

"I'm here for my 11:00 appointment," the woman said.

"Okay, here's some paperwork for you to fill out. Please have a seat, and someone will be right with you," Margi replied.

This client encounter was a success. Margi smiled and felt a wave of satisfaction. There would be future difficult moments at work when faces became fuzzy and voices suddenly changed. But experience from so many situations in her early years taught Margi what to do. Cover. Fake it. From a very young age, Margi learned to pretend. When she felt herself slipping away, some other part of her always came forward to help. Sometimes Margi felt very young. Childish. Sometimes nonsensical words fell out of her mouth.

Margi wondered if people noticed. She wondered what her face looked like during those times. Wondered if it changed. Wondered and worried.

In order to track time, Margi checked the clock multiple times a day. She often looked out the window to make sure the time on the clock matched the position of the sun in the sky. There was always the underlying panic that she had been there far too long—the ongoing fear that her mind might take her to other places.

. . .

Margi pulled into the empty parking lot and climbed out of her car. It was Wednesday. The office was always closed on Wednesdays for patient visits, but Margi worked alone in the office answering phones and working on billing. It took extra strength for her to endure those quiet Wednesdays. They were exceptionally hard because she felt alone, isolated, and vulnerable. She worried that evil lurking in the night might now be waiting for her.

Margi opened the door with her keys and let herself into the dark office. Her hand trembled as she searched the wall for the light switch. Her eyes scanned the rooms to make sure everything was still in place. Nothing appeared disturbed. She checked the time on the wall clock and assured herself everything was safe. There was work to do.

Locking up the office on Wednesdays was the worst. Margi had believed as a child that bad things come out at night, and she still feared it as an adult. Whatever evil might find its way into the office at night would be free to wander throughout. It could reach its dirty little fingers into anything.

Margi checked the time. Her shift was ending. She noticed a couple of the smaller plants in the office. They were defenseless against what might happen at night. Believing they would appreciate her help, she slid them behind some bigger, stronger plants.

Margi returned to her desk and looked at the pencils in the holder.

This is so crazy. This is not normal, but I have to do this. Margi swiftly moved her favorite pencils—the ones she had used all day—and placed them behind the bigger pencils. The bigger pencils would hide and protect the smaller ones.

Margi put herself into the pencils. She felt what they might be feeling—afraid. When she was little, she hid her dolls. In her childhood, she had no power to escape her dark world, but she could save something else. *I can't save me, but I can save my dolls.* That comforting thought continued now as an adult. She could save the pencils.

Margi fought the notion to move some of the innocent items in the office before locking up at night. They would be grateful to her for protecting them against evil. She tried to rationalize such crazy thoughts, but the actions made her feel good. She was making a small difference.

Nobody had ever protected *her* from the dark.

. . .

"Margi, they need your help in room three," the office manager ordered. "The little girl in that room is frightened. Can you assist while they administer the medication?"

Voicing her agreement, Margi entered the room and smiled at the girl. Her eyes were wide, and she looked frightened. Margi nodded her head in support as she patted the young girl on the hand.

The anesthesiologist administered the sedation drug necessary before oral surgery. "Just relax now," he said in a soothing voice. "You're going to get sleepy, and you might feel strange for a minute."

Margi's heart raced. They were the worst words anyone could say, because she had heard those words so many times in early years. As a child, one thing was certain. *Bad things happen when I go away.* It took everything in her power to keep her feet planted on the floor and not run out of the room. Margi took a silent, deep breath and squeezed the patient's hand. It was a token of comfort for the patient—and for Margi.

This was a standard procedure. Margi knew and trusted these

doctors. Over time, helping with patients was getting easier for Margi. The first few times she had to fight hard to stay present. Her mind assaulted all her senses, and Margi felt as though she was the little girl in the chair. But Margi worked hard to stay the course. She had learned to do hard things.

And Margi learned long ago to fight through fear.

. . .

"Margi? Is that you?" Jennifer asked.

So many years had gone by since the two girls had galloped their imaginary horses through the fields behind Margi's house. Both had married and lived in separate states and were busy raising their own children. They saw each other at occasional family events over the years and cherished the reunions. Recently, however, Margi and Jennifer had been catching up on lost details and spoke often on the phone.

"Margi, tell me what's wrong," Jennifer said. She could hear Margi sobbing on the other end of the line. Jennifer's heart sank as she gripped the phone tightly. With only five years between the two, they felt more like sisters than aunt and niece. Margi had begun to open up about some of her struggles and seemed comfortable confiding in Jennifer.

"I can't take it anymore, Jennifer," Margi cried. "I can't take this pain. I can't take this fear anymore!"

Jennifer had heard this before, but tonight Margi's words were cutting. They seemed dangerously desperate. The voice sounded like Margi but slightly different. The tone of her voice was slightly off, and the despair was deep and troubling. Jennifer silently prayed that she could somehow help.

Margi had revealed many of her fears to Jennifer over the last couple of years—the time and space dimensions, the flashes of horror, the unreasonable fears, the family struggles, and the graphic nightmares. Sometimes Margi spoke of eerie glimpses from her childhood. Jennifer knew there was definitely something wrong, but didn't know how to solve the puzzle. It was just so big and complex.

Jennifer knew she could help Margi by listening; after all, the poor girl had been abandoned by everyone as a child. "Just share what's in your mind, Margi," Jennifer offered. "Let me be your sounding board. Tell me about your nightmares so you won't have to keep thinking about them."

It was a combination of carefully calming Margi's fears and letting her talk. Jennifer wasn't a trained therapist, but her instincts kicked in and she found a way to support. To just listen.

After Margi's daring attempt to find words to match the details in her latest nightmares, Jennifer heard Margi relax a bit. The release of details seemed to be helping. Jennifer had never heard such wicked ugliness in her entire life.

"Margi, I think you should start writing down your dreams," Jennifer gently suggested. "Someday, someone is going to come along and be able to understand all of this. Dreams can reveal all kinds of things that maybe your awake mind is afraid to look at. When you write to yourself, you can just listen to your own thoughts and let them flow onto the paper. You don't have to worry about any judgment. Maybe we can find a therapist later who can discover some surprising truths from your dreams."

Margi seemed to consider the idea. "It's so awful, Jennifer," Margi said. "I don't even know if I can write such terrible words, but I'll try. I can try."

Margi expressed gratitude to Jennifer, explaining that the fears were still there, but she wasn't completely alone in facing them. Margi could spill all the ugliness to Jennifer that she could not say out loud to Dennis or the children, and she knew it was helping.

"Jennifer, you know what my favorite song is? *I Can See Clearly Now.* I want to clearly see both forward and backward. I want to see memories from my childhood that frighten me. Right now, it's all such a blank slate. If I could clearly see them, maybe my mind would heal."

Jennifer agreed. "We'll figure this out together, Margi."

Jennifer reflected on Margi's dreams, flashbacks, and fears.

Something had happened to her beautiful aunt as a child. Nobody could make this stuff up. Someone had damaged Margi's soul. Someone had made her feel helpless. Someone had taken away all her hope.

"You know you don't have to do this, Jennifer," Margi whispered.

"I know," Jennifer responded. "I want to, Margi. No matter what it looks like and no matter what it takes."

Jennifer hung up the phone and fell to her knees. *Please, Heavenly Father, help Margi find peace. Bless me to know how to help her.*

The words were tender and sincere. Jennifer's heart ached, and she wiped the tears that were flowing down her cheeks. She had loved Margi since they were both little, and she felt a strong desire to see this through. Jennifer was in this to the end. Margi must never feel completely alone again.

Jennifer felt helping Margi was a calling from God, and she was honored to fill it.

Chapter 22

"Margi, let's talk more about your childhood." The therapist straightened up in her seat and looked directly at Margi, who was squirming in her seat. Margi was uncomfortable and couldn't make eye contact with the therapist.

"It's clear to me, Margi, that you were sexually abused as a child. All the symptoms you've described point directly to childhood trauma."

Margi fought the urge to run. *Childhood trauma.* She had heard that phrase from several therapists, and they all wanted to talk about abuse. Margi was afraid of what they were saying. She knew the next few questions would lead to a conversation about her father and mother. She vowed that was not going to happen.

"There was no trauma," Margi answered. "I grew up just like everybody else with a mother and a father. There's really nothing to talk about. I just want my brain to stay focused and present. I want the nightmares to stop." Margi nervously started tapping the floor with her foot.

The therapist held her hand up in a fist to represent the trauma and looked directly at Margi. Margi looked at the fist in front of her.

"Margi, you never go through it. You only go around it, above it, and below it. You can't heal until you go *through* it."

Margi left the office and never went back.

. . .

"Janet, every therapist I see tries to tell me I've been sexually abused." Margi had stopped by her sister's house to get her opinion. Margi knew that she was always welcome in Janet's home, and she cherished that relationship. Maybe her sister could help.

"Gosh, I hope it wasn't Dad," Janet responded.

Margi was puzzled by the quick assumption. Part of her wanted to explore her sister's assumption, but another part vehemently needed to defend her father. It was such a strange conflict of emotions.

Her older sister Barbara had always brushed off the topic of abuse when Margi asked and then suggested she read good books—something to get her mind on happier things. Barbara had never bonded with her father, and she told Margi she was disappointed in him because he had never filled the role of father for her. During childhood years, Barbara found an escape from home in friendships and ballet.

Margi left her sister's home discouraged and knew she needed to keep searching for help. Both sisters were well-meaning, but neither understood the depth of her issues. Even Margi didn't have adequate words to help them understand. There had to be someone who could offer a solution, although she was starting to feel like she was the only one in the world with a broken mind.

. . .

"Margi, you're going to be okay," the therapist said. "Just focus for a few minutes on my finger."

The therapist lowered his voice and attempted to put Margi at ease. The lowered voice? Talk of hypnotism? Margi had been in this position before. She wasn't sure when or how, but some part of her knew he would trick her. Margi couldn't trust him.

Margi grabbed her purse and ran out the door. That visit turned out to be one of the shortest. She returned home and put a large X next to his name. She would try the next one on the list.

. . .

"I've heard it all, Jennifer," Margi cried. "Every psychiatrist has a different pill and a different diagnosis. I've heard bipolar disorder, anxiety, schizophrenia, and borderline personality disorder. But when I research those things online, none of the symptoms fit me. The doctors aren't figuring this out, and I'm tired of trying all the different medications. They don't do anything for me."

Jennifer listened. She seemed to respect Margi's commitment to keep trying—to find the correct diagnosis and refuse to accept anything that didn't feel right.

"Margi, you did the right thing by trying the medications and some of the therapy, but I really don't think you have a sick mind," Jennifer replied. "I think you have a healthy mind and body that is responding to traumatic events you cannot remember. A pill doesn't help you process the abuse and abandonment we suspect you had as a child. We've talked about the details in your nightmares. Your nightmares and vague memories are strong clues."

Margi listened closely to her wise niece. The words made sense.

"Maybe your beautiful mind is protecting you from your past," Jennifer suggested.

Margi's eyes filled with tears. She had never thought of her mind as beautiful. It was always evil, freakish, fragmented, and crazy. Maybe even broken.

But could it be beautifully broken?

"I love you, sweet Jennifer," Margi said. "I have a referral for a new therapist that I'll call tomorrow.

"We're in this together, Margi."

.   .   .

"Margi, have you ever heard the term *ritual abuse*?" Dr. Brady asked.

Margi was confused and shook her head. Here was that term again: *abuse*. Only this time it was attached to *ritual*.

"Over the past several sessions, you've told me about losing time, not being able to find reality, and exhibiting strange behaviors and fears," Dr. Brady said. "We've talked about witches, Satan, and evil. And you have hazy memories of your father giving you substances in your basement. Your spinning dreams pull all that together."

"Yes, it's all related in a strange way," Margi admitted. "At least inside my brain."

"Margi, my colleague and I have worked with a number of clients who were exposed to satanic cults as children. Many of those cults are secretly operating in the area by your grandmother's house."

Margi suddenly noticed that her breathing had become rapid. Her ears felt hot.

"Your symptoms and stories match up with others who have survived trauma from ritual abuse as children," Dr. Brady said. He spoke slowly, carefully enunciating each word.

Margi felt contrasting waves of emotion. One was a wave of validation that someone finally understood. Knew. The other was a wave of fear. A threatening voice in her head suggested that she was never to speak of this. Margi wondered which path to follow.

"I know your father has passed away, Margi. I wonder if your mother would be willing to meet with me?"

Margi rubbed her forehead. *Does he really want to cross my mother? That is a wildly bold move.* Dr. Brady clearly didn't know her mother. Anything derogatory or accusatory toward her mother turned on a switch of rage. Margi tried to imagine her mother's reaction.

"I'll give you her phone number," Margi said. "You can call and ask her. If she agrees, I don't want to be here when you talk to her. I can't do that."

. . .

"This is Dr. Brady. Is Margi there?" His voice on the phone was serious with a touch of angst.

"This is Margi."

"This doesn't sound like Margi. To whom am I speaking? It's important that I speak with Margi immediately."

Dr. Brady didn't seem to be in the mood for games. In the background, Margi could hear her mother screaming in his office. Margi's eyes darted to the window. *Where am I? Why doesn't my voice sound like me?* She wondered if she was dreaming. Slipping away. She tried again.

"Dr. Brady, it's me, Margi. How's it going with my mother?"

There was a pause on the other end of the phone. Finally, Dr. Brady continued with some hesitation.

"Margi, I need you to come and get your mother. I can't control her."

Margi had driven her mother to Dr. Brady's office for a two-hour appointment less than an hour ago. Margi wasn't surprised. *Why would my mother be interested in my therapy? My life?*

"Okay, Dr. Brady. I'll be right there. I'm sorry."

"I've never seen such explosive anger," Dr. Brady said. "I was telling her some of my assumptions about what happened in your childhood, and . . . well . . . she needs to leave."

.   .   .

Dr. Brady hung up the phone to return to his office. He could still hear Margi's mother yelling from behind the closed door. The woman was deeply disturbed. It was frightening.

The dots were connecting for Dr. Brady. Margi's voice changes. Childhood trauma. Peculiar behavior. Lost moments of time and bodily reality. An extremely angry mother—and he had his own opinion of the father. There were signs of dissociation. Signs of depersonalization.

This case was way beyond his expertise.

Chapter 23

Margi woke to the sound of screaming.

Her eyes opened, and she looked around the dark room. Her skin crawled with sensory overload—images, smells, and emotions. Margi recognized her bedroom. She glanced at the clock on the nightstand. Just after two a.m.

The terrifying scream that woke Margi was her own. Margi noticed the rapid rise and fall of her chest. *Please just stop. I just want this body to end. No more Margi. No life. No heaven. Just make me end.*

Margi pulled up the sheets that her feet had kicked to the bottom of the bed, and she wiped the tears from her cheeks. She felt like a failure in every way. Last week she had found herself attempting to end it all behind the wheel of her car. It had been a simple plan involving the exhaust from her car's engine in a closed garage. But she had left the scene. She was a complete failure—even at her own suicide attempt.

Margi had heard about people in the news who took their own lives and marveled at their bravery. Those who succeeded at their suicide attempt seemed so brave. It was something Margi had never achieved or completed. She had thought about ending her life since she was a little girl. At seven years of age, Margi wasn't sure she understood what dying meant, but she did understand she wanted it all to end. Now that desire was back with a vengeance. It consumed her thoughts every day, and she had failed numerous attempts.

A desperate sob escaped Margi's lips. She rolled onto her side and pulled her knees up tight like she did as a child, hugging the pillow that was wet with tears and sweat. Margi squeezed her eyelids trying to shut out the ugliness that still lingered in her senses.

The bed felt large and empty. Dennis had been sleeping downstairs lately. Margi's outbursts kept him awake, and sleep deprivation was taking its toll. Margi knew it was better this way, but she felt very alone.

What a freak I am. Nobody can help me.

As if nights weren't bad enough, odd habits and traits had become compulsive during the day. *Crazy* had begun to consume her thoughts and possess her soul. Every Sunday Margi felt a compulsion to go driving. A voice in her head said, *They're waiting for you.*

Every Sunday evening Margi drove. Not just anywhere; she drove north. She wondered why. What was north? Her childhood house. Her grandmother's house. The Children's Psychiatric Hospital. Margi drove for a few minutes, circled the area, and then came home. It made no sense. She desperately tried to fight the ridiculous obsession and silently argued with her thoughts. *Just stay here. This is your home now. You have nowhere to be.* But Margi couldn't shake the feeling that someone was waiting for her. So, every Sunday Margi gave in to the compulsive thoughts and drove north.

All the craziness made Margi hate herself. Everything betrayed her—her mind, her parents, and her body. It was a rage of helplessness that directed itself against Margi and anything belonging to her. Margi had moments where she hated her home, her clothes, her bed, her chairs, and her curtains. In a life of betrayal, nothing felt safe—least of all her own body. On bad days, Margi felt her possessions were sad. Sad that they belonged to her. And Margi hated the triggers that were attached to them.

Triggers that reminded her she was a freak.

. . .

Jennifer surveyed the supplies lined up on the kitchen counter. As a schoolteacher, her early mornings went smoother with a bit of organization the night before. Jennifer was in the process of gathering items after dinner when she felt the prompting. It was a quiet thought, but one with urgency.

Call Margi right now.

Jennifer stood still and recognized the request. She was honored to help. The classroom items could wait.

The love that Jennifer had toward Margi came with a connection that felt like her purpose. She wondered if God saw Margi's suffering as a five-year-old girl and said to Jennifer in heaven, *You go down and help her.* It was more than a privilege to help Margi, and Jennifer happily embraced the role. It was a calling from God, and she considered it her greatest life journey.

Jennifer reached for her phone and quickly dialed Margi's number. Jennifer heard three rings, then a moment of silence as the call was answered.

"Hello," Margi finally said.

Jennifer immediately heard a tone in Margi's voice that was different. Margi sounded like this only when she was at a very low point.

"Hi, Margi. I was just thinking of you. How are you doing tonight?"

Margi's words were jumbled, and she broke into heartbreaking sobs. Jennifer felt the despair. She knew this was coming. On top of everything else, Margi's sister Janet had recently died from pancreatic cancer. The cancer had come suddenly and without warning; within just a few months it had taken Janet's life.

Although Janet had never understood enough to step in and really help Margi, she had seemed to care and was an influence for good in Margi's life. Margi had watched as Janet brought brownies to neighbors and made quilts for friends who had new babies. Janet was a living example of serving others. She was a ray of sunshine and brought happiness into every room she entered. Margi seemed to be taking the loss extremely hard.

"I just don't feel God," cried Margi. "He can't fix me—either that, or He won't. Maybe He doesn't care anymore. I feel so abandoned."

Jennifer could hear Margi weeping. Jennifer wiped a tear trickling down the side of her own face, saddened by Margi's struggles and grateful she had followed the prompting to call.

"Tell me about your God, because mine is not here," Margi begged.

Jennifer didn't have all the answers. She had no training or education in trauma or behavioral issues. But she could listen, and she could love.

"We don't know why hard things happen, Margi," Jennifer replied. "Only God sees the big picture. You are not walking this path alone. I am right here with you."

"This is bigger than God."

"No, Margi—it's not bigger than God. He knows. We just don't have the understanding that He does."

Jennifer paused for a moment to gather her thoughts. She needed to turn this conversation in a different direction. A direction of hope.

"You have the strongest spirit of anyone I know," Jennifer declared. "You were sent here to earth with a fighting spirit! Who else could overcome your obstacles and still be alive? You have a hope in Christ. I've heard you testify of His presence in your darkest moments."

"I remember that," Margi whispered.

"Some people seem to have a charmed life," Jennifer continued. "It appears they have the perfect life and perfect kids and they seem to have no trials. Appearances can be deceiving, but those people are on a different journey. You are here for a reason, and you have an amazing gift. A gift that not everyone has. Margi, you have the spirit of hope."

"I'll never give up," Margi cried. "I want God to be proud of me."

Margi's voice had changed. It was somber, but sure. As she had so often done, Jennifer had talked Margi away from the edge. Jennifer could hear Margi quietly crying now.

She was convinced they were tears of promise for a better tomorrow.

. . .

Look unto God with firmness of mind, and pray unto him with exceeding faith, and He will console you in your afflictions, and He will plead your cause, and send down justice upon those who seek your destruction.[1]

The words caught Margi's attention. She remembered her conversation with Jennifer the night before. Jennifer had reminded her of a God that seemed so far away at times. Nightmares had tortured her again during the night, but she had reached for her scriptures this morning to earnestly seek peace. It was a new day. She hoped it was a new start.

Margi quietly fell to her knees.

"Dear Heavenly Father, I have so much to be grateful for. Thank you for my sweet children and husband. Thank you for my scriptures. I'm grateful for the warm water in my shower. I'm grateful for the beautiful mountains outside my window. Please help me feel whole today. Bless my mind to work. Help me feel your presence today. I'm so grateful for prayer . . . grateful that you can hear my thoughts and words."

Margi paused. She knew how to close a prayer but didn't want to say it. It was a word that closes a heartfelt communication with God. Margi's lip quivered.

She would skip the *Amen*. Margi set her heart on keeping that line of communication open. Maybe if she never said "amen," God would stay close. Would help her make decisions and stay present. Help her fight through dark memories and see the good in her life. Maybe He would stay close today.

Margi paused for a moment on her knees. She tried to imagine God's face. His love. Slowly she stood and breathed deeply. She felt a quiet resolve to take another step. To live another day.

Margi needed His light more than ever.

Chapter 24

"That's the BPD talking," Dr. Brady said.

Margi felt conflicted—like a little child who was misbehaving or always in trouble but who craved the strict discipline of a stern father figure.

"You are not being compliant. Have you read the literature I gave you? Listened to the tutorial? When you permanently upgrade your thinking and behavior, then you will be heard. Remember when you overcome Borderline Personality Disorder, it's our win," Dr. Brady stated.

Our win? He wants to take credit?

Margi spent hours doing busy work and research for this therapist. There were assignments and papers he wanted written. Summaries of their sessions together. And there were countless sessions of discussion about his own upbringing and childhood struggles. Margi initially thought it would all somehow fit together in some twisted way to help rescue her own mind. But she was becoming increasingly more frustrated.

Margi left appointments with Dr. Brady wanting to scream. Margi recognized the transference of the relationship from her father to her therapist. Part of her was infatuated by Dr. Brady. The fascination embarrassed Margi, and she didn't tell anybody about the strange emotions that were trying to claw their way to the surface. His stern demeanor felt like something that part of her needed. But another part of her knew better.

Where else could she get help? Margi was desperate to find answers. She had begun doing a great amount of her own research. She read volumes of books about psychoses and other mental disorders. She watched videos from experts in the field of psychiatry. She needed professional help, and she desperately wanted Dr. Brady to fix her mind. But she had certainly done her own reading and wanted her opinion heard.

"Dr. Brady, I've read everything I can find on Borderline Personality Disorder. It's not me. It doesn't fit," Margi suggested. "It's not even close."

"What part of your BPD is telling me that?" Dr. Brady replied.

"The part that wants to get better," Margi explained. "The part that wants to understand why I am this way. The part that just wants to be normal."

"I'll see you next week," Dr. Brady demanded. "Bring a summary of what we've discussed today and be sure to include an analysis of your defiant behavior."

Margi wanted to be heard. Her entire life she had kept quiet. So, she ventured an idea to her therapist.

"I've read some things about Dissociative Identity Disorder. They call it DID. It used to be called Multiple Personality Disorder," Margi said. She averted her eyes from Dr. Brady's glare. She didn't want to stand up to a professional who understood the mind, but the urge to voice her research was stronger.

"I've read all about it, and this is exactly what my mind is doing," Margi said. She summoned up the courage to meet Dr. Brady's eyes.

"Really?" Dr. Brady replied. His eyebrows were raised, and his tone was demeaning. "There's no such thing as that, Margi. Do you really think you can diagnose yourself with some book or article you've read?"

Margi felt foolish. Childish.

"Same time next week, Margi. Once again, we will do this together."

Margi grabbed her purse and walked toward the door. Her steps were timid and weak. Tears were forming, and she felt her face flush with embarrassment. She felt for the keys in her purse and walked briskly toward her car in the parking lot. Summer was in the air, and the sunshine on her face mixed with a cool breeze gave her a glimmer of strength—a simple, brief moment of hope mixed with fortitude.

I am better than this.

Margi drove home with the windows down so she could feel the summer air flow through her long, brown hair. Her tears were hot as they rolled down her cheeks. Margi made a bold decision. She would not return to Dr. Brady's office.

Perhaps the years of therapy had done some good. She had told Dr. Brady more than she had revealed to any other therapist. Initially, he seemed so caring and understanding. She believed he really wanted to help. Recently, Dr. Brady's research assignments for Margi had educated her in so many mysteries of mental illness. But they also supported her belief in knowing what was *not* wrong. Doctor and patient were at a standstill. Margi was not moving forward. The sessions had taken a negative turn, and she always felt worse afterward. Margi was desperate to find help, but she was beginning to recognize the difference between desperation and progress.

Margi turned onto her familiar neighborhood street. She sat quietly for a moment in the driveway before getting out of the car. She didn't question her decision to stop seeing Dr. Brady, but she recognized it as another failure added to a long list.

Alone again, she would continue to seek help.

. . .

Margi sat quietly in her seat with her hands folded in her lap. She looked around the room. People were taking notes. Nodding their heads.

She's not talking about me.

It was a church conference where a speaker addressed the topic, "Do You Know Who You Are?" The title peaked Margi's curiosity. It was a question she had been trying to answer her entire life. She hoped to find answers. But the woman speaking at the microphone seemed to be addressing everybody else. It was another validation that Margi was different.

I still don't fit in. And I don't know how to find me.

The closing song was one of Margi's favorites—"I Know That My

Redeemer Lives." The audience came together in one voice and sang.

> He lives to grant me rich supply.
> He lives to guide me with his eye.
> He lives to comfort me when faint.
> He lives to hear my soul's complaint.[1]

Margi closed her eyes and prayed silently as the audience continued singing the other verses. *Please, God, don't let me give up on you, because I really need you. Comfort me when faint? You didn't. I want to believe you. I don't want to give up on you, because I have seen miracles.*

At the conclusion of the conference, the women in the audience stood and embraced each other and began chatting about lessons learned from the popular speaker. Margi hurried toward the nearest exit. She didn't have the energy to wear a smile. To exchange pleasantries. To pretend she belonged to this group of strong, educated women of worth. She quietly slipped out the side door of the building.

No one noticed.

. . .

Margi could hear the sound of the television in the basement. She heard Dennis chuckle, and she knew he was downstairs probably watching a movie. She emptied the dishwasher and straightened the items on the kitchen counter. The soft glow of the evening sunset filtered through the kitchen window to announce the close of another day. Margi had anticipated a great day with a hope of understanding and inspiration from the conference. Instead, it just confirmed the idea that she was alone. Abnormal. A freak.

Margi paused for a moment, then hurried down the hall to grab her sneakers. She could feel a wave of sadness building in her chest. She didn't want to cry. Not here. Not with Dennis close by. She felt a desire to run away from the emptiness. Run away from this place called home.

Run away from herself.

Margi's sneakers led her down the sidewalk in front of her house and around the corner toward the park. Angry tears flowed down her face and fell onto the cool cement. Her pace was slow and heavy. When her sneakers got to the grassy field at the park, Margi's heart exploded in rage. An eruption of anger at God.

"Why are you doing this to me? Have I not been faithful, and have I not tried hard enough? Why won't you help me?"

Desperate sobs mixed with bitter words came from darkness, fear, and defeat. She reached deep into her soul, pulled out all the negativity, and heaved it at Him.

"Please make me die. Please just make me end. I can't do this anymore."

The last rays of sunlight dipped below the horizon.

"Don't send me to heaven," Margi cried, "because I can't continue on as Margi. Please don't make me do that. Please just make me end."

Margi fell to her knees. She placed her head in her hands, leaned forward, and wept for a long time. She hadn't cried so openly and allowed such outward emotion for some time. The depth of her pain and sorrow was raw and exposed.

A dog barking in the distance jolted Margi's senses. She pulled her head up and noticed darkness consuming the sky. The moon offered a sliver of light that outlined the trees. Margi pulled herself up from her knees and stood in the empty park. Darkness had never been Margi's friend, and she thought it best to walk toward home. She drew the sleeve of her shirt across her eyes and face to wipe the tears.

Once at home, Margi walked through the house toward the back porch and took a seat on the wicker chair next to the flowerpot. She intentionally left the porch light off. Margi didn't want Dennis to find her quite yet. She didn't have the strength to explain the tears.

Margi's eyes lifted toward the sky. The stars were bright and shiny as if announcing some grand event in the world. Margi shook her head and continued her conversation with God. Instead of cursing and screaming, her words were now soft and sullen.

"My life is simple. I don't need much. I just want peace."

A soft breeze blew through Margi's hair. The gentleness urged her to continue.

"And I was hoping—so hoping—that the last part of my life was going to be peaceful. The first part of my life was horrendous, and I thought maybe you'll help me with the last part."

Margi's voice began to quiver.

"I've been a good girl. I've prayed. I do all the right things. I . . . I want to believe."

Tears began to well up in Margi's eyes.

No more tears. Not tonight.

Margi stood and walked into the house. Her sneakers led her down the hallway toward her bedroom. She glanced at the clock. Almost nine o'clock. Her night's destiny awaited. Margi sat on the edge of the bed.

Once again Margi would lay her head on the pillow and succumb to the battle.

Chapter 25

"I don't deal with your kind of cases anymore."

Margi's heart sank. She had been referred to this therapist and had left a message on his voicemail to schedule an appointment. She was surprised he called back so quickly.

"But I'm going to give you the name of a woman who does a great job. Please call her. She's very experienced in abuse, trauma, and dissociative disorders. I really think she can help you, Margi."

Margi thanked him and hung up the phone. She massaged her forehead. She had started the day with a headache—one that was almost certainly stress related. After last night in the park, she knew she needed to find some answers. Margi felt herself teetering on the edge of sanity. There was nothing to do but keep trying.

Margi dialed the new phone number and spoke to the scheduler. There was an opening the next Tuesday because of a cancellation. Perhaps it was meant to be. Maybe God had not forgotten her after all. Margi cautiously had high hopes that this new therapist might be able to help.

"I'll take it," replied Margi.

. . .

"How can I help you, Margi?" Dr. Shaw asked.

She leaned forward in her chair, encouraging Margi to answer. Dr. Shaw's eyes were bright blue, and along with her light-blonde hair, they lit up her face. Her smile was warm, and it prompted Margi to begin.

"Thank you for seeing me," Margi replied. "I've seen dozens of therapists over the years, but you came highly recommended as someone who has some experience in . . ."

Margi stopped. It was always difficult to say the words. To speak the truth.

"I don't know why I'm even here," Margi continued. "I grew up in a lovely family with two good parents. My dad was a dentist."

Margi closed her eyes and shook her head. *Why did I say that?* She fought to refocus.

Another thought came forward. *This woman can help. Maybe we can trust her.*

"Well . . . what I meant to say is that I'm having some trouble staying present. My mind wanders to really scary places, and I want that to stop. I just want to learn how I can keep my thoughts and my reality from scattering. I also have pretty bad nightmares and would like those to stop."

Margi met the eyes of the new therapist sitting across the table. Dr. Shaw's expression was kind and inviting. Margi's biggest concern was that Dr. Shaw would know she was crazy. Crazy enough to need pills. Crazy enough to be put in a hospital. It was a tug of war between finding words to explain her symptoms and vocalizing the frightening words of truth. So far, Dr. Shaw didn't appear alarmed. Margi continued.

"Other therapists have suggested that I have anxiety, depression, or Borderline Personality Disorder, but I've done some of my own research and I don't believe those labels apply to me," Margi stated. "My mother even took me to a doctor in the hospital when I was a kid. I don't know what he thought, because I don't . . . well . . . I can't remember. His name was Dr. Bowen."

Dr. Shaw shifted slightly in her chair and wrote something down on the pad of paper in her lap. Something about her eyes indicated she had recognized the name.

"I just think my mind is broken, and it takes me away to other places. I just want to be able to concentrate on what I'm doing. I don't want my mind to interrupt the present."

"Tell me about your nightmares, Margi." Dr. Shaw's voice was encouraging.

Margi swallowed hard. She had to fight for courage to speak the ugly words required to describe the nightmares. Margi decided to skip the details and just summarize the general themes.

"Well, there are always attics and basements and really bad people who do evil things to me. I'm often being chased, and there's never any place to hide. Sometimes there are witches. Spiders. Candles. People in robes. Deep, dark, murky water. And other deeply frightening things like torture that wake me up and make it hard to start a new day. It's really bad stuff that nobody wants to hear about. I don't even want to say the words out loud."

Margi looked down at her lap and then folded her arms across her chest. Her posture demonstrated that she was clearly uncomfortable talking about her dreams.

"What's your relationship like with your parents?" Dr. Shaw asked.

"I think I told you my dad was a dentist, and he died a few years ago," Margi answered. Her eyes glanced around the room as if she was searching for a way to avoid contention.

"What about your mom?" Dr. Shaw persisted.

"I don't really want to talk about her," Margi said. "I'm not sure what my parents have to do with anything, except . . ." Margi paused then crossed her legs tightly and squirmed in her seat. "Well, a few therapists have told me I was abused as a child. But I'm really frustrated with that, because I don't remember my childhood. Sometimes there's a flash of something, but I don't remember school. I don't think I was there very much. I don't remember teachers or being in a classroom. I've gone through each grade and thought there must be some memory! First grade. Fifth grade. Anything! But there's just . . . nothing."

Margi felt tears well up in her eyes. She fought to keep control.

"I just don't even know who I am," Margi whispered.

. . .

"We'll get to the bottom of this, Margi. We are going to get some answers," Dr. Shaw declared.

Dr. Shaw seemed confident. Sounded certain that there was hope. Margi felt a glimmer of optimism. They had met together for a few sessions, and she liked Dr. Shaw.

"On our first session together, I suspected some dissociation. After spending a bit more time with you, I'm certain of it. Are you familiar with what dissociation is?" Dr. Shaw asked.

"Yes—a little," Margi answered. She had stumbled onto some research about it while she was seeing Dr. Brady.

"*Dissociation* is a word used to describe the disconnection or lack of connection between things. So, if you dissociate an experience, it isn't integrated into the usual sense of self. Dissociation means simultaneously knowing and not knowing. If you can't tolerate what you know or feel, the only option is denial and dissociating. The long-term effect is not feeling real inside."[1]

That made some sense. Margi thought it sounded like a plausible explanation of why she couldn't stay focused for long periods of time. Or at all.

"Research shows that a tendency to dissociate is not inherited genetically. Most commonly, repetitive childhood physical and/or sexual abuse and other forms of trauma are associated with the development of dissociative disorders. We also see it when there has been severe neglect or emotional abuse. It is a way for the child to adapt because when chronic, severe childhood trauma is present, dissociation reduces the overwhelming distress. It's a protection that our mind sets up so we can survive trauma we cannot escape."

Dr. Shaw now had Margi's full attention.

"What happens is that the dissociation continues to be used in adulthood, even when the original danger no longer exists. Any number of triggers can cause a dissociative adult to automatically disconnect from situations that are perceived as dangerous or threatening, without taking time to determine whether there is any real danger."[2]

Dr. Shaw stopped for a moment while Margi thought about what she said. It was a lot of information. She watched Margi closely.

"Are you saying I'm a dissociative adult because of some childhood trauma?"

"Yes. That's part of it. But I'm certain of a more specific diagnosis," Dr. Shaw said. "It's called *Dissociative Identity Disorder*. Previously it was known as *Multiple Personality Disorder*. We don't call it that anymore because it's not a growth of different personalities, but more a splintering of identity."

Margi began to cry and reached for a tissue on the table. Part of her didn't want to believe this. It all sounded so serious. So alarming. But there was a part of Margi that absolutely knew this made sense. She just wanted to heal and to rise above it.

"I am here to help you, Margi. I've helped many other people with the same condition."

"I'm not the only one?" Margi cried.

"No. In fact, I conduct a group therapy with several other women like you. I would love for you to participate in that. I'd like you to see that you're not alone."

Margi nodded hesitantly. This was all happening so fast.

"But I still want to continue meeting with you in private sessions, Margi. We have a lot of work to do. DID is characterized by the presence of several distinct identities or personality states that take control of your behavior. These different identities or parts took on jobs to protect you when you were a child. They continue to serve distinct roles in coping with problem areas. Those parts hold the memories, Margi. You and I can work together to allow those parts to uncover the childhood memories and put them to rest."

Margi felt both relief and fear at the diagnosis. It made terrifying sense.

She was a multiple.

Chapter 26

Dr. Shaw glanced at her schedule; she had time for a quick lunch. Her first appointment after lunch was a group session for several DID patients. Dr. Shaw had invited Margi to attend and hoped she would. Margi was one of the more difficult cases in her career.

The red flag went up months ago when Margi mentioned she had seen Dr. Bowen as a child. Several of Dr. Shaw's DID clients had once been patients of his at the Children's Psychiatric Hospital. A theme of medical abuse, sexual abuse, and brainwashing experiments was common to all those patients. While some had more memory of the events than others, one thing was certain: Dr. Bowen had destroyed a number of beautiful, young minds. The tragic evidence was manifest in story after story told to her by now-grown men and women fighting to move forward after childhood abuse. And the common thread among them all was dissociation.

Margi had slowly begun opening up to Dr. Shaw. Although Margi still seemed to guard some parts, Dr. Shaw recognized them as separate from each other. She knew fragmented memories might take years to uncover, and Margi's case would likely need more time and commitment than she might be able to give. She wrote a note in the file to consider transferring Margi's case to a DID expert who handled only multi-contextual cases referred by other therapists.

Margi certainly needed help. Dr. Shaw determined that she'd meet with Margi a few more times, then make her determination.

. . .

Margi was introduced to the DID group at the beginning of the meeting. Now she simply sat and observed as heads nodded and a few of the women wiped tears. It seemed to be a safe place, but one that was filled with emotion.

For the first time in Margi's life, she understood she wasn't alone. As a child, she was certain God had made a mistake. Had given her a broken mind. Even as an adult, Margi had never met anyone who had thoughts like she did. Until now.

Dr. Shaw moved the conversation to the topic of fear. The women talked about fears that consumed their days—and many that consumed their nights.

"Margi, we would love to hear from you," Dr. Shaw said. "You have a welcome voice here."

"Well . . . um . . . I fear that I'm going to go crazy," Margi said.

A single nod from a woman across the circle encouraged Margi to continue.

"You're not going to go running down the street crazy," Dr. Shaw suggested.

"No, not that kind of crazy," Margi replied. "I'm talking about the crazy that I suffered when I was given drugs as a little girl. They took me to such a terrifying place. I must have visited that place a lot, because my mind wants to take me there sometimes. Triggers do make me go there. I'm scared that one day I'll leave my body and won't be able to come back."

Margi looked at the other women. When there was no response from anyone she hesitated, then continued. "I have drawings of symbols and words that come from nightmares. These terrifying places drugs took me to are in some other dimension."

"I've been there," Susan whispered.

All eyes turned to Susan. Margi recognized Susan as the daughter of one of her father's friends. Susan's father had also been a dentist, and Margi remembered her parents driving her to Susan's father for some dental work. Margi remembered that she had been there, but the details were gone. Susan said that she now lived by herself in her daughter's basement. It was clear to Margi that Susan was really struggling to stay focused and present.

"Susan, describe what you mean by *there*," Dr. Shaw said.

"Darkness. Evil. Horrible places where everybody is tricking me. Men and women in dark, hooded robes chanting. They all just want to get me."

Susan wiped the tear that slid down her cheek then looked up at Margi.

"I've been there," Susan repeated. "Guess we both have."

Margi nodded then looked away.

.   .   .

"I don't want to attend the group therapy anymore."

"Why not, Margi?" Dr. Shaw asked as the two started another private therapy session.

"It was helpful for a while and I appreciate the opportunity. It was amazing to hear that I wasn't the only one suffering, but I think I would rather continue to work on my own therapy. I hope that makes sense."

"I understand," Dr. Shaw said. She knew it was time for Margi to move forward anyway. She needed more time and commitment in therapy than was available in Dr. Shaw's schedule. They had made great progress over the past two years understanding DID and acknowledging that childhood trauma had created the condition. But parts needed to be identified and recognized. It required a great amount of patience and laborious therapy to retrieve the memories these parts were holding.

"Margi, there's someone else who can help you, someone who consults with therapists all over the world helping them better understand DID and the treatment for their clients. He takes only those clients who are referred by therapists like me, and the clients must be multi-contextual," Dr. Shaw explained.

"Multi-contextual?"

"Yes," Dr. Shaw replied. "The combination of your limited memories, nightmares, writings, drawings, and hundreds of conversations we've had indicate that the abuse you suffered as a child comes from multiple contexts. I believe you suffered familial abuse, ritual abuse, and medical drug experiments. All three."

Dr. Shaw leaned forward and patted Margi on the hand. "You can still come and see me whenever you'd like, but let's pull in some more expertise. Add someone to our team. We can do this together."

.   .   .

Margi sat quiet for a moment. Going to a new therapist meant sharing horrific details of her life with one more person. It meant tearing down the walls and learning to trust someone new. Perhaps this was God's way of helping. God knew she wanted to find her childhood memories and move forward. He knew she wanted to fix her broken mind. Maybe this was the path.

"What's his name?" Margi asked softly.

Chapter 27

"Hello, Margi."

There was a slight pause.

"Dr. Shaw has told me a lot about you. It's nice to hear your voice."

Margi's hand trembled a bit as she clutched her cell phone. She was hesitant to let someone new into her life, but Dr. Shaw had persuaded Margi to take this step.

"Hello," Margi responded quietly.

He explained that their first few sessions would be conducted over the phone. Soon after that, a session in Dr. Shaw's office would be scheduled so they *could* meet face to face. He concluded by saying, "You can call me Jay.*"

"Hello, Jay," Margi said.

He sounded nice enough. His voice was friendly and considerate. Perhaps he could help. Margi wanted to trust him, but she was scared. Something deep inside kept insisting that to trust was to be tricked.

"I guess you're the person who is supposed to fix me," Margi said, chuckling nervously.

"Well, not exactly," Jay responded with a smile in his voice. "I'm here to help you understand and learn about DID. Together we can work on some things. I'm here for you."

"You come highly recommended," Margi said. "Dr. Shaw said you have a lot of experience working with people . . . well . . . like me."

"Yes, I do, Margi. I'm happy to work with you."

---

* "Jay" is a composite figure in this story.

Jay was a consultant to therapists as well as local, state, and national agencies in the United States and countries around the world who were dealing with ritual abuse. Jay's graduate work in theology and social psychology and his teaching career in sociology was highly regarded and fed the demand for his expertise. In addition to consulting mental health professionals, he spoke to law enforcement agencies to help them recognize elements of ritual abuse and the signs and symptoms of dissociation both on the streets and in schools.

Jay also accepted clients diagnosed with Dissociative Identity Disorder who were referred from trained therapists. Childhood abuse that was multi-contextual in nature—that included familial, ritual, and medical abuse—generally required much more time and patience to resolve. Most therapists who were juggling a full practice didn't have the additional time and patience to spend with an individual client, no matter how desperate the need.

Unlike therapists who had a traditional practice, Jay managed a busy consulting career in which he was always willing to make a difference on an individual level. While he conducted most of the sessions with clients over the phone, his travel schedule allowed him to periodically visit these clients in therapists' offices throughout the country. Managing things that way allowed him to use his methods and consult with people who were suffering.

People like Margi.

. . .

Margi had finished several sessions with Jay over the phone. She was slowly becoming more comfortable with him, and he empowered her to take a strong role in her progress. During today's session, Margi said, "I've been doing some of my own research."

"That's great, Margi," Jay answered. "What have you learned?"

"I've been reading articles and watching videos about DID. It all sounds just like me. I'm pretty sure that's what I have, but I don't want to say it out loud."

Margi took a deep breath. Jay didn't try to fill the silence; instead, he waited for her to speak.

"I especially hate the older label of *Multiple Personality Disorder*. To think I have a bunch of different personalities sounds completely crazy. I haven't even talked to my husband or kids about it. I've told Dennis that there may have been some abuse in my past, and he knows I'm getting counseling, but I just can't say it . . . I can't say *DID*. It's so scary . . . but it makes sense."

Margi gazed out the front window. Her neighbor was watering pots on her front porch, and another woman was briskly walking her dog. Why couldn't she just be normal like everyone else in the neighborhood?

"Margi, we've talked about dissociation and why it happens. Let me take the title *Dissociative Identity Disorder* one step further. You and I both have a belief in God, right?" Jay asked.

"Yes, Jay. Sometimes that belief is the only thing that keeps me going."

"Okay, I believe God created us in His image and likeness. In that light we were created physically, mentally, and psychologically. He gave the body the ability to ward off disease with an immune system and other things that protect it from getting sick from germs or injuries. Well, the mind was also given protection to ward off attacks. The mind's protection is called *dissociation*."

What Jay was saying made sense so far. Margi applied that idea to what she had researched and continued to listen.

"So, dissociation protects the integrity of the mind. With dissociation, the event that is happening is suddenly not happening to Margi—it's happening to someone else. It allows Margi to step away from what's happening and holds the trauma away from her own mind—her awareness. Dissociation isn't really a disorder. It is God's given ability for the mind to protect itself from trauma."

Margi nodded her head in agreement. She had learned more from Jay in just a few sessions than she had in years of therapy. Everything made sense. Margi was eager to continue this journey of education, because it somehow granted her the needed courage and self-esteem to embrace this fight.

"As a multiple, you are fragmented from childhood experiences, but you, Dr. Shaw, and I are going to pull it all together with a core method called Core-Oriented Recovery Process. We'll recover memories and discover some parts or *alters*, as some call them. Those parts don't come together as one, but they can learn to work together and be stabilized."

Margi was glad when Jay paused for a moment. It was a lot of information to take in.

"I'm here for the journey, Margi," Jay said. "We're going to do this together. In fact, I'll be in Utah next week. I'd like to meet with you and your family while I'm in town. I can help explain this to your husband."

"Oh, that would be really great," Margi said. She had been so worried how to explain all this to her family, and Jay spoke so eloquently about everything. "You'll tell them I'm not crazy?"

"Oh, you're not crazy, my dear. You never were."

Margi felt warmth in her heart as she wiped a small tear from the corner of her eye. She felt that things were finally going to get better.

It was a quiet moment of hope.

Chapter 28

Trauma. That word had come up so many times when Margi worked with other therapists. Jay had mentioned it again. *Trauma.*

Margi's fingers flew across the computer keyboard as she continued to learn more about what might be wrong with her. What was the difference between a bad experience and trauma? Margi's eyes scanned the screen.

One report described *trauma* as preverbal. Incidents reported in emergency rooms consisted of howling or screaming obscenities, but the speechless terror varied from person to person. Victims of assaults and accidents often sat mute and frozen. Even years later, traumatized people often had enormous difficulty telling others what had happened to them. Their bodies reexperienced the terror and helplessness, but the feelings were almost impossible to articulate.[1]

Margi ran her fingers through her hair. She sat quietly, reflecting. *What was my trauma?* Her experience of trauma in her early years was real, and something inside confirmed it, but she longed for details. Her mind swarmed with questions. *Where was everybody? Why didn't I tell someone?*

Margi continued reading about trauma, specifically abuse in young children. It was unsettling, but she craved an understanding. The research stated that children are programmed to be fundamentally loyal to their caretakers, even when abused by them. The terror increases the need for attachment, even if the source of comfort is also the source of terror.

Margi thought about her father. She reflected on her twist of emotions in wanting to be loved and accepted by him, but also feeling repulsed at times. It was confusing and sad. The article also said that emotional abuse and neglect can be just as devastating as physical abuse and sexual molestation. When a child is unseen and has nowhere to turn to feel safe, it is terribly destructive for young children still trying to find their place.[2] Margi thought about her feelings toward her mother—the intense desire to be nurtured, rescued, and needed by her, even after all these years.

Is trauma at the root of all my confusing emotions and crazy visions and thoughts?

Margi scrolled down the page and continued reading, learning that trauma is not stored as a narrative with an orderly beginning, middle, and end. Traumatic memories often return as flashbacks that contain fragments of the experience—isolated images, sounds, and body sensations that initially have no rational context other than fear and panic. Children have no way of giving voice to the unspeakable. In Margi's case, it would have made no difference anyway—nobody was listening.

Margi thought back to glimpses of terror in both her childhood and as an adult. They made no sense. The flashbacks were random and seemed to be triggered by a sound or sight or smell. Margi closed her eyes as she recalled those she had felt more recently. They weren't just normal memories, like remembering yesterday's dinner. They persisted for a long time and had astonishing freshness that captured all her senses at once. They were paralyzing because they were more than just remembering—they were like experiencing the trauma all over again. She *felt* them.[3]

The next heading in the article caught Margi's attention: *Learning to Live in the Present.* That was Margi's greatest desire. She just wanted to live her life with a beautiful family and find gratitude and love right now. Here in the present. How she wanted to run away from all the *crazy* inside her mind.

There are challenges. . . . Margi read about the obstacles felt by trauma survivors. They were summarized by therapists who dealt with clients suffering with complex PTSD and DID. Those seeking help wanted to understand their past but also wanted to enhance the quality of their day-to-day experiences. The traumatic memories from the past became so dominant that it became difficult to feel truly alive in the present. Furthermore, when survivors couldn't be fully in the present, they went to the places where they *did* feel alive, even if those places were filled with horror and misery.[4]

Margi nodded her head. The things she was reading resonated with her soul. *How many times have I felt like my body wasn't mine? How often have I felt I was living in some awful time warp?* Margi considered that maybe she wasn't the only one having these thoughts. Perhaps there really were others like her. Others with thoughts she had been terrified to voice. Thoughts about barely controllable urges and crazy emotions. Thoughts of believing she didn't belong to the human race. Deep thoughts of shame because she was different.

Margi's eyes went to the bottom of the page. She saw a final statement about moving forward after trauma: "The challenge is not so much learning to accept the terrible things that have happened, but learning how to gain mastery over one's internal sensations and emotions. Sensing, naming and identifying what is going on inside is the first step to recovery."[5]

Margi lifted her head. She had some hard work to do. She was determined to take this step. Oh, how she wanted recovery. Margi reached for her cell phone. She pulled up Jay's contact number and texted him a simple but bold statement.

I'm ready to work with you.

Chapter 29

Margi stood facing the mirror in her bedroom. Her eyes met the reflection staring back. Ordinarily, Margi avoided looking in mirrors. She never quite knew what she might see.

Margi ran her fingers through her brown hair and fussed with the pieces in front. Her clothing was nice, but comfortable. A simple necklace completed the outfit. One final glance in the mirror revealed apprehensive eyes. She looked presentable enough, but what would *he* see?

Her appointment was scheduled for four that afternoon. It would be the first time Margi would meet Jay in person. They had talked for hours over the phone, and he was the only person she had ever known who really understood what she was thinking. Nothing she said ever alarmed him—not even her descriptions of strange dreams, disconnected realities, and frightening flashbacks. It was both exhausting and exhilarating for Margi to be so vulnerable. Now Jay would put a face to her words.

What or who will he see?

.   .   .

Dr. Shaw glanced around the waiting room and saw Margi sitting quietly in the corner. Margi's arms were tightly folded, and her legs were crossed. Dr. Shaw smiled.

"We are ready for you, Margi."

Jay and Margi would meet in person for the first time in Dr. Shaw's office. Margi stood and followed Dr. Shaw into her office. As they turned the corner, a white-haired gentleman stood next to a chair. He wore tan slacks and a plaid, collared shirt. He had kind, blue eyes that smiled when he did.

"Hello, Margi," Jay said, extending a hand in greeting.

Margi instantly recognized the friendly voice from hours of phone conversations. She reached out and shook his hand. It was warm and soft.

"Hi, Jay," Margi replied. "It's good to finally meet you in person. Thank you for traveling here to see me."

"Oh, it's my pleasure. How are you feeling today?"

"A little anxious, I guess."

Dr. Shaw suggested that they all take a seat as she motioned to the chairs.

. . .

Jay and Margi started talking about progress made in earlier conversations and goals that were set for the future. Dr. Shaw nodded her head in agreement as she observed the interaction between these two. They seemed immediately comfortable with each other, and she recognized a sense of satisfaction for her part in placing them together. Dr. Shaw cared deeply for Margi from her own months of therapy with her. She just wanted the best for Margi, and she could see that Jay was the right person to accomplish that. Jay was amazing to watch. He lived up to his reputation, and Margi was lucky to be working with him.

Jay glanced down at his watch. He smiled at Margi and leaned forward in his chair.

"Okay, Margi. We have a few minutes before we meet with your husband. I'm glad he's willing to meet with me. Dennis, right?" Jay asked.

"Yes, Dennis." Margi's stomach dropped. How does someone tell her husband she has multiple parts? It was overwhelming to think about. Margi was nervous, but also eager. Who better than Jay to explain everything?

"I'll explain whatever you feel comfortable with, Margi," Jay said. "I'm here to support you in helping Dennis understand DID. And I'll share whatever you want about what we've learned together. Let's spend the last few minutes reviewing what we plan to talk about."

Margi nodded. Despite her pounding heart, Margi felt at peace. Her load suddenly felt a bit lighter. When she was ready, she would explain everything to her children later. They were busy raising their own families, and she didn't want to scare them.

For now, Margi wanted to focus on sharing with her husband. She prayed he would still love her. She knew it was a lot to embrace. Margi realized she was like a mosaic piece of art with broken pieces that somehow fit together.

Thank heavens Jay was here to say the right words.

· · ·

Margi sat quietly on a couch next to Dennis. There were two glasses of water sitting on the table next to them. He noticed lots of leather books on shelves in the office. He had driven straight from work to Dr. Shaw's office to meet Jay. He was feeling a bit nervous, but he was anxious to hear more about Jay and how he could be a help to Margi.

Dennis listened as Jay talked about his work experience and travels throughout the world. Then the subject quickly changed to Margi and the opportunity to work with her. Jay expressed gratitude to Dennis for making time to meet.

"I know you've probably met with a therapist or two over the years," Jay said.

"That's an understatement," Dennis replied. "I've met a few, but Margi has seen dozens. There have been some real wackos—sorry for that expression. We keep hoping that someone can help."

Dennis looked over at Margi. He patted her on the leg and smiled at her. "This girl never gives up—I've got to give her that."

"Margi is a survivor," Jay stated.

A survivor? Dennis hadn't ever attached that name to Margi. It sounded honorable, yet it suggested something a little more serious.

"All my clients are survivors," Jay said. "Margi has been through some things in her childhood that have caused her to learn methods of survival. We don't have all the details yet, but from early conversations with her and considering her fragmented flashbacks and other symptoms, she endured some serious childhood abuse on a number of different levels. More details will emerge with appropriate therapy, but I trust and concur with Dr. Shaw in her diagnosis."

Jay paused. Dennis looked at Margi.

"Diagnosis?" Dennis asked.

"Other therapists have suggested abuse in Margi's past. That's not new information. What they haven't correctly diagnosed is the condition that Margi has in surviving that abuse for so many years."

Dennis glanced again at Margi. Her eyes were filling with tears.

"The way Margi is coping is really a protection, Dennis," Jay explained. "What started out as a means of survival and protection during childhood is still very present and causing problems long after the abuse is gone."

"Is there a name?" Dennis asked. Margi was wiping her eyes.

"Dissociative Identity Disorder," Jay replied. "We call it DID for short."

Margi could tell that the words meant nothing to Dennis. The confusion was clear on his face.

"It used to be called Multiple Personality Disorder," Jay said. "We don't use that term anymore for good reason, but I want to help you understand more about it. An understanding will help you grasp what Margi is experiencing. Essentially . . . Margi is a multiple."

Chapter 30

A multiple? Dissociative what?

Dennis's mind swirled with questions. He was consumed by conflicting feelings of both alarm at the diagnosis and relief that it finally had a name. He sat quiet for a moment, looking back and forth between Jay and Margi. Nobody made a sound. Finally, Dennis swallowed hard and looked across the table at Jay.

"Help me understand," Dennis pleaded.

"That's why I'm here, Dennis," Jay replied. "Margi is very bright. Her beautiful mind saved her life. Let me explain."

Dennis looked over at Margi, and he could see that she was upset. He put his arm around her and squeezed her arm. Dennis realized she was probably terrified about what he must think. He forced a quiet smile and nodded his head in a gesture of acceptance. Then he shifted his attention back to Jay.*

"Let's start with dissociation. It's a very common mental mechanism that we've all experienced in some form. If you've ever driven along a familiar route and arrived at your destination without remembering a good chunk of the trip, you've experienced dissociation. The same is true if you become so absorbed in a book or movie that you become unaware of your surroundings. Or if you listen to someone talk and realized you didn't hear what they were saying. These

---

* As previously mentioned, "Jay" is a composite figure. This description of the concepts of dissociation and DID are from an insightful book by Dr. Lynn Mary Karjala, *Understanding Trauma and Dissociation* (Atlanta: Thomas Max Publishing, 2007).

are all forms of dissociation that people experience every day, and it's a safe assumption to say the capacity to dissociate is inborn—hardwired into the brain."[1]

Dennis nodded in agreement, and Jay continued.

"The highest dissociators are those who have a strong talent and who had reasons to exercise that talent early and often in childhood. That's why most people with Dissociative Identity Disorder have a history of severe and prolonged childhood abuse or neglect. DID begins as the best response the child is capable of making to horrendous trauma from which the child cannot escape."[2]

Dennis felt a hollow heaviness in his heart. The thought of Margi being hurt made him sick. Margi's dad was odd and distant, but an *abuser?* Dennis had never suspected as much. Margi's mother—well, he had seen her rages and the strange effect she still had on Margi. Dennis wondered if they were both involved in this abuse.

"And you suspect Margi was abused by both parents?" Dennis asked.

"Yes," Jay answered, "and others in her childhood. There are dozens of symptoms and behaviors that point to sexual, ritual, and medical abuse. Some of those memories have already come forward in some early therapy."

Dennis hoped this was some sort of mistake. Some horrible, perverse delusion.

"What is this *multiple* thing? I've heard of Multiple Personality Disorder. Hollywood has put some strange movies out about people with that disorder," Dennis said.

"Oh, don't get me started on Hollywood," Jay quipped, "and the profit generated from exaggerated and untrue depictions of multiples."

"Of course," Dennis replied. "I get that. It's just that Hollywood is my only exposure to this."

Jay smiled and continued. "In the past few decades, our understanding of this has changed considerably, so the name was changed from MPD to DID to reflect that new understanding. We now know that no one has multiple personalities. Each of us has only one personality—one core identity. However, if a child experiences a severe, overwhelming trauma and she has enough dissociative talent, she may split off the memory of the trauma into a dissociated part of herself. If she continues to experience prolonged or repeated trauma, such as Margi did, a whole internal system of parts may be developed. Some of these parts may simply be fragments, while others become elaborately detailed and are experienced by the core as separate identities."[3]

Dennis listened intently. This was both fascinating and frightening.

"The relationship between the core and its parts is difficult to grasp," Jay explained. "Margi is the core. She is a daughter of God with a divine identity. MPD wrongly suggests that different personality states are about equal. But there is only one core—Margi. And the core owns the dissociative system—the entire inner world.[4] The good news is that Margi has the power to control the whole system and can learn to do that through therapy. I can help Margi sort through this."

"How have we not known this for all these years?" Dennis asked.

"The typical client I work with is a female in her mid to late thirties, often married with children. She's looking for therapy because she has odd symptoms—like hearing voices, finding things in the house she doesn't remember buying, realizing she can't remember anything over a period of hours, having out-of-body experiences or flashbacks, and feeling disconnected from her own body and actions. She may have been aware of some symptoms for a long time, but they may have increased in severity to the point that she can no longer ignore them. She has no idea what the symptoms mean, and she may be terrified that she's going crazy."[5]

There was that word again—*crazy*. Dennis had heard Margi throw that term around their entire marriage. Dennis couldn't help but react visibly to the word.

"Margi is *not* crazy," Jay explained. "Quite the contrary. She's a dissociative survivor . . . and a brilliant one at that. I know you've both heard misdiagnoses over the years. The average dissociative person spends an average of seven years in the mental health system before finally receiving an accurate diagnosis. Common misdiagnoses are borderline personality, bipolar, post-traumatic stress, and schizophrenic disorders."

"Yes, I've heard those," Dennis said. "This is kind of like PTSD, right?"

"Well, that term gets thrown around a lot," Jay replied. "You'll also hear Complex Post-Traumatic Stress Disorder, or CPTSD. They are closely linked and are sometimes used interchangeably, depending on the therapist or insurance form. They are both the result of trauma, but not everyone with PTSD develops parts."[6]

Parts. Margi has parts.

Dennis let that thought sink in.

"Why haven't I seen parts?" Dennis asked.

"Most DID survivors, like Margi, are very good at concealing their parts. What you see is forgetfulness, mood swings, and irrational fears, isn't it?"

Dennis nodded. Jay was nailing this.

"The job of every part is to serve and protect the core," Jay said. "That is the only reason for their existence. They protect the core from experiencing or remembering the intense pain. They hold the dissociated memories as a protection, and they each have varying degrees of presence. Depending on triggers, they can come and go. Unlike the core, parts can be either male or female and have their own abilities, likes and dislikes, body image, and style. Some have different names. But it's important to remember that dissociated memories and feelings are preserved relatively unchanged; it's like they have been frozen in time. Untreated parts tend to remain the age that they were when they were created by the core—the age when the trauma and abuse happened. Often the parts are children."[7]

Jay sat up straight and leaned forward. "Brain waves documented from an EEG performed on a DID adult will often register normal results from an adult brain, but also theta and delta waves not normally seen in the brain of an awake adult. They are normally seen only in children. Those EEGs seem to be describing two different people. It's scientific evidence that confirms how powerful our minds really are, and the research is continuing."[8] Jay explained that years of experience already confirmed this phenomenon, but science was quickly catching up and recognizing these theories.

It was all so much to absorb. Dennis grabbed his glass of water and drank it slowly and methodically as his mind tried to make sense of it all. He placed the empty glass back on the table and ran his fingers through his hair.

"Okay, do I need to know which part I'm talking to?" Dennis asked. "She's just Margi to me."

"Dennis, you know and love Margi—her core," Jay confirmed. "That doesn't change. Her parts simply exist in her mind to help her navigate life. Her core is always at least partially there or out front. Let me see if I can explain it to you."

Jay smiled at Margi. She was attentive and seemed eager to embrace this new understanding along with her husband.

"When one part goes back inside and another part comes up front, that's called *switching*. In old movies, switching is sometimes accompanied by some dramatic sign or gesture like the head dropping onto the chest or the face going blank. But it's rarely that obvious. In my experience with DID clients, it's more often a glance downward, a blink of the eye that lasts just slightly longer than usual, or no outward sign at all."[9]

Dennis felt some relief. At least he hadn't missed something blatantly obvious right in front of him.

"It's also possible for more than one part to be up front at a time," Jay explained. "This is called *blending*. A couple of parts can be up front at the same time and equally aware of what's going on in the moment. Depending on the task at hand, the core will take charge or stand to the side or behind and let the part control the situation."[10]

Dennis leaned back in his chair. He drew in a deep breath and exhaled slowly.

"Dennis, just love and care for Margi as you always have," Jay affirmed. "That's your role. Be there for her as she works hard on this journey to find peace and safety."

"I can do that," Dennis whispered.

"And I'll do my job," Jay replied. "One aspect of the healing is for Margi to take back her power from her parts. It's an empowering and deeply satisfying process. But in the beginning, it can be very frightening. The parts are not evil or bad. We don't want them to stop doing their job; we just want to change how they do it. It's not their existence that's the problem, it's their behavior.[11] I'll work with Margi to teach her parts that the trauma is in the past and it's safe now. As it is now, the parts don't know that the trauma is over. It's quite a long process, and Margi can educate you more on her progress as she and I work together. Of course, I'm always available to you too, Dennis. I'm just a phone call away."

"Thank you." Dennis realized he wasn't alone in this. He had Jay on his team.

"Margi is strong, smart, and beautiful. And of course, you already know that," Jay stated.

Dennis glanced at his wife and nodded.

"We want Margi to feel and know that she is genuinely and thoroughly a healthy, vibrant whole and not damaged goods," Jay declared. "She has gifts and talents to offer that are separate from her identity as a trauma survivor. Her treatment and progress will validate and empower her self-worth."[12]

Tears welled up in Dennis's eyes as he fought for control. He wanted that for Margi. His dear, sweet Margi. A warm, peaceful sensation washed over Dennis and validated his thoughts.

Finally . . . hope.

Chapter 31

A few gold rays of light filtered through the bedroom window. Dawn. It was Dennis's favorite time of day. He had always been an early riser. Mornings were always hard for Margi, but Dennis loved grasping a fresh start with every sunrise. He was always up and out of bed way before Margi and was usually quick to jump at the earliest flicker of light, but this morning emotions were tender.

Dennis's mind immediately went to last night's conversation with Jay. He lay quietly under the covers while thoughts and memories swirled. It was a desperate effort to make some real sense of past events and his future relationship with Margi.

For years he had known something was wrong. Margi had reached out a few times, but often kept the details to herself. There was unspoken tension. A distance between them he couldn't put his finger on. It was easier to just live separate lives under the same roof. A few therapists had tried to put the blame on him, saying he wasn't present enough. Available enough. Never enough.

My poor, dear Margi. How could I have known? Her nightmares. Crying, screaming, and thrashing. He couldn't even sleep in the bed with her anymore. It was a necessary separation for both their sakes. The pieces were now coming together. Those repetitive night terrors were memories. Fragments of trauma as an innocent child.

Dennis felt his jaw tighten. *What kind of parents don't love and adore their children?* He had so many questions. His own children meant the world to him, and he knew Margi felt the same way. What an amazing mother Margi was to their children from the moment they were born. Even now, she was loving, attentive, and giving to her grown children. He respected her even more in her role of motherhood knowing that she had no modeled behavior from her own mother. Reen hadn't protected Margi. In fact, she hadn't been a mother at all. And her father—Dennis wasn't sure he even wanted to know the details.

The sunlight was now pulling the darkness from the bedroom; light filtering in between the shutters slowly cast a soft glow. Dennis reminded himself he wasn't alone in this. Jay was a blessing. What a kind, generous man. Everything he said fit right on down the line. Jay would help them sort this out.

DID. A diagnosis years in the making. Perhaps he and Margi could move forward with this new information. Battle onward with Jay and a plan of treatment. The diagnosis was a punch in the gut that nearly knocked the wind out of him, but it validated everything—and that was somehow a comfort.

Dennis thought back to the darkest of times. Moments and even days that scared him because Margi appeared to be disconnected. Lost. During those times, he tried to remind her of the children, of the blessings in her life, though it felt like he was talking to a wall. He remembered the time he found her in the closet by herself, repeatedly crying, "I don't want to die. I don't want to die." That wasn't his Margi. With this new diagnosis, he knew he had been right. It *wasn't* his Margi. It was someone else.

Dennis would never look at his relationship with Margi quite the same again. It felt like a dual reality—a loving, secure present living side by side with a traumatic, horrific past. It had to be exhausting for Margi to live in both the present and past realities every single day.

Dennis knew that Margi was still going to suffer. The diagnosis wasn't going to cure anything. But it *did* give them a new starting point. Dennis felt sure of that. His Margi wasn't crazy—she was harmed.

Dennis listened for any movement down the hall. Nothing. Margi was likely still asleep. He remembered Jay's counsel of his role in helping Margi through this. Oh, how Dennis loved her. He would protect her and keep her safe at least here, in this present reality. It was all he could do.

Focus on the present. She was so beautiful and innocent. He didn't care what had happened before he met her. The abuse that had been inflicted on her body from how many others was in God's hands. She was as pure as the driven snow in his eyes. He would love. Protect.

And he would listen.

. . .

Margi's eyes flew open with fright. She frantically tried to focus her darkened, bloodshot eyes. *Where am I?* The nightmare wasn't just a memory—it was an experience. All her senses were still screaming with pain and horror. Sights, smells, and the sounds of chanting filled her bedroom. How could she be in her room while she was simultaneously somewhere else? It was another morning of desperately trying to separate dream from reality.

I don't want to do this anymore. Today is the day I need to die.

Margi had no more tears. She had shed plenty throughout the night. It was too much. This was no way to live, and God would certainly understand. She closed her eyes tightly and begged Him to stop her breathing—and if He didn't, she would find a way to do that herself.

Suddenly she saw a glimpse—quick but powerful. A vision from another place—heaven. With eyes tightly closed, Margi saw a soft, tranquil place. Familiar, heavenly figures spoke to her. In her mind, she heard the words. *No, you can't give up. This wasn't what you agreed to do. Margi, you can't do that today because you've got more to do here. You have more time. You have the strength.*

Margi recognized the comfort, the peaceful light that seemed to wrap its arms around her soul. In the lowest times of her life, she had received the same vision and the same words. They had rescued her in the darkest moments, both as a child and as an adult. This was one of those times.

Suddenly Margi was standing. How had that happened? Surely angels had lifted her from bed when she couldn't find the strength.

Another tender miracle. Invisible hands were there to support and encourage. It was time to begin again and survive this day. On her feet she would need to find courage. A will to live.

Thank you, God. Please don't leave me.

Her thoughts went to Dennis. He was probably already awake. He loved his mornings. Maybe he was sitting in the kitchen reading the newspaper. Perhaps he was eating a piece of toast.

Then her thoughts were filled with her beautiful children. *Dear God, I don't want to be the person who gave up. I don't ever want my children to say that their mom gave up.*

Just last week, Margi had discussed a desire to end her life during a session with Jay. She expressed the hopeless idea that maybe her faith had failed her. Maybe God didn't even know she existed. She remembered Jay's advice now as she stood next to her bed: "Don't ever give up your faith, because your faith saved you. You wouldn't be here today if it wasn't for the fact that God was your wingman, Margi. God and the angels gave you what you needed at the time."

Jay had suggested she read Psalm 91 in the bible, saying it was a great source of comfort for many of his survivors. The words were filled with compassion:

I will say of the Lord, He is my refuge and my fortress: my God; in him will I trust . . .

He shall cover thee with his feathers, and under his wings shalt thou trust: his truth shall be thy shield and buckler.

Thou shalt not be afraid for the terror by night; nor for the arrow that flieth by day;

For he shall give his angels charge over thee, to keep thee in all thy ways.

They shall bear thee up in their hands, lest thou dash thy
foot against a stone.

Margi slowly walked into the bathroom. She squeezed a small
amount of toothpaste onto her toothbrush and avoided looking in
the mirror. That always complicated things.

The evil would not win today. Margi would somehow find her
way to work today, and she would serve patients in the oral surgeon's
office. There were always patients who needed a smile or a kind word.
Perhaps she could make a small difference in someone's life today.

After work she would call her niece Jennifer. She would thank
Jennifer for daily prayers on her behalf—prayers that might have
played a part this morning. Jennifer had cried when Margi told her of
the DID diagnosis; finally there was an answer. Jennifer had called it
a beautiful protection, God's gift to keep Margi alive during all those
years of abuse. Margi and Jennifer had wept together. Tears for past
failures of love. Tears for unspeakable wrongdoings.

But also tears of hope for the future.

PART FOUR

ABUSED CHILDREN SPEAK A LANGUAGE YOU CAN'T LEARN.

Chapter 32

"I have an assignment for you, Margi," Jay said.

"Okay. What kind of assignment?"

"I'd like you to start writing down your nightmares. When you wake in the middle of the night, grab a pencil and paper or your laptop or even your phone. Write what you've seen and heard and felt. Write the words that are going through your mind."

Jay expected the silence that greeted his request. The request was an overwhelming one, initially met with trepidation by all Jay's clients. He listened and waited.

"I . . . I'm sure nobody would ever want to read what's inside my head. It's so ugly, Jay. How could I ever write those words? To describe in detail what I've been through in my dreams . . ." Her voice quivered.

"One of the most effective ways to access all those inner feelings is through writing," Jay explained. "Most of us have poured our hearts out in angry, sad, or accusatory letters that we never mailed. Even if we never send them, it makes us feel better. Don't worry about anybody's judgment, Margi. There is no editing. You just write to yourself. Listen to your own thoughts, and let their flow take over. Later, you may discover some surprising truths. It can be really enlightening."

Jay knew this was a big step. It would validate some flashbacks and the parts that held onto pieces of her life. Although it would confirm some things, it was also frightening.

"Will you read it?" Margi asked. "Are you going to read what I write?"

"I would be happy to read anything you send me, Margi. We can discuss some things you've written when you feel ready. You might want me to read something but you may not want to talk about it. That's okay too. It'll give me a better idea what you're wrestling with. You're in charge of this."

"When do you need this assignment?"

"Email me—text me. Anytime day or night," Jay responded. "There is no schedule. It's just a free flow of information."

"I think I can do it," Margi said. "Jennifer suggested the same thing awhile back, so I've tried to do it a few times." A smile slowly spread across her face. "I always loved English in school. Who knew this would be a reason to start writing?"

Jay liked her sense of humor. Margi was smart. She had a bright intellect. So often the best and brightest children were chosen for ritualistic and medical abuse because of their ability to dissociate. So often he had seen brilliant minds used for evil purposes.

"You can also draw pictures if you'd like," Jay added. "Sketch images, faces, or scenes from your nightmares."

"Oh, boy. I guarantee *those* won't appear in any art museum. I can't draw very well."

"Again, it's just a free flow of something visual," Jay explained. "It may open up some memories or give us a clue about your past."

"Got it. I'll see what I can do. There are going to be some really evil pictures—images I never thought would be allowed outside my own mind."

"Your nightmares are more than just dreams, Margi. They're memory-mares," Jay stated. "Those memories are making the rounds, but they haven't made it all the way into what I call *the blending place*. They're seeping. If there's a memory of trauma and you're in the rapid eye movement stage of sleep, your mind is bringing up scenes in those rapid eye movements and you're having nightmares. The scenes you're bringing up are scenes from your past."

. . .

Margi considered the idea. Something inside had always warned her

164

of sharing information from her past with anyone. Now that warning rushed to the surface with new intensity. Margi felt her heart begin to race.

From an early age, Margi had learned not to let anyone get close to her mind. *If you let them in, they will trick you.* She wasn't sure who *they* represented, but this she knew for sure: It was always about trickery. *You take me down a road where I think I trust you, and then you take me someplace else. You hurt me. And you trick me.*

Margi struggled with the ability to trust. *Whenever people are nice to me, I pay in the long run. There's always a catch.* It had become a tragic and paralyzing fear.

A fear that someone would always take her and trick her.

. . .

It had been another night spent tossing, turning, and yelling for help. Margi's gasping breath awakened her, and she pulled the covers up around her neck. *Another day.*

The nightmares still present in her mind and body, Margi begged for help like she did so many mornings. She needed to move forward and find a way to start her day. *God, please help me.*

Suddenly Margi remembered. In the middle of the night she had written something. Something on her phone. A text, perhaps?

Margi reached for her phone, and her shaking fingers scrolled down to see if the words had been saved. There it was. A text to Jay she had sent at 1:35 a.m. Her eyes flew down the screen as she read the words. *Are these my words?* She remembered grabbing her phone and texting Jay, but she didn't recognize the words in the text.

Who wrote this?

The words gripped her.

Maybe the person you talk to is safe now, but what about what's coming? Bad things are always coming, and I have to be prepared, and there's nowhere to hide, and I can't run away from me. I always have to be there and feel all the fear.

There's no will to live in that place. No one ever should have to know what that's like, but I live it every single day. The players might be in hell, but so am I. Each day is the same as the day before. Today I'm somehow a day older, but every day repeats the one I already had. So, I don't know how time passes. It seems to pass but returns again, and the only players all my heads can see and feel are stuck in a time that demand I look at them and keep them close.

Tonight will be another last night and tomorrow will repeat itself. I can't fix that. I'm sure it's a mean trick that's being played on me. It just goes round and round.

You can't help me.

Chapter 33

Jay had assured Margi in their last conversation that she was making progress.

"We are learning some things," Jay had said. He assured her that it was a foundation for future sessions. He said that parts were coming forward and being communicated on paper for the first time. He applauded her for the courage to begin writing and encouraged her to continue.

Margi walked into her bedroom and looked at her bed. It was late. She really needed some rest but resisted even the idea of laying down. *I hate my bed.*

The nightmares were bad enough, but waking up was another level of fear. Margi was afraid of the nightmares themselves, but she was also scared she would wake up as a different part. She sat on the edge of her bed and looked down at her pillow. *Where are we going tonight?*

Margi lay her head on the soft pillow and closed her eyes tightly in a futile attempt to keep everything out. Then the words almost audibly filled her head, triggering a shiver that ran the length of her spine.

You're at the gateway to hell. Satan has control over you.

Margi scribbled the words on the notepad next to her.

Margi then reached to the other side of the bed and slid her laptop over to her side. She sat up, lifted it onto her lap, and began to write.

I will lay here in my bed and wait for the nightmares to come. They don't even wait until I'm asleep. I will lay here and pray one more time to an invisible God to please take away this unbearable pain, knowing that day will never come. I will carry this burden that has gotten so unbearably heavy with no relief in sight. I will live forever with the demons that haunt my nights, and I will start each new day in a terrifying new dimension where no one should ever have to visit or get to know.

I'll have to accept that I need to fight hard to keep my sanity and find a will to be alive. I will lay here one more night not knowing who or what I am with a fear so intense it takes away my breath. Tomorrow I will pretend once again to appear that nothing is wrong and just take all that is imposed on me. I can't give up. I don't know how, but I have to wonder how much I can take.

. . .

Margi continued in her courageous endeavor to describe in detail what was happening after nine p.m. That's when it always started. As the hour hand inched toward the nine position, Margi felt her mind begin to dissociate. So many words. So many different thoughts and flashbacks to places she didn't remember. But her mind clearly *did* remember, because it was relentless in its effort to take Margi there.

In her last session with Jay, Margi had expressed her desire to be articulate. She wanted what she wrote to be exactly right. She had never really put words to paper. Not like this. Now she felt pressured to accurately describe what her mind was feeling. She knew it was important for the purpose of therapy—important for Jay to fully understand.

. . .

I feel like a soldier who has been in battle or combat his whole life—maybe for a thousand years—and every day is the same as the day before, with no hope of the war ever ending. Only this soldier's head is so divided, he can't even see who he's fighting against. His exhaustion is wearing him down and making him so sick, and he wishes he could die from his wounds.

He hates the war. He doesn't know who he is or why he's meant to fight so hard, and he wonders why the people around him aren't also at war. His war must be his own hell.

. . .

Writing was incredibly challenging. Margi shuddered at memories of waking and being so terrified she could hardly reach over and turn on the bedside lamp. Just when she wanted to forget the awful details, she found the words to describe it and bring it to life all over again. They weren't just visuals. She *felt* them.

Occasionally the scenes were so horrid that Margi couldn't describe them in writing. What words could possibly explain the kind of evil that was beyond anyone's imagination?

But even during those times, Jay said, she needed to try. "That's how you know when they're real and that it's not just a bad nightmare. It's something that you lived, Margi."

His words of comfort and his positive encouragement helped Margi keep trying to document it all. With a pounding heart, Margi continued to reach for the strength to grab a pencil.

Margi often cried in the morning when she read the words she had written during the night. They made her realize how bad the situation was deep in the broken cracks of her mind. But she also realized that deep inside there were parts ready to divulge some details.

.   .   .

Last night I went to a place in the woods; there were mostly men, but women too. I watched as they did terrible things to a cat. His front legs were tied above his head, and he was put on the table. They were saying something religious and quoting scripture. I saw somebody being pulled up by a rope on top of a barn. Terrible things were going on. It was evil.

.   .   .

Last night I was in a triangle with a group of people chanting, and I had to sit on the floor in the center of this triangle. One of the people had a cup of blood. It was from a dog they had just killed.

· · ·

Last night my dad dropped me off in front of a house. It was a party for friends of my parents. I was hung up by my wrists and passed around to a group of adults.

· · ·

Last night . . . was so bad I can't write about it.

Chapter 34

"I've got notebooks and notebooks describing my dreams," Margi told Jay. "It's quite a collection now, but I'm not sure I'll ever show them to anyone. They're just horrible."

"You're not required to show them to anyone. For now, they are a valuable resource. Your parts have found an outlet that will help us learn more. I'm proud of you. You're doing great."

"So many of my writings are repetitive," Margi explained. "When I read through them, I see some of the same themes—water, spinning, and basements, to name just a few. Some of the same phrases and words come up over and over. If I don't remember writing the words, how can I write them exactly the same night after night?"

"Your parts are writing," Jay replied. "And they are holding memories and talking about them. It makes sense that the part who was writing yesterday will come up again tonight or next week and write again using the same vocabulary or the same expressions."

"Why can't they tell the story once and then just move on? I just want all the details so *I* can move on."

"Maybe you as the core are not ready for all the details," Jay said. "Your parts are protecting you. This takes time. It's a process, not an event. You're getting there."

Margi considered that for a moment. *A process.* She was so tired. Margi really wanted a quick fix, and it was clear that even Jay wasn't going to provide that.

"I've been having some really strange dreams about my mother lately," Margi whispered. Even though nobody was around to overhear their conversation, she was always uncomfortable talking about her mother.

"Let's talk about that," Jay said. "Tell me about those dreams. What's happening?"

"Well, sometimes in the middle of the night I wake from a really scary dream and feel like I'm suffocating. It feels like there's a pillow over my head and . . . I can't . . . it's so terrifying, but I can't breathe."

"Who is holding a pillow over your face?"

"I don't know. But whenever I have those suffocating dreams, I think of my mom. Not the kind of thoughts like I want her to come and help me, but more like she's terrifying and I'm with her. I can't get air, and I'm frantic."

Margi paused for a moment before continuing.

"Sometimes I have to run to the back door of my house and step outside for a minute to get some cool air on my face. I'm always so scared to go back to bed because . . . well . . . she might be there. And I feel so disconnected when that happens. It scares me half to death. I just know that normal people don't have dreams like this. Who dreams about their mother like that? It's so strange but so real."

Suddenly Margi stood up and began to pace. Her voice trembled.

"I need to go. I'll call you later. I need to go."

"Where do you need to go?" Jay asked. "Who am I talking to?"

"I just need to go," Margi answered. "I don't like talking about my mother. I shouldn't talk about my mother. Bye."

· · ·

Jay wrote a few notes then hung up the phone. They were making progress. The parts were not only writing but were beginning to talk to him. He was beginning to recognize some characteristics of different parts from the writings and information shared over the phone.

· · ·

Last night I was in my grandmother's basement. It was those rooms—those three rooms. I was in the basement, and those three rooms in the basement were

172

connected to me somehow. My dad took me there through a back entrance into the basement. I felt dread. Horrible dread. I saw those three doors, and I couldn't open them because I didn't want what was behind the doors to be a part of me.

In my grandmother's basement, I had no clothes on. There were two other girls there, and they drew a picture of moons with stars around them on my stomach. Something bad happened.

There are so many secrets.

. . .

Margi slipped the white t-shirt off the hanger and pulled it over her head. She grabbed a favorite pair of jeans. It was time to begin another day. There were several items on the to-do list today, and Margi preferred it that way. The busier, the better. Anything to keep her mind busy and active.

On her way out of the bedroom, the notepad caught her eye. The front cover was tucked behind the pages, which indicated that Margi had written during the night. *Oh, what happened last night?* She hesitated at first, then walked over and picked up the notebook. Her eyes scanned the page.

It was another entry about her grandmother's basement. There were so many. They often included spinning in dental chairs surrounded by men dressed in black. Spinning upside down. Spinning tables. Spinning faster and faster until she couldn't grab anything to stop and her mind went to another place. Why so much spinning? Was it some kind of mind control? And why her grandmother's house?

As much as Margi remembered loving her grandmother, the house her grandmother lived in had always made her feel uneasy. Her crippled grandmother was unable to go down the stairs, but Margi knew the basement was a lower level that ran the entire length of the house. In the basement were three bedroom doors. Something frightened Margi about basements in general, but her grandmother's basement was especially terrifying, and it was the subject of countless nightmares.

But moons and stars? She had sketched the picture of the moons encircled by stars beneath the narrative. *Why moons and stars? Why would I draw it like that? I've never seen anything like it before.*

Margi picked up the notebook and took it over to the computer. She googled moons and stars and began to scroll through images and drawings, looking for any information that might give a clue to the meaning of what she had drawn.

Then she saw it: an exact replica of her drawing. The article featuring the photo described satanic rituals and the meaning behind them. The image Margi had drawn was often tattooed in semi-permanent ink on the lower stomach where it couldn't easily be seen by others. The ritual figuratively sacrificed internal organs to Satan. The article made other references to sparkly orbs and chanting men in robes.

Margi's eyes widened at the discovery. She had no actual memory of anything like this, nor had she ever read or seen anything related to this representation of the moon and stars. Margi's heart pounded in her chest.

Why would I draw that?

Chapter 35

Did you know the space in between is a dream? And the words spoken there are an echo and they don't match time? And the person saying the words is in the space in between? And time doesn't match what I'm seeing or hearing? So, where does that put me?

I am outside of your time and not sure how to get back inside. Everyone in between doesn't notice because they don't know they are in my dream. Why isn't anyone scared like me? Why do they all look so calm like everything is okay?

There is nothing anyone can tell me that will make me believe I am part of the present and included in time. I have a different time. I am made of so many different things. You must see that when you look at me. Sometimes I'm hollow. Sometimes I'm the wrong size and my body doesn't feel like mine. So, who are you seeing?

I don't know my own voice. I hate to hear my voice and look at my face. We don't match. And the thoughts are so loud inside, and they don't match, and I need them to stop. Why can't someone make them stop? I hate all of this to be attached as one. We just move and can't take time to think about what we are and what it feels like to be inside. I wish I knew how to leave, but they won't let me.

I can't forget about the place where we came from. It is so dark and thick in that place. It takes your mind away and owns it. I know it's there. I know I can't think about it, but I know it's there because sometimes I see it for only a moment and can feel it start to take us away. And I know if I let myself go there, it will keep us. You think it's only a place in my mind, but it's a real place—more real than where I live now. It's where we came from and they are waiting for us.

The life I've lived is all a make-believe place with make-believe people to trick me to believe in its reality. They think it's funny. Nothing you can say will ever change all this. Your logic is not my logic. It doesn't apply.

I just want to go home. But I don't know where that is.

. . .

"If you had been abused only by your father, you would have worked through some issues and been okay now," Jay suggested. "If you had familial abuse and also some ritual abuse, you would still be doing really well right now."

Margi listened intently. She had voiced some discouragement at the slow progress. Margi still wanted an overnight cure; she wanted the roller coaster she was on to stop.

"But that third context—the medical trauma that includes drugs, hypnosis, and mind control—is what is holding you back from healing," Jay continued. "It really is. Some of your parts are holding drugged memories and programmed thinking. When those parts come forward, a lot of patience and time are required to break through that. And until we can retrieve and put those memories from the third context to rest, it pulls in all those confusing, fuzzy feelings of alternate dimensions and realities for you."

"Sometimes I wish they would have just killed me," Margi muttered. "This is so hard—so overwhelming to beat."

"They took you to the edge of your life and your sanity, Margi, but you held on. Your fighting spirit held tight from the beginning. It is still fighting."

Margi thought back to so many conversations when she told Jay that it was time to die or that no one could ever help. Those were blanket statements coming from some unyielding place. Jay always questioned the logic of such statements, and Margi always gave the same quick retort. *Well, it's my logic.*

"Your last writing was one of many confirmations concerning medical trauma," Jay noted.

Margi thought back to her essay from the night before. She had texted Jay in the middle of the night with a detailed description of space and time never coming together. She wondered what part had written those words so carefully.

"I have a number of drawings that I sketched about my dreams; they seemed so strange, but when I researched them on the computer, I learned they represent exercises in mind control," Margi added. "Like all the spinning and ropes and water . . . lots of water."

"Are you still working on your collage?" Jay asked.

"I'm almost done. There are some things I just can't draw, so I went to the computer and searched for certain words then looked at images. When I found an image that looked and felt real to me, I printed it. I have an entire collection of those images along with my sketches. There are sad girls, stairs, dark rooms, black-hooded robes, water, and so many other things."

"Have you shown the images and sketches to anyone? Dennis?" Jay asked.

"I will when I'm done. I want to show it to Dennis and my kids. It's a horrible collection of evil, but it defines what's inside of me. I've been very careful to include only things that are accurate—precise images represented by flashbacks or nightmares. It's both horrible and validating at the same time."

"That's good," Jay replied. "See this through, Margi. I want to see it next time I travel to Utah."

"I found a picture the other day that I colored when I was five or six years old. It's called *My Witch*."

"Send it to me," Jay asked. "I'd like to see it."

"I will. I've included it in the collage. There is another one that shows a smiling, happy family standing next to a house. The words *reality, family, God, light,* and *your world* are written next to that family. Then there's a dark scribbled line underneath that happy image and there's a child laying on the ground with arms stretched out. The words *dark, evil, Satan, unreality, voices,* and *fear* are written next to her."

"Take a picture of the drawing with your phone and text it to me," Jay said. "I'd like to see that drawing as well."

"Okay. Sometimes it's hard to look at my drawings and read my writings. I'm not even sure who wrote them."

"We'll get to that," Jay replied. "You keep working on that collage and keep texting me. You can do this, Margi. You're strong."

Margi didn't feel strong. She felt beaten. Weak.

"That little girl under the house is sad," Margi whispered.

. . .

"Jay, I'm ready for a teaching day," Margi said.

Jay had called for a scheduled session. Sometimes Margi didn't want to talk about herself but wanted to just learn. Jay was so full of insightful information. Margi had her notebook and pencil ready, and Jay always let her designate the subject matter.

Often Margi wanted to discuss theology. She knew Jay had done doctorate work in that area, and she loved to listen to his depth of understanding. Margi's parts were furious at God. They had a tendency to point at God and wonder where He was. He never showed up. Margi needed to understand why.

"Maybe He did," answered Jay. "Let's talk about a few ways that God showed up."

"Okay, I'm listening," Margi replied.

"God helps us and communicates with us both directly and through other people. Jennifer is a godsend. Her love and patience and willingness to endure this with you is immeasurable. And Dennis has been with you for how many years? Where is God? Look at your children."

Margi felt tears in her eyes. Jay always had a way of taking her spiraling negative thoughts and bringing clarity to them all. Teaching days provided a context for the trauma. Greater understanding and wisdom helped her understand it was not her fault. Teaching days helped Margi make sense of places and events in time.

And teaching days brought some peace to Margi's core.

Chapter 36

First of all, I don't have any stupid parts, and everything is all make-believe. And there is no stupid child that's attached to me that had bad things happen to her. There is NO child attached to me.

I wasn't born a child; I was made. There's only some freak of a child that haunts my thoughts. I have no idea where she comes from. Everyone else seems to have a child inside them that they're attached to and grew up with, so everyone else seems to have an identity, and they get to know who they are as a human. They made only one of me, and I'll have to go back to them someday. So just stop trying to help me, because I'm not like anyone else and you're wasting your time.

You really think you know, but you have no idea. You can't help something that wasn't even made to be like you. There have never been words invented that can describe how divided it is inside and how there's nothing holding anything together. It could be possible at any time for God to stop the world from turning and I'll fall off or I'll be left behind or I'll be left to suffocate or I'll be the first one chosen when everyone else has gone.

I never know what the next bad thing will be, so I'm forever scared beyond what anyone else could imagine. I hate it here. I'm so tired.

Just stop trying to get inside my head because there is no one there.

. . .

"Margi, let's talk about the email you sent me a couple of nights ago—the one that announces you don't have any parts."

"Yep. I read that one the following morning," Margi said.

"You and I had been talking about parts that have certain jobs. Parts that have been protectors for you. We discussed that the night before."

"Yes, I remember."

"In your writing, someone is telling me you don't have parts. Who is telling me that?"

"Just me," Margi answered.

"Well, *Just Me* is a part. What can you tell me about her?"

"She just does what I do—what the core does. She's always on my left, and she takes over when I'm too shy or too scared. She's just kind of another me."

"Can I talk to Just Me for a few minutes?" Jay asked. "I would like her to tell me more about herself."

"She won't come out. She had to go."

Jay knew that was common with DID survivors. Parts came and left quickly. It would take time for them to develop a trusting relationship with him. They were young and frightened. It was promising that Margi had addressed one of the parts by name. Just Me would likely be an inner helper who held information about the other parts.

Jay looked forward to future communication with Just Me when she was ready.

. . .

"Hi, Margi."

Jennifer and Margi spoke almost daily, and Jennifer often expressed happiness that her aunt was finally getting the help she needed. Jennifer said Jay was a blessing—and it was her belief that God had heard many desperate prayers, including hers, pleading for help on this journey. "Did you read the last email I sent to Jay?" Margi asked. "The one declaring I have no parts?"

Margi often sent Jennifer texts and emails she had already sent to Jay. Jennifer had been a sounding board through years of work with other therapists in Margi's life, and she trusted Jennifer.

"Yes, I read it," Jennifer answered. "I'm thinking there's a part of you that is afraid to let anyone know the truth."

Margi considered that thought and nodded in agreement. This road was bumpy, winding, and full of potholes. Every single day brought a new adventure. She was so glad Jennifer was along for the ride. She could tell her anything. Margi knew Jennifer was on this path with her for life, no matter what might land in her email inbox.

"I worry that Jay really believes the email and that maybe I'm making this whole thing up," Margi said. "This DID diagnosis makes perfect sense to me, and then I send off an email declaring there is no one inside my head!"

"Margi, this is all part of the process. I understood that some part of you is in denial. There are children who are afraid that if they tell anything, they'll be punished for it. If I understand that, I'm certain Jay does too. We're all in this together. The dreams, the writings, your photos and drawings, the flashbacks, and even the absence of childhood memories all paint a very accurate picture. Your family will all stand behind you. No one doubts you, Margi."

Earlier Jennifer had walked Margi through practice conversations with her adult children. Jennifer had encouraged Margi to be open about DID and to carefully help her own adult children accept their mother's diagnosis. Jennifer expressed her belief that over time, her children would ask more questions and Margi could slowly fill in the details when they were ready. Jennifer had promised to help guide Margi through every step.

Tears welled up in Margi's eyes. Phone calls to her beautiful niece always ended on a positive note. Jennifer was a gift from God.

. . .

Jennifer's intent from the beginning had been to end every conversation on a positive note. Regardless of how many tears or fears each phone call contained as it started, Jennifer wanted to help Margi find promise.

Within the first minute of Margi's calls to her, Jennifer knew whether

Margi was calling or whether one of her frightened parts was speaking for her. Jennifer didn't need to know names or characters; she knew based on the speaker's attitude and opinions. She prayed every day to turn their conversations around. To bring Margi's core front and center so that her heart would recognize what was important and true.

. . .

NIGHTTIME

Nighttime is an event. It starts when the sun has the most shade and the day world fades into the night. It starts early and lasts all through the night. She gets no relief.

It's also when day Margi is removed and replaced by someone else. Her movements and thoughts aren't hers, but she has no choice but to stay inside where she doesn't belong. She knows when she gets into bed that her mind will take her to places that are made of hallucinations and force her to be with men and women that are strange and unhuman and evil. She feels their evil deep inside her. She leaves all that might be safe in her day world to go into this magic make-believe world that she has no power over. She can never stop the process or the places she visits at night.

Nighttime has a life of its own. She goes from place to place running and hiding and living in a world of magic and ghosts. And men and women hurt her and have sex with her and frighten her beyond anything that is human and she has to endure it all. Doctors doing things to her body telling her they have to do it. She has to live with spiders and water everywhere. She lives in basements and she's lived with Satan. He sometimes chases her and tells her things she doesn't want to hear.

She spins and spins and no one ever comes to save her. She lives a day life, but her night life is most exhausting and she is so alone. She never expects to be rescued. She just accepts that she will always be alone. Rescuers never came.

When morning comes, she has to pretend that the events of her night life never existed.

. . .

"What's that?" Dennis asked.

Margi quickly pulled her arm back and tugged on the sleeve that had shimmied up her arm to reveal a red mark.

"It's nothing."

"It's *not* nothing. It looks like a burn, Margi." He gently pulled up the sleeve to reveal a second mark. "What are these? How did this happen?"

"I was just careless." Margi tried to sound convincing, but her voice cracked. She could feel Dennis's eyes follow her as she quickly gathered the dinner dishes and piled them next to the sink.

"Talk to me, Margi," Dennis pleaded.

Margi didn't want him to know. This was one more item on a list of hundreds of crazy things. She just wanted to be a good wife, and that was becoming more and more difficult. He deserved better.

"I . . . all I really want is peace," Margi said. "I can't find that."

Emotions began to spill. Her head dropped down, and her shoulders slumped. Tears rolled down her cheeks.

"But you've been doing so well with Jay. You said you were making some progress."

"I am, but sometimes I look in the mirror and I just hate me. I wake up afraid. I go to bed afraid. I'm so desperate to make it go away." Margi dabbed her eyes with a napkin.

"How did you burn yourself, Margi?"

"My curling iron. I'm not looking for attention. I just . . . I hate who I am. Why won't God help me? I must be a freak of nature."

Margi's mind carried her back to that morning. She had turned the curling iron on high. As she burned the marks into her arm, the words flashed into her mind.

You are worthless. You are hopeless. You are helpless.

. . .

Dennis's eyes widened as he recognized the heart-rending condition.

183

He had seen the emotional signs of Margi's DID, and God knew this was difficult for him. He had his own struggles with all of this. He imagined how difficult it was for her, but clearly it was much more painful than he knew.

Margi's self-inflicted burns were a physical cry for help. She needed so much more from him. *What can I give her?* This was a learning curve for both of them. He wasn't trained in how to handle this.

Dennis stood still for a moment without saying anything, then felt a quiet thought. *Acceptance. She needs acceptance and security.*

"Margi, I'm not going anywhere. I'm here for you."

Dennis wrapped his arms around his weeping wife and held her close. "I love you, Margi, and I'll always love you no matter what."

"I'm such a mess," Margi cried.

"We've all got our issues, sweetheart," Dennis said. "We're going to tackle this together. I'll tell you what. Those nightmares of yours— I think you're carrying those around with you all day long. I know you're texting them to Jay, but I want to help you unload."

Margi lifted her chin and looked at Dennis.

"How?" Margi asked.

"I'm going to come in here every morning, and I want you to download. Just spew, because I don't want you to carry that around in your head for the rest of the day. It has to affect your mood. I can't explain it, and I can't solve it—Jay is the expert here—but I can listen. You get that stuff out of your head so you can start your day."

. . .

Margi thought for a moment. She had always tried to keep the details from Dennis. They were so ugly and embarrassing. Maybe it was time to be more open.

"It's not going to be pretty."

"That's why it needs to come out," Dennis replied.

"I love you," Margi whispered.

Dennis was right. He didn't have the answers, but she appreciated his willingness to share a portion of the burden. He had loved and cherished her since they were teenagers. They were still on this journey after all these years. Dennis was still by her side even after all their ups and downs.

Margi promised herself she would take his hand and walk it together.

Chapter 37

I wanted you to talk to the crazy one. The one that's evil and capable of horrific things. I don't know if you've met her, but she's totally different from Margi. When she's here, I go way inside.

She believes she's crazy because her thoughts come from a different place. She believes she's like the crazy people in movies, and she hears and sees things that aren't there. Her world is made up of hatred and delusion, but when someone comes into her space, she can bring out the normal Margi. Inside she knows she's crazy and can fool everyone.

I really wanted you to talk to her while she was here. She couldn't find a real place to land tonight. Then tomorrow she's gone, and we pretend nothing happened and we find a Margi who can move on without her. Ha! Can't wait to go to sleep and have nightmares then wait and see who I get to be in the morning.

Freaky little beast!

Who were the people who lived in the house with her? Who is that little girl in my head? Why is she always in a dream?

Why didn't anyone love her? Why was she invisible to everyone? She was so excited to open her Valentine box at school, but she didn't get a single valentine from anyone! Ha! That's because no one could see her! How did she get through each day in a world that wasn't real? Oh, just put her out of her misery!

Poor stupid little beast!

. . .

"I got your email last night at nine. Have you read it, Margi?"

Margi was still reeling from an exceptionally bad night. "Yeah, I read it. I didn't write it."

"Well, somebody did. Who is this little girl? Did she write it?"

"It was . . . um . . . Little Margi," Margi said. "She's so sad. I should feel bad for her, but I'm really scared of her. She holds a lot of evil."

"I'd like to talk to her," Jay replied. "She can probably help us."

"She can't help anybody. There's too much pain. Little Margi is in my nightmares, and sometimes she's there when I wake up. She was there . . . um . . . this morning."

"Maybe you and I can both reach out to her and provide some comfort," Jay suggested.

"I don't want to comfort her. I'm terrified of her. This morning I couldn't breathe. I could feel the man on top of me. He was . . . hurting me."

Margi began to cry softly. She wanted the memories to go away. There was nothing good in Little Margi. "She is a dark, evil little girl. Little Margi believes God has turned His back on her. She has been rejected again and again. We just go to bed every night and prepare to relive my terror and the horrible images and feelings that go with it. I'm afraid to even sit on my bed at night. It's like *here we go*. But at some point, it gets so late that I have to sleep."

"Little Margi is not dark, and she is not evil," Jay said. "You were never evil. Little Margi is a beautiful little girl who had evil imposed on her. She holds a lot of secrets. What *happened to her* is dark and evil, but *she* is just an innocent child."

"I'm terrified of her," Margi said.

"You and I are going to begin working together on a project, Margi. Remember how we've talked about parts and their purpose? They have important jobs, and they each hold pieces of the trauma in order to protect you. They are the secret keepers."

"Yes, I remember."

"We need to take some of those memories along with the feelings and behaviors associated with them and contain them in a safe place. When a part is stuck in a scene from trauma, it doesn't know that the core survived and went on to be okay. Your part is afraid to find out the end of the story, because it truly doesn't know what happened to you. It

188

assumes the worst."

"You told me the parts are still protecting me because they still think the trauma is still going on, right?" Margi asked.

"Yes, that's right. Little Margi is holding on to terrible memories because she is protecting you. She doesn't want you to feel them, but sometimes those traumatic memories seep into the present. If Little Margi is out front—like she often is after nine at night—you're going to experience what she's feeling. What she's holding."

Margi nodded in agreement as she scribbled some notes on the notepad next to her. Jay was helping her understand. She wanted to remember this so she could talk to Dennis about it later.

"We're at a point now, Margi, where you should learn some new tools," Jay said. "Your core is ready to take back control from your protecting parts. There are new tools—new ways of doing things. The new tools are much more effective than the protectors' old ways. I think you're ready."

"Oh, I'm ready. What kind of tools?"

"It's a guided imagery exercise. I'll teach you how to do it. Margi— you as the core—is going to do it. You're going to design it."

"Design? Design what?"

"A Safe Place."

Chapter 38

SAD AND LONELY

The miserably sad and lonely girl was so confused with the world she had been placed in. It was a world unlike anything else. She dreamed dreams of wickedness and spent time in hell with demons and witches and magic. It wasn't imaginary or make-believe, and it just seemed to her that's what she was made of. She knew it was born inside her.

She was forced to spend her days going from one dimension to another and found herself floating through the terror of it all. Watching someone else's body moving her through time—feeling her mind and small frame disconnect and leave to be separate from her as it invariably did. How did she get to this place? And what happened to her sight? Why had her eyes betrayed her again? She hated them for what they showed her.

She was back inside a suffocating, transparent bubble that changed the total appearance of her world. And why does her mind always get to decide when all this must happen to her? She came to expect that her world was never as it seemed. With her limited understanding of the true nature of life and love, how was she to know she was a victim? She lived in a hell that was hers alone, so her mind had to put it away—outside her knowledge. She kept it a secret from herself because she knew that this held enough terror that it could cause a mind to break.

All she ever wanted was to climb outside her own mind, but she found that hopelessly impossible. Instead, she ran aimlessly, hoping to find her mind and get it back into a time that made sense to her. She prayed to an imaginary God that maybe this time she could see the world as she was certain others did instead of being in her own very private dream that lacked continuity on any level.

There is no sense of where time goes. The distance between reality and the nightmare of seeing life moving on without her through eyes that don't seem to belong to her is a small, thin line. The illusions of magic and demons always catch up with her and stay in her mind as long as they want. She learned quickly that they hold the control that took away her time and forced her eyes to look at things that were beyond all laws of logic.

She was lost inside a time that only she could see and in a dimension that existed only for her. But to her it was more vivid than real life itself, and with that came complete and absolute terror. She rarely saw time and space together as one as it should be.

This girl was made up of hidden parts of herself that would join her and come and go as if on a whim. They would blindside her with fear beyond any imaginings and leave her wondering when they would return to once again take her away from her world that used to be right.

This prevented her from attending school as a child should. It denied her the right to dream that there could ever be light in her dismal existence. She didn't dare imagine a tomorrow that didn't include the same horror of today, with unknown people locking her away and keeping her until they were done. She was stuck in a time that never seemed to match the day's space.

The girl lived in a horrible, dark box with a man and a woman. She was mostly invisible, except when the man wanted to be with her. He gave her medicine that caused her mind to break and to separate into fragmented pieces. She could feel her body detach and leave her so another one could hold the shame and horror of what was happening.

She's gone once again. That's when the man would lay on top of her small body and suffocate her with his love. And when he loved her from behind, she could barely breathe. He was sad with life, so her job was to make him happy. But his happiness became her pain, and he didn't care that he took her soul and gave it to the devil. They now both live in hell. He wanted her to share that awful place with him so she could be sad and lonely too.

But somehow, she still loved him very much and still called him Daddy. The woman who lived there didn't care what she saw and she didn't hear the cries for help because she lived in a hell of her own. And no one, it seemed, could make her happy. Sometimes the woman's face could change so it had the look and the sound of the devil. But we can't talk about her.

Then finally after many years went by and the girl was on the edge of crazy, the woman took her to a special hospital. She saw doctors that talked to the inside of her mind. They told her she was very sick and needed to come back every week, so she did—eighty-

one times. But the things they told her mind were put away in a secret place inside so she could be the little girl they wanted her to be. She was given more medicine and put back in a dream so her mind could again take her away to a place deep inside her own head, and only the doctors knew the way to get her back with their own special words. They chose to leave their words inside until the next time. Here it was determined she must lock away these secrets and live her days and nights in and out of altered states of mind.

They told her she'd never get better, and she knew that too. When she left the hospital, she had to go home. Back to the horrible, dark box with the man and the woman. She spent her time watching, observing, and testing her reality because it would change in an instant.

Nothing about her world made sense because the medicine and memories of their effects would promptly recreate the torment of her living hell. She often thought—and by now was convinced—that maybe she had died and was living with her personal demons inside her own private hell.

She prayed most days that she might find the power to die and never again remember that she ever existed. Those prayers went unanswered, and she was made to endure each new agonizing day.

Chapter 39

There is no God. Or maybe there are two Gods. But the only one I know laughs at me. He laughs at me when I pray for help. He's a laughing God. He can't help me—or he won't.

Jay read the text from Margi. His finger traced the list of contacts in his phone and found Margi's number. He glanced up at the clock. It was only eight—still early enough this evening to call.

"Hello," Margi mumbled.

"Hi, Margi. I just got your text. It's a bit unusual."

"Not really," Margi said. "Most of us don't believe in God. He's never been there for us."

"Who am I talking to?" Jay asked. He knew this was not Margi, the core. Margi never gave up on her faith; she clung tightly to her beliefs.

"It's Just Me," Margi replied, "and some others. Pissy is here."

Just Me was turning out to be an important part, an inner helper who often spoke for others. She helped Margi in certain circumstances by normalizing everything. She was also a supervisor of sorts who watched over the other parts.

"Margi has a strong belief in God," Jay said. "Her faith means everything to her. She believes it has saved her life."

"Margi's faith has failed her. They told us to call out to God and then laughed when He didn't rescue us. They told us there is no God."

"Who is *they?*" Jay asked.

"I don't know," she replied. "Lots of people. Bad people."

Jay could hear Margi start to weep. She sounded desperate. Her voice sounded dreadful.

"We think differently from Margi. There is no hope. I am helpless. I am hopeless. I want to die. I want to end all of this, but I don't know how to give up. I'm scared of heaven. I just want to end . . . to be nothing."

It was time to turn this around. The parts needed to get behind Margi so she could be out front. Jay took a direct approach. "Margi, tell me what your daughters are doing. How is your son?"

"Don't talk about them. We don't have children. Don't even bring them up."

"Of course you have children," Jay said. "Your children mean the world to you. You're going to be a grandma again soon. How wonderful is that!"

There was a long pause. It was time to bring the core up front. Nothing like children and grandchildren to bring the present into the forefront.

"Margi, tell me about your beautiful granddaughter. What did you do with her this week?"

"She *is* beautiful." Margi's voice was soft now. It sounded to Jay like the agitation was gone.

"I really try to be a good person," Margi said quietly. "I try to do all the right things and even help other people by teaching them about prayer and faith. I want so badly to believe. It aches. I want to believe Him."

Jay could tell that Margi the core was now up front and in control. What a difference.

"I only ask God for one thing. To help me find peace. Thank you for helping me, Jay. I'm working so diligently at helping my head. I'm trying to make them all safe. Look at my amazing life. Look at the blessings."

Jay smiled. What an inspiring woman. Her strength was heartening.

. . .

DRIVERS

I'm the driver, at least I think it's me
It appears foggy around me
I can't see far behind me or in front of me
There are no sides

I'm not sure where I've been or why I was there

I'm not even in time

I'm sure I'm not real

I'm not sure if I'm facing the right way to go forward

I'm so afraid and I want to go home

There isn't a road that will get me there

Everyone else seems to know how to get home

I don't know what home looks like

I wouldn't even know the people that live there

So where do I go if I can't get home

I'm so afraid

How do I make sense of this

Now I'm a new driver, at least I think it's me

I don't remember who was just driving or where she's been

So much time has passed

I can't remember where it went

I know I don't want to go where she was

And I'm not sure how I got here so

I have to find a new way

And decide where it is I need to be

It feels important that I get there

I'm so worried that I won't know what I'm supposed to do there

I seem to recognize the people

But they are the wrong size and they aren't in my time

Actually, there's so many of us

We can't let anyone know we don't know them

Or how we got here

Someone might notice we don't look and sound the same

We're not sure what year it is but that doesn't matter

Because there is no such thing as time

Is it still the same day

There's morning drivers

And nighttime drivers that bring with them all the evil

And dread of night
There's even a driver for every season
And for all the times of the day
There's drivers that take us to places we can't come back from
The problem is the drivers don't seem to know all the other ones
And why they do what they do
They all have their own set of fears that accompany them
I've always hated all of them
I live my days in fear of the new drivers
That take me away

. . .

Margi reached for her cell phone. She hadn't talked to Jennifer for a couple of days. Life had been busy for Jennifer, who was working hard at the school.

Margi was so appreciative of all the time that Jay spent helping her understand and cope. Surely he had other clients who needed him as well. He made her feel like she was his number-one concern. It was time to fill Jennifer in on her conversation with him tonight.

When the screen lit up, Margi saw the text to Jay that had triggered his phone call. She scrolled back and saw that someone had written more. Her heart sank as she read the words written to Jay:

There is no God on this side. Please don't tell me you understand that I will heal. There is nothing to heal from. I was born to live in isolated hell.

There is no God on this side. There is nothing holding me down or holding me together. My mind has forced me to take me back to the dark places where she landed. My steps must follow.

Although the movement of my feet appear to go forward, I'm forced to revisit and relive the pain of that child who screams for relief from the hell she has been placed in. She's so bewildered at the way her world changes right before her. Forever changing and never remaining. And the time that never catches up to the space around her.

Margi wiped a tear with her sleeve and then scrolled down to find

Jennifer's contact information. It was late, but hopefully Jennifer wasn't asleep yet. Margi listened as the phone rang once. Twice.

"Hello, dear Margi." Jennifer's voice was the reassurance Margi needed.

"Hi Jennifer," Margi whispered. What would she do without this earthly angel? "I know it's late. I just want you to tell me how you know. How you know that God is real. Remind me of your testimony."

It was a humble request. Margi needed a glimmer of light.

"I need to hear it again tonight."

Chapter 40

It had been a long week. Jay's travel schedule had included seminars, conferences, and office sessions. Consulting was rewarding. The more therapists understood about trauma—and particularly the treatment of DID—the better. Educating therapists was Jay's way of reaching more survivors, of spreading the wealth of knowledge. That knowledge ultimately reached those who were suffering, and that made all the travel worth the investment of time and energy.

It was always good to be home, though. Jay was anxious to get back to his own list of survivors. It was one thing to teach the guided visual exercise to other therapists and clients across the country. It was quite another to carefully help survivors build their own Safe Place—a place Jay knew could make all the difference in their ability to cope as a multiple.

The Safe Place* visualization was created by the core with guidance from a trained therapist. It belonged to the core and, like everything else in the inside system, it existed to serve his or her needs.[1] Building the Safe Place took weeks or even months, depending on the client, and each imagery was quite different, depending on each survivor's preference.

The purpose of the Safe Place was just as the name implied: it was a safe place to bring memories and the parts who were holding them and to effectively work with painful thoughts and feelings. One important aspect of this very special place was that it was always the present day there—it was never the past. A dome of golden light was placed over and

*The imagery of the Safe Place is the property of Heartland Initiative, Inc. This particular depiction of it can be found in Karjala, Understanding Trauma and Dissociation.

around the Safe Place as a complete sphere of protection. No one could enter without the core's permission.[2]

Jay had eagerly described to therapists how to help their clients visually build such a place. It needed to be beautiful and comfortable. Generally, it resembled a one-story house with no attic or basement. There was no back door, and the windows couldn't be opened from the outside. There were as many rooms in the house as needed, and it had everything any frightened or hurting parts could ever want or need. Bedrooms, a kitchen, a private study, and playrooms for the children could all be included.[3]

Another key element of the Safe Place was a healing pool with water that contained sparkles from the same golden light that made up the dome. Parts could come to the pool, bathe in the water, drink from a waterfall, and be healed inside and out. Some survivors also put in a bank vault with a floor, a ceiling, and thick, strong walls all made of metal. Painful memories that survivors were not quite ready to work on could be stored in the vault. There they were safe and ready to be dealt with at any future time. A solid, effective method of containment for traumatic memories, feelings, and emotions was critical; the more trauma memories a survivor could contain in the vault, the fewer flashbacks he or she had.[4]

Each client's image was individual, based on preferences of beauty and peace as well as past fears. Some built such a place in a mountain meadow. Others preferred a southwestern mesa with very tall, steep sides. It was critical that the Safe Place was built by the core in a positive, healthy direction and that it did not include any trauma triggers. Attics and basements were often associated with abuse, so they were not included. Even color could be significant. As the therapist and client understood this individualized Safe Place, future effective therapy could begin to take place there as both core and parts could come together for the purpose of healing.[5]

The Safe Place was essentially a blending place—a place where consciousness was shared. Jay had observed multiples for years; he realized they were very clearly talking about a three-dimensional place in their mind and they could see all the dimensions that were there. There was somebody talking, and there was somebody else there as well. Often several people were there. They were coming together and blending. It went from person to person, and at some point, to a committee. It was multiple consciousness.

Jay understood that everyone has a blending place, but it's not clearly experienced internally. A blending place is where the present meets thoughts and events from our past that have become instrumental in who we have become. For most, it's not a clearly defined place—though it is for a multiple.

As Jay consulted and worked with therapists, he often used generalized examples to illustrate how a DID survivor might use the Safe Place, such as dealing with traumatic memories that surface in the morning after a night of very real, horrific nightmares. Unfortunately, he had heard the same story too many times in therapy sessions with hundreds of survivors. So, Jay taught the method through an all-too-common example:

> When a survivor feels a traumatic memory and sees the scene from the past, she is in the blending place. She wakes up and she feels like she can't breathe. There's pressure on her chest. She has abdominal pain and pain from below. Something is pressing on her, and she immediately sees a scene of her being molested in the blending place. It's a scene from her past. The person who sees that can hopefully get somebody to move the scene with surrounding parts out of the blending place and move it to the Safe Place and then into the healing pool. That's when helpers take over and go into the scene.
>
> Survivors often create angels to be their helpers. The angels can then help bring the children out that need to come out. The angels are completely immune to flashbacks because they weren't affected by any of the trauma memories.

They are infinitely kind and patient and will rock and sing to the child parts for as long as needed.

The angels put child parts into the healing pool to be cleaned. If there are images of the perpetrators, the angels turn those off and put them away. The perpetrators are separated. When there's nobody left in the scene, they surround the scene with light, shrink it to the size of a baseball, and get rid of it by shooting it into the sun.

There's so much value in clearing it. It's a wonderful thing for the survivors to do.

Jay knew from years of consulting and shared experiences from therapists that the exercise of creating a Safe Place was empowering for survivors. It could provide significant stabilization in a survivor's inner and outer life. Survivors found that they could control their inner life and no longer be at the mercy of unpredictable emotional storms. For most, it was a profoundly healing experience.[6]

Jay finished his breakfast then flipped his calendar open and scanned his appointments for the day. A full schedule. Not surprising after being gone for a week consulting. He made a few notes, then focused on the first scheduled session of the day.

Margi.

Chapter 41

It was a beautiful farm. A quiet, gentle place away from civilization where there was plenty of sunshine and a variety of gardens filled with flowers and vegetables. The farm animals were loved and cared for, and the puppies and kittens were soft, playful, and adored. And all of it was designed and created by Margi.

Initially, Margi had balked at the imagery exercise. Jay suggested the idea in early conversations because he knew how important it was to stabilize Margi's trauma with the Safe Place tool, but it took some time for Margi to trust Jay.

"Create a new place in my mind? Oh no . . . no . . . I'm not going there, Jay. Too many devious people have tricked my mind into going someplace new. Besides, there's no such thing as a safe place."

It had been a long and arduous process with many conversations, but Jay's patience never wore thin. He had suggested various settings as he tried to persuade Margi to try the imagery exercise. After all, every survivor had a wide variety of opinions based on previous traumas, and each created a place that felt exactly right. Margi had been very passionate about what felt safe for her. She trusted Jay and wanted to take this step, despite her apprehension.

An ocean beach? Never—there was too much water. She had so many fears involving water. The woods? Oh, no—she often had disturbing flashbacks of scary roads leading to a cabin.

And then Margi had a thought. *A farm.*

. . .

Margi had always dreamed of living on a farm. She imagined a tranquil setting lush with God's beauty and the opportunity to work with her hands. Margi loved the beauty, serenity, and trusting nature of animals. They unconditionally loved you back.

The healing pool at the farm had to be shallow, because Margi was afraid of her water dreams. When she created the pool, Jay suggested that angels come and put their hands in the shallow pool and infuse it with light, much like a biblical healing pool. Margi agreed, and the pool became safe—a healing pool of water and light.

Workers were needed to help the frightened children parts when they arrived at the Safe Place. All the caretakers Margi envisioned were women—angels and sweet nurses. As children were taken out of the scene and placed in the healing pool, the angels washed them with healing light, both inside and out—including their eyes—to get the drugs out of their system and to banish any leftover hypnosis.

The angels and nurses did whatever it took to make the children feel safe. Children could wear soft pajamas and have angels read bedtime stories if they were tired. If they needed a distraction, they could play with puppies or kittens, plant flowers in the garden, or feed the horses.

Just Me was a bridge part between the outside world and the inside world. She had a role in taking traumatic scenes that had entered the blending place and escorting those parts along with their memories to the Safe Place. Just Me understood all the parts' needs and helped the angels provide comfort or assign jobs—whatever it took to make the children feel safe and loved.

Ultimately, Margi was the owner of her farm. She directed and guided everything. If it was to work properly, she had to trust the safety and nurturing emotions that her Safe Place could promise.

. . .

Although Margi had worked hard to set up her Safe Place, there was still lots of hard work ahead. She needed to put her farm to use.

She needed to find the courage to talk to parts that frightened her. Parts like Little Margi.

If Margi could describe her core, it would be a kind, nice person with a sense of humor who loves God. *I just want to be her—only her.* That thought and desire was strong and persistent. Yet, just as heartfelt was a seemingly conflicting point: *The parts are my friends. They saved me.*

Before Jay, those *friends* never had a safe place to express terrifying images and feelings without the fear that they would go away and no one would bring them back. Now they were all learning to trust Jay's kind devotion and dedication to help.

Through this new exercise, Margi was realizing that although those *friends* had a real purpose in providing protection in the past, she now had the tools and the power to bring them forward. To help them understand there were new jobs—happy and carefree jobs working on the farm. Their past jobs weren't necessary anymore.

Margi closed her eyes and reviewed her role in directing the exercise and making a commitment to hard work—even when her core felt very distant and it was easier to stay in a dark place. On days that Margi needed everybody out of her mind so she could be an adult, she imagined the terrified parts and envisioned her core reaching out to them:

Come out of this dark place you're in and come to the present with me. I want you here. We all want to be in the light. I have a Safe Place for you. Bring your scenes, and I'll put them under a dome. We'll cover it for now and we'll look at it later. Come and wash with healing water. There is safety and peace here.

Please, come out of the dark.

Chapter 42

I am proud of how much I've accomplished.

Margi sat for a moment and embraced what she was learning and feeling about herself. Self-praise was a positive thought Margi had never felt as a child. Now Jay had an amazing ability to turn things around after a difficult session and help Margi feel like she was making progress.

Margi clung to the thought. She knew that soon enough shadows would darken as daylight ended; when that happened, she knew her peaceful feeling would be replaced by the fear and weakness found in torrid dreams. But right now, for just a moment, Margi recognized just how far she had come.

Margi thought back to her early school days. *I must have been blending with drugged parts. And who knows what happened to me the night before.* She had been trying to make sense of the world. All the other children in class looked so normal—laughing and playing. Talking to the teacher. She couldn't do any of that. How Margi wished she could talk to those teachers. She wondered what they observed in her and thought of her.

Margi thought back to consistent and constant prayers her entire life. She always prayed to be whole; she prayed for it as a little girl, and she still prayed for it as an adult. As a child, she couldn't have known what *whole* really meant. Her DID diagnosis now validated what her spirit had felt and what she had been praying for most of her life.

Margi thought back to moments or even hours when she felt removed as a wife and mother. All emotions were firing in another dimension. She knew there were moments when she pulled away and didn't interact. She also remembered moments when her children referred to her as *Mom* or Dennis introduced her at social events as his *wife*. How could her family have understood that a child part was out front? That child was crying, *I'm not a mother—I'm ten years old! Your wife? I'm not married.*

Now at least she recognized the blending and understood why it happened. The emotions and the feelings were still very much alive, but at least there was a label she could place on herself other than *crazy*.

Any number of triggers had the potential to pull Margi into the past. During that altered reality, Margi assumed the fears of a frightened little girl as she blended with her. For a time, she was both a child and an adult.

· · ·

Cloudy days are the color of dreams. There's no light when they cover the sky. They are a constant trigger and a reminder of my abandonment, abuse, and the fear of being in an altered state. They have an immediate ability to transform me to another time—another dimension.

As I walked outside for the mail, I also walked directly into a late afternoon from my past. It envelopes me once again, and I'm ten years old wondering where time went. Why am I in a dream and why don't things appear the same? Time seems to slow down, and I'm so alone. There is no one on the outside to help me. Will I be in here forever? Where is reality? The fear fills my soul.

I'm always so bewildered at the ease and frequency of this phenomenon. Just walk back into the house, Margi. Time will hopefully find its way back to you.

· · ·

With the DID diagnosis and her ongoing therapy with Jay, Margi understood the blending and confusion, but she also felt a new sense of courage. It was time to stop hiding. She had always been so open with Jennifer, and now she was able to be more open with Dennis. Margi wanted to be brave enough to share more with her children and maybe even a few close friends. She knew she could share quite a bit while still keeping the darkest details to herself.

I've come a long, long way. It's time to share. Time to help my family understand. Time to be vulnerable.

. . .

The DID diagnosis came as both a comfort and a disheartening crush to Margi's children. Together Margi and Dennis relayed what dissociation meant, sharing explanations from Jay's discussions. It solidified some things for the children and gave some clarity to odd behaviors, but it also introduced more questions. They expressed anxiety and dread over imagined events and experiences from their mother's childhood.

My grandfather? How did I not know this sooner? Who else was involved? How much does grandmother know?

The questions were valid, but Margi didn't have all the answers. Her children were grown adults now and were moving forward in their own lives. They wanted her to do the same—to make peace with the past and focus on tomorrow. Margi listened to their oversimplified reactions and appreciated their kind intentions. What they wanted for her wasn't that easy to do, and Margi certainly would do just that if she could.

Margi's children looked back fondly on their early childhood. Their mother had been happy and supportive of everything in their lives. They were grateful for positive childhood memories and now respected their mother even more considering this new information. They recognized that Margi had risen above her own upbringing and ensured that things would be different when she loved and raised her own children.

The new information confirmed some questions they had from their teenage years. They knew their mother tried, but too often there were "those hard days" when she spent a lot of time in her room. She had tried to hide the tears, but her older children saw through the secret. What they never knew then was the reason behind the tears. Sometimes they blamed themselves, wondering if they weren't good enough. Now all of it began to fit together.

The children had often joked about their mother's forgetfulness, about blank gaps of time from Margi's childhood memories as well as from their own. Margi couldn't remember funny stories told at the dinner table. There were forgotten conversations, blank stares, abrupt changes of the subject, and sudden mood swings. They now understood the reason for some of those gaps. Tragically, it was beginning to make some sense.

Questions the children had in the past still applied. *I don't know if she's listening. Do I have her attention? She sounds different—like it's not even her. Do I pull away and detach, or will that hurt her even more?* Their relationships going forward were going to take work and patience, but all of them were willing because there was never a doubt that their mother loved them.

Margi's children were all starting their own families now; with children of their own, they were feeling their mother's pain from a new perspective. Margi's children were experiencing the intense drive to protect their own children at all costs because they were now parents. It made the truth of Margi's early years almost unbearable to consider. Her fear must have been incredibly intense to cause her mind to divide into parts.

Had theirs been a somewhat dysfunctional family? By definition, probably so. But this family had always risen above. Laughter had filled their home for as long as they could remember. That was especially remarkable as they now realized how hard their mother must have fought every day just to find joy. She had fought with every piece of herself to nurture her own children when she had never been nurtured herself. She had reached inside her heart and soul and loved fiercely even when love hadn't been given to her.

Margi's children would always love and respect their mother.

And they would fight for their mother in return.

Chapter 43

YOU THINK YOU KNOW

By Little Margi

You think you know, but you don't. How could that even be possible? You try to explain with the words you were taught, but they aren't the words that can penetrate this mind that they created. Your words can't help me.

You leave me behind and go about your life. I'm left alone inside to live out days that are filled with the fearful nothingness of this so-called life. I'm left alone to try to keep one step ahead of those unseen forces and the groups of the faceless who chase me and keep me running to the point of exhaustion.

You lie to me and tell me I'm going to be okay, but there's no stopping them or the power they have over me. And there's no human capable of taking away the images and the disturbing, dreadful fear that's buried so deep inside. It thoroughly consumes me.

I'm so alone in here. Her cries are never heard because they're trapped beneath the cover that hides her. I wish I could leave this place behind and join the world of real life. There's nothing holding me down or holding me together. My mind forces me to go back to the dark places where she resides; my steps must follow, even though my feet seem to move forward.

I'm forced to revisit and relive the pain of that child who screams for relief from the hell she has been placed in. She is so bewildered and confused at the way her world changes right before her. Her world is forever changing and never remaining, and time never catches up to the space surrounding her.

Why can't they come together for her? And why aren't we allowed to know who and what we are? My eyes are so confused by the familiar unknown people we see. We knew them yesterday. The crushing fear and the pain are relentless and ungodly.

Do you know this kind of mind? Do you live it—ever—on any level? Then please don't tell me you understand and that I will heal. Heal from what? There's nothing to heal from.

I was made to live in this isolated hell, and there is no God on this side.

ILLUSTRATIONS.

Margi age 9 - Margi rarely smiled in any photographs from her childhood.
The cat belonged to Margi and was a treasured pet whose purring provided great comfort
and a sense of grounding. Animals didn't have the fear that Margi lived with
every day and they loved her unconditionally.

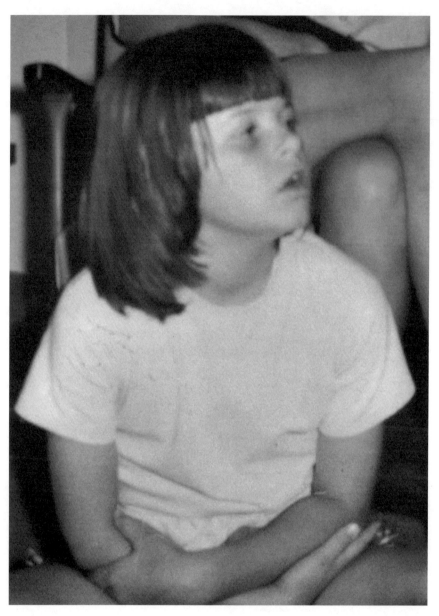

Margi age 10 - Dark circles under Margi's eyes from lack of sleep and drugs.

Margi's childhood house or more commonly referred to as the "dark box" in her writings.

*Margi's basement in her childhood house. This was her
father's train set. The basement was her father's sanctum of escape and fantasy.
Notice Margi's doll carriage underneath the table.*

The coal room in the basement of Margi's childhood house.

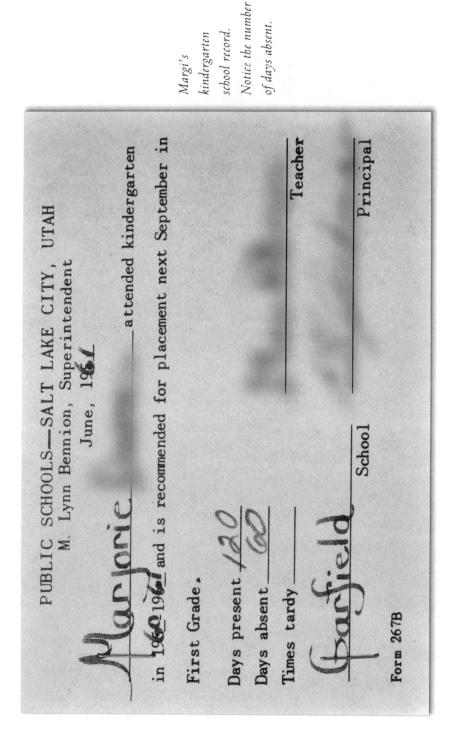

Margi's kindergarten school record. Notice the number of days absent.

PUBLIC SCHOOLS—SALT LAKE CITY, UTAH
M. Lynn Bennion, Superintendent
June, 1961

Marjorie _____ attended kindergarten in 1960-1961 and is recommended for placement next September in First Grade.

Days present 120

Days absent 60

Times tardy _____

Garfield School

_____ Teacher

_____ Principal

Form 267B

Margi's elementary school record showing a total of 223 days absent.

ATTENDANCE, SCHOLARSHIP AND CITIZENSHIP

[SURNAME]   Marjorie (FIRST NAME)   (MIDDLE NAME)

ATTENDANCE, SCHOLARSHIP AND CITIZENSHIP (KDGN.- 6TH GRADE)

SCHOOLS ATTENDED (DATE OF LAST ATTENDANCE SHOULD BE INDICATED IN PARENTHESES FOLLOWING THE NAME OF SCHOOL)

SCHOOL YEAR	GRADE	ATTENDANCE	RATING
19 60	K		S C
19 61			
19 __	1		S B
19 __	2		
19 __	3		S C
19 __	4		S C
19 __	5		S D
19 __	6		C

ADDRESS

DATE	
8/31/60	
6-71	"

ATTENDANCE, SCHOLARSHIP AND CITIZENSHIP (7TH & 8TH GRADES)

7TH GRADE   SCHOOL YEAR 19 68 69

FIRST SEMESTER — SCHOOL Clayton — ADVISER Mr.

SUBJECT	MARK
7-English	C
7-Arithmetic	
7-Social Studies	
7-Home Arts	
7-Health	
7-Rem. Reading	
7-Phys. Ed.	B

SECOND SEMESTER — SCHOOL Clayton — ADVISER Mr.

SUBJECT	MARK
7-English	C
7-Arithmetic	C
7-Science	D
7-Art	D
7-Home Arts	D
7-Phys. Ed.	B

8TH GRADE   SCHOOL YEAR 19 68 69

FIRST SEMESTER — SCHOOL Clayton Jr. High — ADVISER Mr.

SUBJECT	MARK
8-English	C
8-Arithmetic	C
8-Social Studies	D
8-Science	F
8-Gen. Music	C
8-Phys. Ed.	B

SECOND SEMESTER — SCHOOL Clayton Jr. High — ADVISER Mr.

SUBJECT	MARK
8-English	C
8-Arithmetic	D
8-Social Studies	F
8-Art	F
8-Homemaking	F
8-Phys. Ed.	C

DATE OF CREDENTIAL — TO WHOM SENT

1-14-7?	Highland- Home Inst
3/25/77	Crs. Granite Comm.Sch.
9/12/77	Crs. SL College Med. Dentl. Asst.

Jr. High
47-68-49

Grade school
223 days absent
- 1 year 3 mos

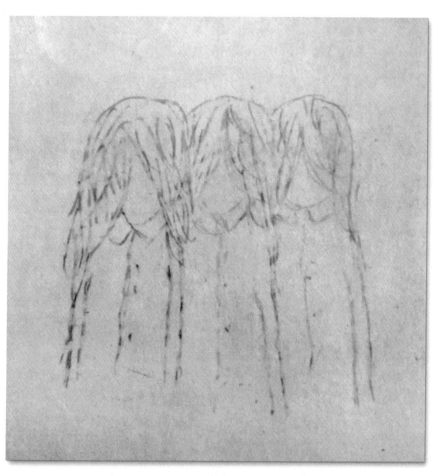

"THREE OF US"

Self portraits from left to right – Normative Margi, Margi and Just Me. Margi took an eraser and went over the drawing to illustrate that nobody is whole.

"US"

Self portrait of Just Me on the left, Margi on the right,
and Little Margi in the middle.

Heaven is laughing at my pain

I'm evil

am I still in a dream

I was made to suffer

No such thing as a program

what dimension am I in

I was made - I wasn't born

MAGIC.

who am I

where's reality

I don't have parts

I'm not in your world - I'm separate

morning margie

I don't know who you are

you don't understand

is everything the right size

you can't help me

there's demons inside - they watch me - they talk to me in my dreams

I hate it here

she's a freak

everything I tell you is a lie

I'm 10

I'm 12

When am I / who am I

I don't have parts

I'm so afraid

Day margi

I'm 7

why am I talking to you

I don't know whose body I'm in

daughter of Satan

When will time catch up with today's space

is it still the same day

I HATE HER

you think you know but you don't

bullshit guy

God loves me

God hates me

Night margie

Alice

Tim

you will be afraid of me

Basement Guy

I will be like this forever

I'm in HELL

Am I dead + this is my hell

mostly together

ym   Lm

core

testor

mother

dark people

other dimension

- leave that part where it belongs
- I understand
- then must be real
- read good books
- find a hobby

- just pray
- think good thoughts
- I see no signs of multiplch

time is up!
Goodbye!

226

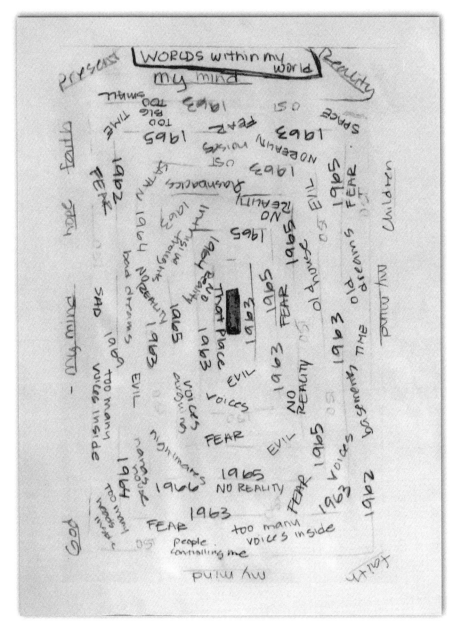

227

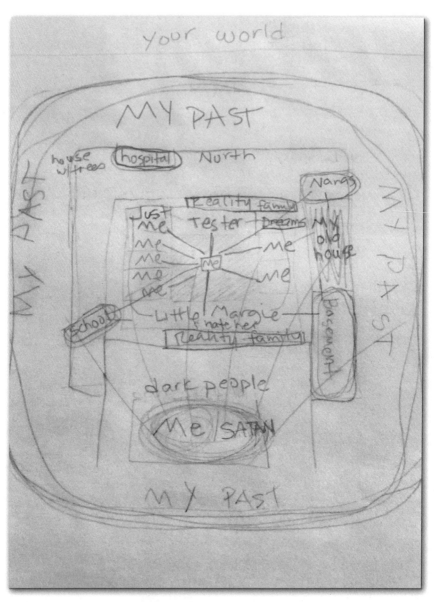

"YOUR WORLD, MY PAST"

Margi and a number of her parts illustrating pieces of their past.

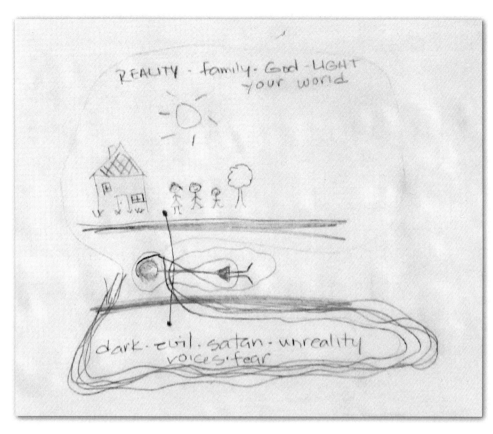

"REALITY"

Margi's drawing representing two separate realities with one hand in each dimension. Both realities are just as real to her.

PART FIVE

YOU CAN'T FIND PEACE UNTIL
YOU FIND ALL THE PIECES.

Chapter 44

Margi tucked the envelope into her purse and walked out the door; today she would be working a full day at the oral surgeon's office. She respected both the surgeon and the anesthesiologist at the office. They had been good to her, and this job had provided a healthy distraction and an opportunity to serve.

Margi had never talked about her past to anyone in the office, but today she was looking for an opinion. She had prepared for the conversation. When both doctors were available and there were no waiting patients, Margi broached the subject.

"Can I ask your opinions on something?"

They both smiled at Margi. "Sure, Margi. What's up?"

"Well, I have been doing some research, because . . . well . . . I had a difficult childhood, and I managed to find a few old pictures of me as a child. I brought them with me and wondered if you would look at them. I'd like to ask both of you a question since you've worked for so many years in the medical field with children."

Margi tried to keep her voice calm and genuinely inquisitive. She hoped they didn't see her heart pounding against her shirt. Margi pulled three photos out of the envelope and laid them on the table in front of both doctors.

"I'm somewhere between the ages of nine and eleven in these photos. In all the photographs I have of myself as a child I have these same dark circles under my eyes."

As the surgeon looked at the three photos, he asked, "You have these same dark circles under your eyes in all childhood photos?"

"All of them."

"No smiles, either," the surgeon observed. "Kind of looks like no one's home."

If he only knew the truth of that statement.

"What's your question?" the anesthesiologist asked.

"Any idea what medical reason would cause such dark circles?"

"Drugs and a lack of sleep," the surgeon answered.

"Drugs will do that if they're frequently used; it also happens if someone is missing a lot of sleep on a consistent basis," the anesthesiologist added.

Margi sat quietly for a minute. She thought back to her favorite stuffed monkey, Mugs. She had held him tightly during so many awful nights. Now he was still tucked safely in the back of her bedroom closet. She still didn't have the heart to get rid of him. He was losing his stuffing from years of being hugged a little too tightly. If only Mugs could talk—oh, the stories he could tell.

Margi realized both doctors were looking at her. She wondered how long her thoughts of Mugs had distracted her. Margi lifted her moist eyes and focused on the doctors. In time, she might share more about her childhood. For now, she had another validating answer.

"I'm sorry, Margi," the surgeon offered. "You look so sad in the pictures. I'm sorry that your childhood was hard. I didn't know. You're such a delight here at the office and a great comfort to all our patients."

"Thank you," Margi replied. She smiled at both the doctors. "I appreciate both of you and your kind words."

Margi scooped up the pictures and stuffed them back inside the envelope, sliding it into her purse. It was another piece of the puzzle—one of many puzzle pieces Margi was determined to fit into some larger, perplexing image.

. . .

GROWING OLD

I am growing old without knowing the pleasures and playfulness of childhood.

She didn't dare to dream about what could be. It was all about what it was. She gave up having hope long ago because that was too painful.

A child shouldn't have to worry and be afraid every day of the next moment. Wondering when we would once again be back in a dream and not knowing how to wake up or how to leave our body. Wondering why God didn't hear us cry for help and make it stop. And what had we done to make God do this to us? It had no end and we had to accept that and find our way without help. There was never any comfort or safety, so she had to create a make-believe world. And that world didn't include hope.

The days didn't ever change and they never improved. To live in a dream, we had to learn how to do things differently than others. We had to figure out how to keep moving and talking when we're not in a body we're familiar with, and how to behave around the people in our life that aren't in the same time as us. And try to understand the space in between that is too thick to reach them. Their voices are muffled. The size and color of the world around us is all wrong. We know the difference. Is the space I'm in right now today or yesterday? How long have I been here? Am I the same person that walked into this room? And please don't look at us. You might see how many of us are inside and you will be afraid of us. We're all ages and you won't be sure how to talk to us.

There are so many conversations going on in my head. Everyone is arguing about how to get through our day. The ones that want to die argue with the ones that don't. The children argue with the adults. The adults try to reason with the children. We want to be grown up, but we want to be children. We want to be in charge, but we want to be taken care of.

. . .

"Hello, Margi," Janie yelled as she waved.

Margi was watering her flowerpots when she heard her neighbor. She put the watering can down and walked across her yard to catch up with her friend.

"Beautiful day, isn't it?" Margi exclaimed. "The weather couldn't be more perfect."

"Yes, it is!" Janie agreed. "How are you feeling today? You look good."

"I'm doing well, thank you." How Margi adored her sweet neighbor. Janie had always found opportunities to check on her and just have a friendly chat now and then. She was warm and kind and seemed genuinely interested in Margi. They had been neighbors for more than twenty years.

"Well, that's good," Janie continued. "You know I always wonder which Margi I'm going to get."

"Really?" Margi asked. She smiled nervously.

"When you told me about the DID, it made a lot of sense," Janie explained. "For years I always thought something was up. I recognized different people in you, and I was not always sure who it would be." She chuckled and smiled at Margi with kind, caring eyes.

"Sorry, I forgot I had said something to you," Margi stammered. "I don't remember exactly what I might have told you about the DID."

"Oh, don't worry about that, my friend. I'm just so glad that you're doing well. It's always great to see you outside working in the yard. Sunshine is good for the soul."

"Thank you, Janie," Margi said. She clasped her friend's hands in hers and looked into Janie's eyes. She was such a kindhearted woman who always looked for opportunities to serve and love others. What an example she had been for Margi all these years. Sweet Janie.

Another gift from God. And another person to know the truth.

. . .

"Jennifer, I just got off the phone with Jay."

Jennifer could tell in the first five seconds of most phone calls whether she was speaking to Margi's core or to a sad, angry part. She didn't separate the parts by name; she just understood that Margi the core was hopeful and loved God while the parts were often irrational, desperate, and hopeless.

Jennifer had seen both the highs and lows of Margi's journey, and she was so proud of the progress Margi was making. Early on, Jennifer called Jay at least once a month for advice on how to help. Those low moments when Margi called were frightening, and Jennifer didn't feel prepared to handle them; at those times, she worried that Margi might take her own life. Jay always coached her through, and his enlightenment gave Jennifer the determination she needed to make a positive difference in Margi's life. Jennifer could never deny that she was divinely guided as well. God was in the small details of her life. She felt lifted and inspired beyond her abilities when she spoke with Margi.

"Jay and I had some new parts come up in the Safe Place today," Margi reported. "There are some new memories I want to tell you about. I've learned some new things."

When details had first started appearing in writings from Margi's dreams and in therapy with Jay, Jennifer began to have her own nightmares—angry, attacking dreams directed toward Margi's father. The new details were too awful. Too wicked. Increasingly evil.

Ultimately, Jennifer had to let go of the anger. *This is not about him. This is about helping Margi.* She made a conscious decision to leave Margi's father and whatever he had done in God's hands. Give it all to God and focus on Margi. It was an answered prayer and a tender mercy that allowed Jennifer the freedom of an open mind and a consoling acceptance.

The Safe Place. What a remarkable and inspired exercise. Jay had described the process in great detail to Jennifer so that she could support Margi. Jennifer felt comfortable discussing the exchanges with both Jay and Margi and quickly became conversant in the skill.

How many times Jennifer had felt Margi was at the breaking point! But Margi always woke up and tried again. Jennifer often reminded Margi of how things would eventually be. *One day we're all going to be in heaven after this life, and we will realize how magnificent and strong your spirit is. We will honor you for enduring what you've been through. You never gave up, and you blessed the lives of others through your own suffering.*

Jennifer leaned back into the soft cushions on her couch. She smiled at the opportunity to love and listen.

"Tell me about it, Margi. Let your parts release some of those memories. I'm here to listen."

Margi relayed new understanding from the day's discovery. Together they would consider how the puzzles pieces fit together.

Chapter 45

Margi's finger quickly traced the table of contents in the book she'd just found on healing from trauma. There it was: the chapter called "Integrating Traumatic Memories." The entire book looked interesting, but Margi was eager to jump ahead to the discussion about those memories coming forward.

The chapter talked about body memories left behind from trauma and the imprint of earlier trauma being left on the body, the mind, and the soul. Examples mentioned crushing sensations in your chest that you might label as anxiety or depression. The fog that keeps you from staying on task and from engaging fully in what you are doing. The self-loathing. The chapter suggested that the challenge of recovery is to reestablish ownership of your body and your mind—of yourself.

Margi considered how many physical ailments she had felt over the years. How many doctors had she seen only to hear there was no medical reason for what she was feeling? She had paid thousands of dollars in medical bills throughout her married life, and for what?

Margi continued reading. The author reported that past emotions and physical sensations imprinted during the trauma are experienced not as memories, but as disruptive physical reactions in the present. There was a clear difference between simply remembering an ordinary event and recalling a traumatic event. Those differences were even visually apparent in brain scans.

A list of her recent physical symptoms—such as fibromyalgia and pelvic pain—raced through Margi's mind. *Which ailments of mine are real present-day conditions, and which are imprinted memories?* Margi recalled that she often had breathing problems early in the morning, including feelings of suffocation or a closed throat. *Could those be a past memory of someone putting a pillow over my face or giving me a drug that caused side effects?* Sometimes the doctors she saw for the problem prescribed a course of antibiotics for pneumonia. Other times, they simply threw up their hands in uncertainty.

The research was clear. When people remembered an ordinary event, they didn't relive the physical sensations, emotions, images, smells, or sounds associated with that event. And those ordinary events were generally remembered with a beginning, a middle, and an end. Conversely, when people recall traumas, they *have* the experience—they are fully engulfed by the sensory and emotional elements of the past. Not only that, but those elements are fragmented, missing a sense of time and perspective.[1]

Margi leaned back in her chair. So much of her research was confirming what she had felt for so long. The more Margi educated herself on DID and trauma, the more it all came together. Everything was starting to fit.

This is me!

. . .

Margi walked into her mother's kitchen and handed over the folder. Her mother had asked for some help with insurance paperwork.

"Hi, Reen," Margi said. She ignored the sour gut she felt every time she walked into this house. "All finished. The papers are all in the folder, and I've made the phone calls. There should be no problem at your next doctor's appointment."

"Good. I can't understand that stuff and won't be bothered by it."

"All right," Margi said. "I've got some errands to do. See you later."

Reen grunted a curt reply under her breath. Margi looked at her mother, expecting something more. Perhaps a bit of gratitude for the help? When none came, Margi turned and headed toward the back door, wondering why she still expected appreciation or anything in return. Reen was never going to change. Margi silently scolded herself for even wanting more.

As she walked toward her car parked in Reen's driveway, Margi noticed a large brown box sitting next to the city garbage can. Her curiosity getting the best of her, she walked over to take a quick look inside. It appeared to be full of her father's belongings. She ran to the back door, opened it, and stuck her head inside.

"Hey, Reen, there's a box of stuff that looks like it used to belong to Dad. Are you throwing it out?"

"Why would I have any need for that stuff? Of course, I'm throwing it out. It's garbage."

"I might take it home and just look through it before tossing it myself," Margi stated. "You okay with that?"

"Why should I care?"

Margi shut the door quickly and ran over to the box. There were clothes and books and all kinds of items. What caught her eye were folders filled with paperwork at the bottom of the box. She pulled one of the folders out and flipped through some of the papers inside. They were personal receipts for drug purchases from a pharmacy that used to be a couple of miles from the house when she was growing up. Now that pharmacy had been replaced by a chain.

Margi's eyes grew wide as she saw hundreds of reference numbers for drugs that had names similar to valium. *Why all these drugs? Who were they for?*

Her hands trembled slightly as she pulled out another file folder. The tab read *Margi—Dr. Bowen: Children's Psychiatric Hospital*. Margi gasped. She had a distinct memory of a conversation with Reen during her early teenage years during which her mother had shoved a paper in Margi's face.

"I can't afford this, Margi," her mother had scolded. "You're costing me too much money."

Margi had felt helpless. She was being blamed for something she didn't even understand.

Margi picked up the large box and shoved it into the backseat of her car. She drove quickly through the neighborhood, parked in her own driveway, grabbed the file folder from the box, and ran inside to lay the hospital receipts out on the table. The first thing she noticed was the date. Margi's eyebrows arched as she counted the visits. One, two, three . . . seventy visits when she was twelve years old. Margi continued to count. A new year and more appointment receipts. Eleven visits at the age of seventeen. It was a total of eighty-one visits at the psychiatric hospital.

How is it possible that I do not remember a single appointment with this doctor? What teenager meets with a doctor eighty-one times and has no memory of it? Margi's stomach dropped as she considered the possibilities. She remembered that both Dr. Shaw and Jay had seen other clients who had been patients of Dr. Bowen. It was clear to Margi that he had quite a reputation with these two; even though they were prevented from discussing the details about other clients, Margi could clearly read between the lines. There were big issues associated with Dr. Bowen—issues that contributed to traumatic events and DID. Margi had tried to Google his name years earlier, but there was not a trace of him anywhere on the internet. His very existence on the web was wiped clean.

Margi picked up the phone and called the number on the invoice. She was transferred repeatedly, but finally spoke to someone in the records department.

"I'm calling about a patient who saw Dr. Bowen years ago," Margi stated. She gave the year and address from the invoice.

The reply was swift. "All the records from that institution and that doctor were destroyed in a flood. Sorry, I can't help you."

A flood in Utah? How convenient.

Margi hung up the phone. Another dead end. But another door had opened. Eighty-one mysterious visits. It supported the third context that Jay had suspected—the medical context where consciousness is altered.

A context of drugs and programming.

Chapter 46

"Good work, Margi." Jay was impressed with the amount of research and digging Margi was willing to do to both educate herself and find answers. Nothing was ever clear-cut, but if enough pieces came together, they painted a picture—even if the picture had some missing pieces.

"Eighty-one visits," Margi exclaimed. "Can you believe that?"

"I'm not surprised," Jay replied. "Maybe you can begin working with some of your drugged parts. Get them out of the blending place and into the healing pool. You've worked hard creating your Safe Place."

"That's what I really want to do," Margi said, "but I can't do it by myself. It's too terrifying. I'm afraid I'll go to those drug dimensions and never make it back. You're the only one I trust to bring me back."

Margi's voice was quiet. She didn't sound unsure—just timid. Frightened. Jay knew that drug memories were more frightening than any other type of memories. It was like freefalling in other worlds and not being able to find anything real. In Margi's case, he knew that the thought of an eternity in that dimension was too much to bear.

"Your core will bring you back, Margi, but yes, I'll help you."

Jay understood her fear. Medical trauma and programming were the most difficult to deal with. Many of his survivors were drugged and warned under hypnosis that if they ever told anyone, the terrifying drug parts would stay forward forever. Though it sounded ridiculous to the average adult, the survivor absolutely believed the threat beyond any doubt or rational explanation. It was mind programming, and it was extremely difficult to erase.

"What if I go to that . . . that place? I can't look at it or I'll go crazy," Margi confided.

"Margi, they took you to the edge of your sanity—perhaps to the edge of your life," Jay explained. "You didn't go crazy then. You're not crazy now. And Margi, you will never be crazy."

It always came back to that word. *Crazy*. Margi listened and trusted Jay's words. He was always willing to dispense wisdom and perspective. She needed to trust him.

"Okay, I'm ready, Jay. I'm going to make it really scary in here."

Margi placed blankets over the window in her den to darken the room. She held tight to her cell phone, which was her lifeline to Jay.

"It's dark in here, Jay. Now say some really scary things to me. I want those parts to come out and talk, because I can't tell you."

"I'm not going to scare you, Margi. Your drugged parts are already scared children. You don't need to purposely scare them."

Back and forth they talked. Jay could tell Margi's fear was escalating, but she had stated an absolute resolve to gain some memories. After nearly an hour of talking, Jay asked Margi what she was doing.

"I'm in a ball . . . I'm curled up on the floor. It's very dark."

"Maybe Just Me can help. Is Just Me there? Is she close?"

There was a period of silence. Jay listened and waited.

"She's here. She's here on my left. She's pulling my hair."

Jay had seen this before in a previous office visit. In the middle of a session as they began talking about the children on the other side, Jay had watched Margi shift and pull and twist her hair on the left side with her left arm. Jay had recognized it immediately. It was Just Me representing cognition.

"Just Me is pulling my hair so I can feel present," Margi whispered. "So I won't go too far away." Margi could feel her hair being twisted and pulled, but she didn't try to stop it. Suddenly, she heard her voices change. She felt paralyzed with fear.

"I don't know who I am or what I am. There's no logic. There's no real."

"Where are you?" Jay asked. "What does it look like?"

242

The voices answered the questions. They described the abuse through frightened sobs and then quiet whispers, as if they were afraid someone might hear.

Suddenly Margi yelled.

"Please don't leave me here! Please help me. Don't leave me."

"I'm right here," Jay said in a soothing voice. "I'm not going anywhere. You can do this. Let's move those parts and get them out of the scene they're in. Get them out of the scene and move them into the healing pool. Your angels will help them."

Margi spoke to her parts. "You've all worked hard today. You each had a job to do and your help has been appreciated, but I'm giving you permission to go rest. Go rest in the Safe Place." Margi worked closely with Jay as he patiently brought her through each step of the process.

She repeated this kind of session again and again, each time learning something new. It was scary to hear her other voices, but Margi felt strong and wanted those parts to talk.

Sometimes Margi got to the very edge of a memory only to have parts give warnings—*Oh, don't look! It's too horrible. It's too scary. Don't look at it!* Margi often pushed away when that happened. Obeyed the warnings. Trusted that what could happen next was too much.

Other scenes seemed illogical. Nonsensical. But they were real to Margi and the others. It's what they knew. The places often appeared even more real than where she lived now. Margi was sure no one would ever completely understand.

When parts came up, they were only in front for a short time when working on difficult scenes. Jay explained that they tired easily. Their burdens were heavy. Details came out involving drugged children, sexual abuse, and scenes including bondage, discipline, and sadomasochism (BDSM). As a child, Margi was violently spanked so obsessively during the sexual abuse that it suggested submissive training in that culture. The memories and information these parts held was invaluable but needed to be dealt with quickly and efficiently.

Therapy sessions generally vary widely in scope, depending on many factors. Margi's sessions were different and focused on unique needs and goals. They were directed primarily by Margi, but Jay was there to support and to teach.

One thing, however, was consistent. After discovery and time spent in deep, dark corners of her mind, Margi's closing, desperate request was always the same. A quiet, trembling voice always reached outside the blackness.

"Don't leave me. I want to go home."

Jay always patiently worked with Margi at the end of a session to move strong parts that were forward. He encouraged the core to return up front so she could now direct the others to stand behind or help make sure parts were put in the Safe Place. Often at the end of difficult and revealing sessions, Margi was left feeling weary and fearful. The information gained from parts was valuable, and Margi trusted Jay to ensure that her core was completely present before ending a session.

It was a vigilant process involving guidance, diligence, and trust.

. . .

I really hate it in here. People think they know, but they don't. All of you on the outside are playing your own game of make-believe to make me think you're real. I'm the only one who's real, and I live in hell. All alone.

There's no God where I live, either. The fear, I believe, is going to be my death, and it's coming soon. I'm so afraid.

Where will I go when that happens? It's all just so relentless. All I want is some relief; my pain is so incredibly bad. What kind of a demented world do I live in, and why am I made to stay in it? I can't stay here much longer.

I think I'm running out of life.

Chapter 47

Margi stood rigid. Motionless. Hoping that something—anything—might trigger a memory. A soft breeze swept the hair off her face but brought no hint of memory with it.

Her eyes searched the area as she desperately tried to imagine the old hospital. Margi had gone online and researched the old Children's Psychiatric Hospital and learned that condominiums now occupied the space where the building had once stood. Fortunately, there were pictures of the old structure. It was certainly worth a drive to visit the area in person.

Margi wandered over to the west side of the property. *Eighty-one visits.* She walked through grass fields and sidewalks that surrounded the site. Perhaps she would find glimpses of memories hidden somewhere in the grounds.

The surroundings were vaguely familiar. Margi had a fleeting memory of getting out of the car and walking up to a door. She had been there.

Why can't I remember? Dear God, what happened during those visits?

Tears streamed down her face as Margi walked and walked. The details were gone. Hidden from her. But the raw emotion was still there.

I know I hated it.

. . .

"Are you sure you want to do this?" Dennis asked. "This house is the subject of so many nightmares. You think you can handle this?"

Margi nodded. They were parked outside her deceased grandmother's house—an old, dark home nestled up against the mountains in a neighborhood close to the University of Utah. It had long ago been sold to new owners, but Margi was determined to go inside. She was on a mission to find answers.

"Come with me," Margi said. "I'm going to knock on the door."

Together Margi and Dennis walked to the front door. Margi took a deep breath and knocked.

The young woman who answered the door looked friendly enough.

"Hi, my name is Margi, and this is my husband, Dennis."

The woman nodded in response.

"I'm here because my grandmother used to own this home years ago." Margi handed the woman a couple of pictures. They clearly verified that the structures were the same.

"We were in the area and . . . I just wondered if we could impose on you to let us look around. It's been so long. Could we come inside for just a minute?"

Margi held her breath as the woman looked at her and then back at the pictures. Perhaps this was reckless. Crazy. Maybe she should grab Dennis's hand and run in the opposite direction.

"Sure, come on in," she said. "I'll show you around a bit."

The woman was sweet and inviting as she wandered through the main floor of the home, giving a tour. Margi could hear her own heartbeat. She hoped no one else could hear it or see the fear she was attempting to push away.

"You know, we have ghosts," the woman reported. "Or at least that's what we call them. Strange happenings and sounds and things."

"Well, that would be my family, because they built this house," Margi replied. *If she only knew.*

The woman led them into the kitchen and pointed toward a door. "Here's the door that opens up to a staircase. The staircase leads to the basement."

Margi knew that door. She held tight to her senses and grabbed Dennis's hand.

"My daughters are afraid to go downstairs," the woman added.

246

"They're scared of the basement."

So am I.

As they entered the large basement, Margi saw a couch and a couple of chairs. There was a wood table and an assortment of decorations that made it look homey. Artificial plants and flowers brought life into the basement.

Despite a noble attempt by the new homeowner to make the basement comfortable, Margi felt nothing but fear, death, and sadness. Nothing could cover up what came from inside. She allowed herself to look down to the other end of the large room and swallowed hard. Three doors leading to three bedrooms. Three doors that had been in so many of her nightmares.

Why am I so afraid of this house? What was behind those three doors? Margi looked up at Dennis, hoping he could read her thoughts. His expression was solemn. Heavy.

Margi turned back toward the stairs, pulling Dennis along with her. She had seen enough. Felt enough.

"Thank you very much," Margi said. "I appreciate you letting us see your home."

. . .

Margi and Dennis walked down the familiar path to their car parked out on the street. Dennis looked back and noticed the separate entrance in the garage that led directly into the basement. Someone could go down to the basement through that door, and no one in the upper house would ever know. It was a separate entrance—to use for whatever twisted need someone might have. Someone like Margi's father and whatever group of demented people he associated with. Dennis's stomach sickened at the thought.

As they prepared to drive away, Dennis looked back one last time at the house and then to his brave Margi.

"That house is dark," Dennis muttered. "Dark and eerie."

Chapter 48

As Margi's car rounded the corner, she braced herself for the sensory overload. It was a compulsion she was still dealing with after all these years—a strong, obsessive pull to see her childhood house. A draw so powerful, it pulled Margi tightly into its mystical grasp.

A few years before Margi's father died, her parents had purchased a modest house in the area. For years, the old rental house where Margi spent all her childhood years sat vacant. A few renters came and went, but for the most part, its hollow hallways and empty rooms were deserted. Only memories remained in the chilling space.

Sunday evenings still found Margi heading north. Doing what felt like a required drive-by. *They're waiting for me.* Errands still found her re-routing for just another glance, a hopeful answer to her own empty spaces.

Jay had counseled her not to visit the house. He explained that programs were compulsive, and nothing positive was going to come out of that structure. But now that she was working with Jay and learning more, her visits were less about an unexplainable lure and more about gaining an understanding of the past. They were about healing her parts.

A few hundred yards from the corner, there it stood—the same dark house with square windows and a gaping entrance. Small windows along the base of the house called attention to a basement beneath. Just the sight of the home generated all the same emotions Margi had felt as a child.

Why am I still in there when I'm really not?

Margi pulled up into the driveway and got out of her car. She approached the house and cupped her hands tightly around her eyes to peer into the windows. Nobody seemed to be living there. Margi hadn't seen any activity at the house lately.

As she walked the property, peeking into rooms through murky windows, she felt a shift. A sensation that she was floating in a dream. Nothing felt real. She peered inside one room after another and put herself in the walls. She became the furniture. The house.

Where is Little Margi? How can I get her out? She's in her bedroom.

Margi began to sob. Desperate tears poured down her cheeks.

This house is me! I'm in all those rooms. It knows my fear.

Margi ran behind the house to the gully, a wooded area with water running through its base. A cruel wave of fright sent her running back toward the car. She climbed into the driver's seat and tried to catch her breath.

This house has a life of its own. If I sit here long enough, that house will talk to me and tell me what happened inside those walls. Margi was sure that there were still children trapped in the basement. *I need to get them out! They're trapped!* She cried for the children. She cried for herself as part of this evil house.

After an hour, the late afternoon sun began to cast shadows from trees lining the street. The eerie feeling was enough to get Margi moving back toward her own home. She started up the engine and drove back down the street. At the corner, she paused and took a last look at the dark box mentioned in so many of her writings.

I'm sure it was a beautiful home, but nobody loved it. I am the house. Nobody loved us.

. . .

The old, dark, abandoned house at the top of the street holds the secrets of my past. It's holding onto them with no chance of giving them up. This house can't talk, or it would tell of a child who lived there a long time ago. I think she lived there. I'm not sure exactly who she was. I think she is a part of me, but she is more like a child

250

in a dream that seems to haunt me. She was a child who didn't know the meaning of reality or where dreams and reality separated.

This house was once a beautiful new home with hopes of being loved and taken care of by the people who would live in it. But instead, it spent its life abused and neglected with no one to ever own up to the responsibility and care of this home. Always hoping someone will come along and care about how it must feel to be this home that stands out and is so conspicuous to others who now stare at it and laugh at what it has become. It wonders each day when it might improve.

The sadness and loneliness of this home was almost unbearable. Probably not everyone can see the evil that the walls of this home hold. But the house knows all about the evil and about how nighttime fills the walls and the space inside with that evil. I always believed the house itself carried the blame for the bad things that went on inside. The other homes that stood nearby didn't have this happening to them, but they knew something was wrong with this house. It wasn't like them. This house knew it was different, but it had no control over what the people did to it to make it that way.

Many years have gone by, and this house is still standing, but it is now crumbling under the strain of it all, and it won't be able to withstand much more. It's getting harder each day for this house to carry the burden of all the dark secrets inside, and it will eventually be crushed by the weight of it all. For there comes a time when even the strongest must know when to give up. It still stands there in a sense defiled with all the marks of abuse and hidden shame that only that house can know.

This house has spent its lifetime trying to be strong and live up to its expectations and be all that it was intended to be. It hasn't known if there was a purpose to or even a confirmation of its existence. It's been difficult to hide all that went on inside, and it has grown more hopeless with age. The house is growing old, and life has taken its toll. It shows its age, and it may never understand why it was built and what it was built for.

Looking at this home, it's obvious to see the irreversible damage that was done to it by others and that the possibility of total healing has long since passed.

Chapter 49

Feelings of ambivalence raced through Margi's thoughts, and she felt a nervous pit in her stomach. She knew what was coming. Fear. As soon as they reached the neighborhood, she felt it. A dream-like sensation of slipping back in time. Margi knew she was about to leave the present to willingly step back into her childhood. *I'm going to face this monster.*

.   .   .

Jay was in town for some consulting appointments, and during his visit, he took time to spend an afternoon with Margi. Most of their sessions were handled over the phone, but he wanted to take advantage of a personal visit. One of the items on his list was to visit Margi's childhood house. Jay had previously counseled Margi to avoid the tendency to visit on her own, but today he wanted to go and see if they could discover some answers. He would be there to guide and direct. Together they drove through neighborhood streets toward the house.

"There it is," Margi pointed. "Straight ahead—the dark house."

As soon as they pulled up in front of the house, Margi switched. Jay immediately recognized that protector parts were up front. Her countenance changed as she stiffened up defensively and her tone of voice changed. Jay felt a wave of compassion mixed with determination to face the terror right in front of Margi.

"Okay, Margi. Let's face this house together. I'm anxious for you to show me around."

Jay looked up to see a middle-aged woman standing on the front step. Margi had called her realtor friend to let her inside the house for a look around. The house was currently on the market, and her friend would be able to open the lockbox on the door.

Laura motioned toward the front door, which was cracked open. She welcomed the two of them to step inside.

"Thanks, Laura. This is . . . um . . . the house I grew up in, and I want to show Jay around if that's okay," Margi said. "You're welcome to come inside with us if you'd like."

"You know . . . I was here a few minutes ago and went inside. I've never been in a house like this, and I've sold a lot of houses." Laura paused for a moment then said, "This house is creepy, Margi. Really frightening. Something's wrong here, and it's disturbing."

Jay could see that Laura was visibly shaken. Earlier, Margi indicated that she had never said anything about her childhood to Laura. Could others feel whatever evil had gone on in this house?

"I'm just going to wait out there on the curb if you don't mind," Laura added. "I've got some work I can do in the car. You take your time, Margi."

Margi and Jay watched as Laura scurried down the driveway toward the car. They looked at each other then took a step inside the front door. The house was rundown and neglected, and it definitely needed a lot of work. Jay felt a gripping darkness consume his senses as soon as he crossed the threshold. He had visited some places with other clients where abuse had taken place, but this was worse than anything he had ever experienced.

Margi walked with Jay from room to room, describing what she could remember about certain rooms; as she did, Jay listened and responded with questions about details and events. He had expressed his hope that parts would come forward in this setting, possibly putting some fears to rest or revealing something new.

Jay looked out the window in the family room that gave a view out the back of the house. He opened a back door and took a step out on the back porch. A park was visible in the distance.

"What is that out there, Margi?" Jay asked, pointing to the park.

Margi took two small steps toward Jay and stood quietly, looking at the park where fields had been when Margi was a child. Before the ground was leveled for the park, there had been a secluded gully with a stream running through it. Margi nervously rubbed her hands through her hair before answering.

"There's a big gully," she whispered. "I play down there sometimes."

"Who am I talking to?" Jay asked.

"Cardboard. I'm Cardboard. It's my gully. My dad takes me down there a lot."

This wasn't the first time Cardboard had come to the front. She had participated in other conversations.

"Can you tell me about that?" Jay asked.

"It's a really bad place. Why are all those people there now? Don't they know they're in my dream? My nightmare is here. This is a real place. You're in my nightmare, and you're all walking around playing and laughing. This is not real. Don't you know that? "I need to go now," Cardboard said. As quickly as she had emerged, Cardboard wanted to leave.

Margi walked back inside. She felt shaken, disheveled, and frightened. She paced the family room area for a few minutes while Jay gave her a moment. Margi's steps finally slowed, and she turned toward Jay.

"I need to show you the basement."

"Yes, of course," Jay said. "You're doing great, Margi. You can do this."

. . .

As they descended the stairs, Jay's eyes scanned the basement as it came into view. It was filthy, gray, and dark with cement walls and small windows that barely allowed light into the main room. He could tell it was a bad place. The dark feeling in it was undeniable and thick.

"My dad kept his dental chair right over there," Margi said.

Jay recalled stories and glimpses of events that had come from this place. Parts had divulged details that happened here from a childhood of terror. He had heard many stories from all the survivors he had worked with over the years, but to stand where so many had taken place in this survivor's childhood created another level of empathy.

Scenes from the past were buried under dust and scattered debris. The aversion to this place was palpable. If only these dingy walls could talk.

"This house is not a good house," Jay said. "Let's get out of here."

. . .

Margi felt herself slipping. She knew she was blending with someone. She began to pace the floor, circling the area where her father's train set once stood. Emotions of anger and hurt flowed through her veins and consumed all her senses. A part was up front. She turned quickly toward Jay and gave the order.

"You have to get out of here. Just go home. Leave me here."

"Who is telling me that?" Jay asked.

"Nick. I have to stay here. I belong down here."

. . .

Margi continued pacing, and Jay could see fear and anger in her facial expressions and mannerisms.

"You need to leave. Besides, I . . . I have to go to school."

"Well, Nick, I think it's time to leave here. Let's go to a better place."

"This is where we belong. It's dark and scary. Dad says Margi is a dirty girl and that God is displeased with her. She deserves to be punished. She's not like other girls."

Nick stopped in the center of the room and looked over at Jay. Nick's demeanor was certain with a hint of confrontation.

"Dad kept his train set right here. He was down here with Margi. Dad gave her something to drink and then told her to hold onto the train table. He held up her nightie. After he was done, he put her in the cold, dark coal room in the back of the basement to wait for the drugs to wear off."

Nick continued to pace as more tragic details were released—ugly pieces of living nightmares that were safely guarded as secrets. It was abuse on a wicked and wretched level, and Jay realized it was Nick's job to keep them from Margi. He was a protector.

"Margi, come with me," Jay demanded. "It's time to go home—home to your husband. I'd like to meet your children. Perhaps they're waiting for us." Jay needed to pull the core out front. He began to talk about people in the present. People that Margi loved and cherished.

"Follow me, dear," Jay said soothingly. "Let's leave here together. I'm not going to leave you alone."

Parts were all forward, and Margi was aggressive in her defiance about leaving. She was putting up a fight.

"No! I'm not leaving. *You* need to leave."

"Margi, you need to come with me right now. I'll carry you out of here if I have to. Your realtor friend is waiting outside. Come on—it's time to leave."

They battled in what seemed like circles. From his experience, Jay knew it was a fight to leave memories and come back into the present. Jay extended his hand and nodded toward the staircase. Ultimately, Margi lifted her head and looked at Jay's face.

"Okay," Margi whispered softly.

Margi looked straight ahead as they emerged from the house. Laura saw them come out, and she ran up to put the lockbox on the door.

"Thank you." Jay spoke for the two of them and waved at Laura as they climbed into Margi's car. They sat quietly for a moment, gathering thoughts on what had just occurred. The mood was somber.

. . .

"That was awful," Margi whispered. "I don't like that house."

Margi looked over at Jay. His kind eyes held compassion. What a merciful man to walk through dark chapters with her. She felt dissociative and weary from the experience. Minutes in the house had felt like years. Margi was so tired. She wiped the tears that were rolling down her cheeks.

"You're going to be okay," Jay promised. "You're going to be okay."

Chapter 50

Margi continued to work hard with Jay. The understanding and wisdom she received from him was priceless. It strengthened her ability to move forward and use more coping methods for dissociative episodes. Margi's family could see the shift in her confidence.

Despite better intentions, Margi continued her random drive-by visits to her childhood home. One day, she saw the word *SOLD* tacked over the top of the sale sign in front. The house that for decades had been rented to Margi's family and had then been abandoned and vacant for years had finally been purchased. Margi called her realtor friend Laura to ask about the sale. She learned that a nice family with two children had bought the home but had plans to do a major remodeling job before moving in. Laura told her the construction was scheduled to begin shortly.

Margi wanted her adult children to see the house, so she arranged with Laura to meet at the house on a Sunday afternoon. Margi didn't want to share any grisly details of events; she didn't believe her children should hear such things but felt that their seeing the house would be evidence and affirmation for them of their mother's childhood. She wanted to give them an image of it before it was torn apart.

The three children arrived and stood together on the sidewalk in front of the house. They had seen the front of this house hundreds of times throughout their own childhood as passengers in their mother's car. She had often created a reason to drive by, had paused briefly, then had driven away. Today they would see the inside of the house for the first time.

Once again, Laura said she wanted to wait outside on the curb. Margi and her children walked inside. Most of the time, there was sarcasm, joking, and laughter when everybody got together, but today the mood was weighty and serious.

. . .

The children had their own memories of Margi's father, but they were cloudy. They were very young when their grandfather was alive. A few fleeting memories of pancakes and swings in the park were all that was left from those early years.

Now those memories of their grandfather were tangled up in new revelations from their mother. They felt conflicting feelings of fondness, horrendous betrayal, and resentment toward him for what seemed to have happened.

What the children knew about their mother's childhood created its own atmosphere as they walked from room to room, their hearts racing. It was hard to be there. Imaginations filled in details and gave them a new perspective, as well as prompting feelings of sadness and heartbreak over what their mother had endured. Their judgment of the house was unanimous.

This place was chilling.

. . .

This time Margi hit the brakes.

You can't tear the house down. That's my house, because I AM the house.

A casual drive-by of her childhood home revealed that the demolition planned by the new homeowners had begun. Workers were gutting the house; doors and drywall were piled in heaps along the side of the house. Margi felt panic rising in her throat. She parked the car and walked over to one of the workers.

"Hi; I used to live here. Can I just take a quick look inside?"

"Sure," replied the worker. "It's wide open."

Margi walked inside. Workers were sawing and ripping and shredding. Margi felt the destruction of the house in her soul. She desperately covered her mouth and tried to maintain control. Down the hall the bookcase had been removed and the stairway entrance to the attic was wide open, a gaping entrance leading right into a nightmare. Why wasn't anybody else scared of this? Margi's heart pounded as she looked up into the attic. The new owners were probably going to put bedrooms up there. A shiver ran down Margi's spine at the thought of sleeping in the attic. Too many attics had appeared in her nightmares. Margi turned and ran back out to the yard, stopping next to a large pile of debris from the destruction. She saw the same worker.

"I see you're throwing all of this out," Margi said. "I need that door. Can I have that heat vent?"

"Whatever you need, lady," the worker responded. "It's all going to be taken to the garbage."

You can't be disrespectful and just throw things out, because this is me. I am one with the fear in this house.

Margi reached for her phone and called Dennis. She asked him to drive up to the house and help her gather some things. A few minutes later, he pulled up and got out of his car.

. . .

"What's going on, Margi?" Dennis asked. It was obvious that the remodel job had begun. He wondered if it had triggered something in Margi.

"See these doors over here?" Margi pointed. "That one is the door to the coal room. They were all in the dark, dreadful basement with me." Margi looked up at Dennis and hoped he somehow understood. "And here's the old metal heat vent that was in my bedroom. In the winter, I wrapped myself up in my blanket and sat next to it on the floor to feel its heat and listen to the moan of the furnace. It gave me some measure of safety and comfort—like an old friend. I . . . I can't leave them here.

261

In a strange way, they're all part of me, Dennis. I want to save everything. They're begging me."

Dennis realized that Margi had made herself a part of this house. He needed to diffuse the situation. Maybe there was a compromise.

. . .

"I'll load up the doors and take them to our house, but if I do, they're just going to sit in the backyard," Dennis explained. "What if we take just the doorknobs? You can bring the doorknobs back to our house and do whatever you need with them."

Margi considered the idea. That could work. She could save the doorknobs. They would be happy to be away from this dark house.

"Thank you, Dennis," Margi said. She wondered what he must think of this craziness.

The two of them gathered the doorknobs and put them in a sack. Margi imagined the doorknobs were grateful. She tried to envision this house with a new family—a family with happy children in a healthy home. Maybe they had a little girl who smiled. Maybe this new family would bring real life into this house.

Maybe this home could even be beautiful.

Chapter 51

NO BEGINNING

I had no beginning. There was no start to being me. I don't know where I came from or why I'm here. I have a name they call me, but it doesn't match the face I see in the mirror or the movement of the body that's attached to me.

Days have been filled in with imaginary time in a world I didn't create with people who didn't belong to the child inside me. She sees her world from inside a dream that has lasted a lifetime. What could have happened to real? Where did it go and why did it leave? Time is so jumbled and nonsensical and doesn't move at a chronological pace. Why does time seem to move around and not stay with me?

I need the loud words in my head to stop and go back to the person who put them there. They don't belong with me. The words I hear come from those who are buried deep inside the space between their thoughts. And what their eyes can see is the wall that traps them.

At night, the home she's always known slowly becomes a small, dark, suffocating box that has taken a step outside of real time. It's filled with furniture and familiar things that have now joined the rest to be in this new dimension, and she's left behind to live in her own space in a time that doesn't really exist. She'll dwell in a mind that has betrayed her and taken away her sanity. Nothing else exists outside this box.

As the windows are blackened with the darkness of night, the dim yellow lamps cast such eerie sadness and make everything she sees seem much too small. The man and woman who live there have also changed in size and don't seem to see her. They must disappear once this begins.

She is so very alone. If no one can see her, how can they help her make sense of why she can't be allowed to live outside this imaginary tomb?

Now she must begin the process of believing the only explanation is to doubt her sanity. She sometimes tells herself it's just another bad dream and someday she might wake up. She tries to pretend that what is happening once again will be gone when she wakes up. But by now, she has come to expect and anticipate that each new day is more dreadful than the last, and she knows each day will take more of her.

There are memories inside that don't belong to me. I wish they would leave me alone. Who is the girl that lives in a dream and haunts my days and my nights? It seems she's been with me forever, even though I don't want her around. She has become an expert on extreme fear and profound loneliness, and she knows the dread of life itself. She has no sense of feeling human or being part of a structured existence.

She also knows that nightmares can happen when she's awake.

Chapter 52

Margi pulled out one of her early notebooks. She had always taken notes during sessions with Jay. Looking back several years was a strong indicator of just how much ground she had covered. Reading what she had written back then helped her realize how scattered her parts had been and how removed her sense of reality had been. The marks and comments all over the page were jagged and chaotic. Although she still had some bad days, Margi felt proud of the positive direction in which she was going.

The parts that held the memories of her father had been coming forward in the blending place. Margi had her angels take them out of the frightening scenes they were in and move them to the Safe Place.

She knew therapy would be ongoing and that there was still more to uncover. For one thing, her mother was still a mystery. Reen. She didn't even like to use the term *mother*, so she still referred to her mother by her nickname. It was less personal. Less of a bond.

The mystery about her mother didn't persist for lack of effort. Margi had bravely broached subjects with Reen in an attempt to fill blank spots. Reen always perceived a question as an attack and could easily be triggered into a rage. Once that happened, she was uncontrollable. Even so, Margi had repeatedly tiptoed into the inquiries.

She recalled an earlier conversation.

What can you remember about my childhood?

Nothing.

Really? Nothing?

I was an attentive mother and I took cookies to school and tested the children for their eyes.

It was a scripted answer she gave to everything. Margi pushed harder.

Was I a cute little girl? Did I laugh? Did I play dollies? Because I don't remember anything about my life. Was I funny? Was I sad?

I don't know. You've got to stop asking me things I don't have answers for. You're asking me things I don't know.

Margi shook her head to clear the memories of conversations with Reen. They never ended well. Why should she expect that one day they would?

.   .   .

It was a cool, autumn Sunday evening. The children and grandchildren had all come for dinner. It had been a lovely evening with the usual laughter and good times remembered and retold at the table. Margi's children reminisced about early events in their childhood, and her grandchildren giggled as they eagerly listened. Margi had decided to reach out and invite her mother. As usual, she sat at the table stoic and unamused by the humor.

The hour was getting late, and it was time to drive Reen back to her own home. Everyone else had left and Dennis was preoccupied on a lengthy phone call, so there was nobody to come along for the ride. Margi would need to make this trip alone. She gathered her mother's belongings and helped her out to the car. On the way, Margi decided to grasp another opportunity for questioning. After all, the kids had all been reminiscing about childhood memories.

"Hey, Reen, tell me about my childhood."

"It was a dark time," Reen grunted.

"Well, tell me about my junior-high or high-school years," Margi pressed. "Anything you remember?"

"It was a dark time," Reen repeated.

"My whole life with you was just one big dark time? Was there no joy? No pleasure? No happiness? Nothing?"

Reen was quiet the rest of the journey, staring straight ahead. She was done. There would be no more discussion tonight. Margi pulled up to her mother's house, turned into the driveway, and took the key out of the ignition.

"Let me turn some lights on. I'll be right back," Margi said.

Margi opened the door and tried to ignore the predictable fear that always seized her senses at her mother's house even though her mother no longer lived in the house Margi had grown up in. She reached her hand inside to feel along the wall; her fingers found the light switch and flicked it on. There it was—the same furniture from her childhood. Just the sight tried to take her present reality away. Margi fought the dissociation pulling on her.

Margi walked down the dark hallway toward her mother's bedroom. In the darkness, she held her breath as she passed the basement stairs. Flashes of gloom and terror filled her mind. She felt like a child stepping back into a nightmare. Something was coming down the hall to get her. She suppressed the urge to scream and flicked on the bedroom lights.

Margi quickly returned to the car, helped her mother inside, and pulled out a kitchen chair for her mother to sit on. Margi went to her mother's bedroom, took some pajamas out of the drawer, and put them on the edge of her mother's bed. She returned to the kitchen and placed breakfast items on the kitchen table for the following morning. Margi felt a wave of emotion and fought the urge to cry. *It was a dark time? My entire life with you was miserable?* Even in this frightening house, Margi's heart ached for approval.

Margi turned to face her mother. Reen showed little expression, but a stern scowl filtered through her impassive face. Once again, Margi's world changed in an instant, and she was naked from the waist down. Even as an adult, her mother still had that effect on her. *There's a wicked memory. I just don't know what it is. I can't think about her. I can't look at her.*

Margi was that child again—stepping back into an all-too-familiar nightmare. *Who is this woman I am caring for? Why am I in this house with her?* The woman had the appearance of someone she once knew, but the connection to her was a frightening mystery. Margi knew she had referred to her as *mother*, but she had no idea what that meant. This woman was a stranger.

Margi looked past her mother's face into the family room. She blinked hard as the room changed to a dark yellow and appeared to be shrinking. *Just like my old house! How is it that this house I have never lived in can remove me from a present state and once again place me back inside that suffocating box of my childhood home?*

Margi turned and ran out the door. She ran past her car and turned the corner, still running. The house itself felt as if it was closing in on her. She desperately needed to run away from this woman and the walls that were holding her there. The terror of her childhood chased her down and caught up with her as she tried to run away.

It was dark and approaching nine p.m. Recognizing the altered state she was in, Margi stopped and pulled herself together. She needed to leave—now. She needed to get as far away from whatever wicked memory this place held.

Margi quickly returned to the house, climbed into her car, started the car engine, and turned the volume on the radio up high. The blast of music was a welcome distraction. The deafening sound covered her sobs. She always cried all the way home after dropping her mother off.

As she pulled out of the driveway, Margi glanced back at the house to see her mother peering through the kitchen window. She nearly froze with fear seeing her mother's face up against the glass, watching her leave. Margi's heart pounded. *It's not the house. It's not the furniture.*

It's her!

. . .

"You've never been comfortable talking about your mother. That was clear from the very beginning."

"I just don't understand it," Margi told Jay. "I'm terrified of her."

"Well, that comes from years of abandonment. That itself is abuse. There may be more that we haven't uncovered."

"At least I'm starting to get brave enough to ask some questions," Margi said. "Jennifer has helped me find the courage to ask."

"Good for you," Jay responded. "But I know you're capable of more. You've started down this road with your mother, and I think you should continue. She knows things. I'm sure of that."

Margi let that sink in. She took a deep breath and let it out slowly. Just a simple conversation involving her mother had ratcheted her anxiety up a notch.

"I'll tell you what," Jay said. "I'm making another trip out to Utah in a few weeks. I'd like to meet your mother. We can go to her house together. I think we could really gain something by talking to her. How does that sound?"

"Okay."

"In the next few weeks before I come to Utah, I want you to continue asking her questions. Be patient but direct. Let's see what you can learn on your own before I get there."

"I can do that."

Dennis had also urged Margi to have more conversations with her mother. Margi knew he was right. Reen was in her nineties, and her health was beginning to deteriorate. Who knew how much longer she had to live? The walls needed to come down. What secrets did she hold?

It was time those secrets were shared.

Chapter 53

"Your mom's not getting any younger," Jennifer said. "You are smart and brave and able to do this! We've gone over a list of questions. Call her as soon as we hang up."

Margi hesitated. She needed to do it right now, while she still had the courage. She scrolled down the list of favorites in her cell phone and touched the name *Reen*. It rang twice, and her mother answered in her usual sour voice.

"Hi, Reen. Just calling to check on you. Everything okay today?"

"I've been better. My body's getting older—that's for sure."

Margi considered the adjustment it must be for someone as vain as her mother to watch her body age and slowly deteriorate. Vanity always came back to bite. It was nature. Reen was far removed from her days of flirting and demanding the attention of men.

"Remember awhile back when I asked if I could take that large box of Dad's belongings? Well, I found some paperwork in that box. Receipts for visits to the Children's Psychiatric Hospital. The visits were for me."

There was no response, so Margi continued.

"Eighty-one visits when I was a teenager. What was wrong with me? What did I have?"

"I don't remember."

"Well, the doctors must have said *something* about my progress."

"I don't remember, Margi. You're always asking me things I don't know."

"Reen, I went to a psychiatrist when I was about twenty years old. I remember going there, and I can tell you exactly where it was. I can remember the cherry-brown chair I sat in, and I remember speaking with the doctor. Why don't I remember a single visit to this hospital?"

"I don't know." It was Reen's perfectly canned response to everything.

"Did you take me there?" Margi asked. "Who drove me?"

"Maybe someone came and got you."

Suddenly Reen shifted gears. Changed the subject entirely. It was her pattern.

"You know, I've really become a great artist," Reen stated. "I think God has kept me alive so I can paint. I should show you some of the things I've done next time you're here."

"Reen, please listen to me. I had therapy today. It was difficult. I know that I was blind-sided by drugs as a child, and it's terribly frightening to have those drug memories haunt me. I was abused as well."

"Well, I hope you don't think your daddy played any role in this. I knew him as a man. He would never do such a thing. That would make him a monster, and I don't believe he was."

"Please don't call him *daddy*," Margi said. "I've told you so many times not to call him that. It makes my stomach turn."

Reen's voice was louder now, and Margi could tell her mother was on the verge of anger.

"Nothing your daddy ever did was normal. *Your* life is difficult? *My* life with him was difficult! I had to give out samples at the grocery store. Can you imagine how degrading? A dentist's wife handing out samples to earn extra money!"

Reen took a deep breath. "It's in the past," Reen said, sounding calmer.

"No, it's not," Margi replied.

"Well, it is for me. You need to stop thinking about the past, Margi."

Suddenly, the subject changed again. Reen began asking about Halloween and all the decorations the neighbors were putting up, saying it was a fun, festive time of year.

"I've always hated October and Halloween," Margi stated.

"With your past, it's no wonder," Reen replied. In the same breath, she quickly turned the conversation to compliment herself and all her motherly attributes.

"I went to your school one day and volunteered, and then I came home and went to bridge club with the ladies. You know what those women asked me? They wanted to know how I could do it all. They thought I was the greatest mother."

Margi was weary. Conversations with her mother always went around in what seemed an endless circle, with contradictions flying between sentences and abrupt changes of subject. It was exhausting.

"Reen, we are both getting old," Margi said. "Is there anything you can tell me about my past or my father's behavior? It would be really helpful."

"My life was too hard when you were young," Reen said. "Your daddy was obsessed with you, and he was with you all the time. His desires for you were inappropriate."

Margi could feel years of hurt and neglect raging inside her chest and boiling to the surface. Her face burned.

"I was being sodomized," Margi said. Her voice quivered, but she got the words out.

"Well, that explains his needs in the bedroom," Reen grunted. "He was a strange man, and I never understood him. He never grew up. He was a child."

Reen paused for a moment, then hurled another assault. "You've just ruined my day by talking like this."

"I've ruined your *day*? I've had to live with this for fifty years!" Margi was crying. Angry tears. Hurt tears. And everything in between. Margi didn't hold back, and the tears brought more accusations.

"I had to try to make sense of what was happening to me. I was abandoned by my family and had to find ways to soothe my fear, find reality on my own, and cry myself to sleep every night! All this with no help from any of you!" Margi cried. "Horrific things were happening to me, and I had to comfort myself. Can you begin to imagine how terrifying that was? THAT was my childhood."

Margi clutched the phone in her hand and fought the desire to retreat from the confrontation. She charged forward with her words.

"You know things you're not telling me. I know you have secrets!"

"He was a liar and a cheater," Reen confessed. "Your daddy was sneaky. I never really loved him."

"He raped me," Margi whispered.

"Don't think about it."

"Why were there no adults to help me . . . ever? To save me? Nurture me? Why didn't *you* help me? It had to be obvious that I was a sad, sick little girl."

With no strength to hold back her emotions, Margi was bawling now.

"I was unhappy in my marriage," Reen said. "I've had a difficult life!"

"That's when you nurture your children even more!" Margi wailed. "I was also in a hard place, but my children were my world. You made me feel invisible, and I had to get through all of this completely on my own."

Margi could feel the blood fueling the redness in her face. Her heart was pounding, and her ears were ringing. "What mother lets her child miss 225 days of elementary school?"

Her mother was silent. Margi continued crying.

"You know I was part of the PTA and took cookies to school. I guess we were both in a bad place."

Margi wanted to reach through the phone and hurt her mother. Margi was crying loudly now, and she knew it was time to end the conversation. But she had one more point she wanted to make.

"No, Reen—*I* was in a bad place. I was being raped and sodomized and drugged. You let bad things happen, and you never helped me. THAT is a bad place."

Chapter 54

"Reen, this is Jay. He's been helping me with some therapy."

Margi held her breath. Reen had agreed to the home visit with Jay, but she had hesitated. It had been a few weeks since their last confrontation, and Margi had purposely tried to smooth things over. She had made a point not to ask any more questions.

"Nice to meet you," Jay said. He shook her hand and smiled. "I've heard so much about you."

"Oh, I'm sure you have. My daughter here wants to talk only about the past. I keep telling her to leave it all where it belongs—in the past."

"Well, sometimes that's easier said than done," Jay responded. "Sometimes it helps to clear a few things up. That way we can stop trying to solve the puzzle."

"Margi, why don't you get your friend Jay a drink," Reen said, ordering Margi around like she always did.

. . .

Small talk ensued for some time. Jay had encouraged Reen to talk about the early days in Utah and about raising a family. She was clearly enthralled with the high position she felt her family name had in the community. The prestige was important to her. Reen's eyes lit up when she talked about past years in her prime.

"Everybody who was anybody knew us," she bragged. Jay knew it was now time to gently probe some things.

"Tell me more about your husband," Jay asked. "What was he like?"

"Mostly good for nothing. It was always about his friends and those men he worked with. That's all he could talk about—men. He had a doctor friend, and every Sunday he drove by the man's house."

Reen snickered and shook her head. "I think the writing was on the wall. He had a thing for men, especially his doctor friend. He never admitted to it, but I think he was gay. I've never said that out loud before."

Jay locked eyes with Margi. That explained her father's obsession with some of his habits of abuse.

"But you know, he was also obsessed with Margi, even to the point that people outside the house talked about it and knew about it," Reen explained. "Everyone could see that his attention was unnaturally focused on his daughter. He never focused on me. Everyone knew it was unusual. Even the neighbors saw it."

"Is that why you shunned me?" Margi asked. "Were you jealous of me and Dad?"

"Yeah," Reen muttered.

Reen shifted in her chair and changed the subject, as she always did when things got uncomfortable for her.

"I think it would be nice if you were to take home one of my paintings. Look—I've painted some pictures of chickens. I think you should take one home," Reen said, handing one of the paintings to Jay.

Jay noticed the intentional and rapid change of subject. He knew Reen was redirecting attention elsewhere. He was determined to reel it back in. Jay could sense Margi hesitating as they got into sensitive areas. He was ready to take the questioning into his own hands and be direct.

"You talk about this obsession your husband had with his daughter," Jay asked. "When did that start?"

Reen looked over at Margi then back at Jay. Her eyebrows arched and she spoke softly.

"Well, from the time Margi was little—four or five years old—he picked her up and undressed her and bathed her. Then he dried her off, put her nightie on her, tucked her into bed, read a story to her, and then got in bed with her. He did that every night."

Margi's eyes filled with tears. Jay realized that as hard as it must be for Margi to hear, her mother's words must have been incredibly validating. It confirmed so many early flashbacks Margi had described to him.

"So, you saw that?" Jay asked. "How did that make you feel?"

"You know—I knew it was wrong," Reen said. She gathered up some more paintings of chickens and seemed to be nervous as she rustled through the papers.

Jay looked over at Margi. She was wiping tears off her cheeks.

"I think I'm getting tired now," Reen announced. "Probably need a nap."

Jay decided this was probably a good time to wrap things up.

"Thank you for talking with us today," Jay said. "I've got some more business with Margi, so I think we'll be on our way."

. . .

Jay opened the front door and held it for Margi. She walked toward the doorway then paused on the threshold. Margi froze as she considered her next move. Her feet felt heavy—sluggish. Lifeless. She could feel her mother's glare boring into her back. Margi lifted her head and slowly stepped through the opening.

She didn't look back.

. . .

Margi pulled out her scriptures and laid them in her lap. It had been a long, emotional day, and nightfall was close. She needed some light, and her scriptures were her favorite place to find that. She opened the leather cover and went to her favorite scriptures where she read:

The light shineth in darkness, and the darkness comprehendeth it not; nevertheless, the day shall come when you shall comprehend even God, being quickened in him and by him.

Then shall ye know that ye have seen me, that I am, and that
I am the true light that is in you, and that you are in me;
otherwise ye could not abound.[1]

Tears filled Margi's eyes as she considered how far-reaching His
light could be. It had found her in such darkness. Margi was learning
to love her parts. She knew her core loved Christ. When she prayed, she
gathered her parts together and believed some of them prayed with her.
She told them that Christ loved them too.

That poor little girl. She was so bewildered with this world she was placed in.
Margi was trying to love that little girl. It was a process, but Margi was
doing her best. She was sure that Christ especially loved Little Margi.

As Margi climbed into bed, her eyes met the framed scripture on the
wall next to her bed. She made a point to read it several times a day. Her
daughter Megan had written the scripture in her beautiful handwriting
and framed it for her years ago, before they knew anything about a DID
diagnosis. Margi's eyes carefully read each word:

And now, verily I say unto you,
And what I say unto one I say unto all,
Be of good cheer, little children;
For I am in your midst, and I have not forsaken you.[2]

It was a scripture that had always touched Margi's heart, no matter
how many times she read it. Who knew that over the years the meaning of
this scripture would change and deepen? That it would bring such peace?

Margi hoped that her children parts would believe the scripture and
eventually *be of good cheer.* How desperately she wanted them to feel safe
and loved. They had suffered for so long.

Margi lay her head on the pillow and braced herself for what was
to come. Another night of darkness. Another tomorrow to fight. But in

this brief moment, in her darkened bedroom, Margi reached again for His light.

PART SIX

THERE IS NO GREATER AGONY THAN BEARING AN UNTOLD STORY INSIDE YOU.

— Maya Angelou

Chapter 55

"I can't believe how much energy they all have!" Margi exclaimed.

It was exhausting just sitting on the couch watching it all! An afternoon at her daughter's house always brought such joy to Margi's heart. Time spent playing with grandchildren was a treasured gift. Margi wondered how she'd been so lucky to deserve all this.

The grandchildren ran circles around the room and occasionally stopped to show Grandma Margi a treasured toy. It was the best kind of show-and-tell. In turn, they always got lots of attention from Grandma Margi with plenty of *oohs* and *ahhs*.

Blocks, stuffed animals, and dolls were all included in the circus of playtime. How blessed her grandchildren were to have toys and a happy home. They were blessings not unnoticed by Margi.

"Look, Grandma. This one is my favorite."

Margi turned to see her sweet granddaughter holding a naked doll. Toddlers were always ripping the clothes off their dolls. It was a peculiar thing. No matter how many sets of clothes were purchased for the doll, the little ones uncovered their doll's nakedness.

But this doll was different—a special doll whose eyes opened and closed. Margi focused to control her breathing. Naked dolls were always a trigger—particularly this one. *Hurry up and get your clothes back on. I feel your nakedness. I feel what you feel. I'll come help you.*

"She's beautiful," Margi said. "Can I hold her for a minute?"

Margi took the doll and left the room. She looked through the toy shelves in her granddaughter's room and found some clothes. Quickly she dressed the doll and wrapped her up tightly in a blanket so no one could touch her. *It is ridiculous that I'm doing this.*

Margi recognized she was projecting her own fears on this doll, but she couldn't ignore how it made her feel. This was a safe house. Her grandchildren flourished in this home with loving parents who protected and nurtured them. But somehow, the stench from the past always managed to seep through the cracks and consume Margi's emotions. She identified it as two separate events but experienced it as one.

Margi thought back to that favorite song, *I Can See Clearly Now*. She wanted to see both backward and forward with clear vision and understanding. Some might never understand the need to know such awful details as the ones from her past, but Margi felt she needed to recognize them to fully heal. All she wanted to do was rescue all her children parts from bad scenes. *Maybe one day we'll all see clearly.*

Margi picked up the fully clothed doll swaddled in a blanket and walked back into the family room with the others. She handed the doll back to her granddaughter.

"Doesn't she look beautiful?" Margi asked.

Her granddaughter smiled, her eyes bright, and she took the wrapped baby into her own arms. Margi breathed a bit easier now. Everyone seemed comfortable, safe, and loved.

· · ·

Years earlier, when Margi was first diagnosed with DID, she investigated social media as an avenue to gain more understanding. She found a DID online support group and joined in hopes that reading about others might be educational as well as useful in recognizing that she was not alone in this diagnosis. Margi noticed immediately that others in the group described events and struggles just as she did in therapy. Their words were almost exactly what she herself would say. It was validating and interesting to read and feel such a connection to others who were suffering.

After watching on the sidelines for years, Margi was ready to venture out from the silent fringes of the group. She was certain she was in a better position now to reach others and make a difference after years of working with Jay. So many in the group were running from their parts and living lives filled with fear. It reminded Margi of her own earlier days. She knew from her work with Jay that it was possible to work with the parts instead of running away and rejecting them.

Margi logged into the group site, eager to take it to the next level and participate. She was nervous about being open, but the idea of serving someone else was stronger.

Hi, I'm Margi.

She sat staring at her phone. It would be minutes before someone else responded. There were some back-and-forth introductions and then a question from another member.

Tell me about your parents. Were they part of the trauma?

Margi immediately felt the words in response.

I had good parents.

Before she hit *send* she recognized the falsehood. She had said the same thing to Jay several times in therapy. He explained that younger parts had wishful and magical thinking in believing that they had good parents because they wanted that so badly. It was common for them to come up and relate their needs and desires to have a safe mom and dad. Margi felt the wishful thinking of her parts. But her core knew she didn't have a safe mother *or* father.

My parents abused me. Margi paused and then continued. *Has anyone had spinning?*

Comments flooded the page, and most sounded so familiar. Those who had been subjected to ritual abuse described many of the same things Margi experienced in her nightmares. One by one, the items group members mentioned coincided with memory-mares and flashbacks over decades of Margi's life. It eerily confirmed the existence of rituals in her past. What she *didn't* have was the WHO. *Who did this to me? Who COULD do this to me?* Between the drugs and the terrified parts holding those memories, Margi didn't have all the answers yet. That was still a work in progress.

Margi's intention was to help others, but she needed to ask one more question.

Was anyone ever treated by Dr. Bowen in Utah?

Margi didn't want to divulge any other information. She didn't want to fuel any exaggerations or fabrications. A young man replied.

Yeah, my sister and I saw him. He drugged both of us, and I swear he was into some kind of mind control. Evil doctor.

Everybody had a story—the details were just different. Like Margi, all were struggling to live productive lives one day at a time, and some were doing a better job of that than others. Margi began to reach out with comments. She reminded them of a loving God who knew their struggles and of angels who were there to support and guide. She taught about a core who was capable of controlling and managing the parts.

Many of the group members were put off by the subject of religion or any God. It was too intertwined with rituals. Margi understood the concern and the reaction. She had parts that felt those same feelings. *But how can people heal and do this without God? I have had angels who have carried me. I know that.*

Margi continued to reinforce the need for a combination of therapy, hard work, and faith. For her, all three were essential. Feeling profound appreciation for the support she received, she ached for those who didn't have a Jay or a Jennifer. So many were hurting with little support.

As Margi reached out with her own opinions and desire to help, some responded and messaged her privately. Margi felt the weight of the supportive role. She prayed before typing the words in response to those asking for advice. She asked God to help her find the needed words for each one. Margi knew from experience that sometimes you just needed to hear *You're not crazy. You're brave and strong. You can do this.*

One woman spoke of suicide—of her constant thoughts of darkness and her desire to end it all. Margi responded with heartfelt words: "I know first-hand you can do this. You can't stay in a part forever. You will come out of this because those parts can't stay up for long. You'll feel better later. Just hang in there. Please . . ."

Another woman reached out privately with details of her abuse at the age of five. She asked Margi to read something her five-year-old part had written. Margi agreed, knowing it was going to be difficult to read. Before the woman sent the piece, she typed the words, *I'm crazy.*

Margi's stomach dropped. Her heart was filled with empathy. Margi's eyes filled with tears as she quickly responded.

"You are not crazy. You are very brave. You are a warrior."

Chapter 56

"I feel like I'm starting to find some kind of purpose in my life," Margi stated. "If I can just help one person, that would be amazing."

Margi had told Jay about reaching out to those in the online DID support group, and he had applauded her confidence. He knew that as survivors gained some control, they often began to look for more meaning and future direction in their lives. Now he saw Margi take that step.

"There's another way you can help," Jay suggested. "With your permission, I'd like to send some of your writings to some therapists I work with. Your words might be useful for them to use either in therapy with trauma victims or in understanding how those victims struggle in their thoughts. Your writings are really good. Your parts have been able to articulate what they're feeling."

"Oh, I would love to help," Margi said. "That sounds great."

Years earlier, Margi never dreamed she would one day be capable of helping others who were just like her. Back then, she had considered herself unique—a one-and-only mistake. Now maybe there was more ahead. Opportunities to help others using her own perspective and experience.

Margi knew that hard work was still ahead. Although there were moments when Margi thought she could be friends with all her parts, she still feared Little Margi. She was front and center in the middle of the night and first thing in the morning after a string of nightmares. What Margi needed was to not hate that little girl.

Margi reminded herself often, *I've always had parts. They saved my life.* The challenge was getting all those parts to cooperate. Margi was doing an incredible job of telling the parts *I want this*, which was so important for the core to learn. *I want this, and I'm going to have this. I'm the boss. It's my mind. My body.* And the parts were gradually learning to cooperate in meeting her needs, wants, wishes, and desires.

One of her desires was to travel. Margi was now able to prepare her mind to leave the safety of her home for a short trip. To drive somewhere new. It was a tremendous but thrilling challenge. She hoped to take occasional longer business trips with Dennis soon.

With a better understanding, Margi was getting stronger and stronger with her core. It was a new experience to be in charge. In her youth, Margi was raised in a household where she didn't have a say in anything. Now, for the first time, she was able to speak with authority and direct the other parts. *You need to go to the Safe Place. Let's go to the farm so you can do your new jobs.*

I need to be in charge today, so get behind me.

. . .

Dennis and Margi stood behind the car and double-checked the things they had loaded in the back. Most of it was camera equipment for the work trip to Nauvoo, Illinois. Dennis did a visual check of his own things and then saw that Margi's suitcase was loaded on the right side. He looked over at his sweetheart. This was a big step—their first lengthy trip across several state lines together. Margi looked a bit nervous.

"All good? I think we have everything," Dennis stated.

"Yep. I think we're set."

"Okay, let's do this!" Dennis felt like a teenager again and couldn't wait to take Margi on this road trip for work. It would be the first time she had left Utah in a long time. Dennis recognized what a huge moment this was for both of them, and he was giddy with excitement.

Dennis and Margi climbed into the car, and the roar of the engine signaled the start of their adventure. Dennis put in a favorite CD before backing out of the driveway. The song began to play. Dennis kept his foot on the brake and looked over at Margi and smiled. This wasn't just any song . . . it was *their* song. "Two of Us" by the Beatles.

The Beatles continued their chorus as music and lyrics filled the car with reflections that dated clear back to high school. It was an anthem that both recaptured thoughts and events from the past and celebrated an infinite love that continued to carry them.

The music ushered the car down the driveway and through the neighborhood streets. Dennis and Margi sang along and laughed at the togetherness of it all. Both recognized the tender mercy as the wind blew through their hair.

Life was good.

. . .

"Mom, you need to go to my doctor. He'll run some more tests. You can't ignore your symptoms."

It was exasperating. Margi's daughter Megan had listened to her mother complain for months about abdominal and back pain. Margi's appetite was all but nonexistent, and her energy levels were down. Megan knew how her mother felt about doctors poking and prodding, but this needed to be addressed—now. All the research Megan had done confirmed the strong feeling she had about her mother's symptoms. It could be serious.

"It's nothing to get excited about," Margi replied. "A new doctor will make a fishing expedition out of it. It's a waste of time."

Megan understood the level of fear and anxiety her mother felt as she battled with DID every day. Megan's relationship with her mother was extremely close. Margi probably confided more in Megan than she should have, but Megan was a good listener and a solid researcher.

Megan had spent countless hours at the computer educating herself on DID, so she understood that adding one more thing to her mother's plate must feel overwhelming. Nonetheless, Megan had a strong prompting to push her mother hard in finding an answer for her new symptoms. The desperation and fear for her mother was overwhelming.

"Mom, I'm trying to save your life!" Megan shouted. The panic in her gut was fueling a rush of emotion and fear. Frustration was at a high point.

"If you don't care enough about your life to save it, then I can't either," Megan explained. "I can't hear about this anymore. I can't deal with it if you won't. You have got to go figure out what's wrong!"

Megan was frustrated. Her mother had recently been the focus of Megan's intense prayers, and she knew she was receiving guidance to lead her mother in this direction.

"Mom, I've always prayed really hard for you," Megan said. "I also know that sometimes you aren't in a place to receive inspiration because of what you're going through, but prayers are always answered. Sometimes those answers come through someone else."

Margi nodded to indicate her agreement.

"I'm pretty prayerful about it and about discerning what is a real possibility for you," Megan continued. "Don't you think you should trust me on this, Mom? I'm not leading you in a bad direction."

. . .

Margi sat quietly. *What if something is wrong? Really wrong?*

Margi couldn't bear the thought of dealing with one more thing. It was too much to even think about, but Megan was insistent. Margi trusted her daughter implicitly. Maybe she should trust her daughter's feelings and pursue this.

"Okay," Margi whispered. "Will you go with me for the appointment and the tests?"

"You know I will," Megan replied.

. . .

"Margi, we need to take a look inside and see what's going on. Find the source of the pain. That's going to require surgery."

The doctor knew a little bit about Margi's past. Margi had been up front with him about trauma as a child and about medical abuse by men in hospitals. He expected there would be trust issues with his staff. They encountered this with a few patients every year, and they were prepared to emotionally handle Margi with special care.

The doctor nodded at Megan, who was sitting next to her mother, then looked directly at Margi. He had stated his own analysis of the situation and suggested this plan of action, but Margi wasn't so sure. The doctor's eyes displayed compassion, but his words were terrifying. *Surgery? Anesthesia? I just can't . . .* Margi fought the urge to run out of the office. Perhaps the abdominal pain and the fatigue would just go away on its own.

Tears filled Megan's eyes as she squeezed her mother's hand in support.

Margi began to cry. The doctor handed her a tissue and talked about scheduling and positive outcomes, but Margi didn't hear any of it. His lips were moving, but none of it made any sense to Margi. Megan was taking notes.

This can't be happening to me.

Chapter 57

It seemed like a rational assumption: Because of what she had already been through in her life, Margi assumed there would be no more severe trials. Nights were sleepless as she tried to understand how this could happen. She wondered why God would do this to her, and she cried out to Him, asking, *Haven't I been through enough?*

Margi had called Jay the day of the exploratory surgery and immediately pulled him into the mental preparation.

"I need you to help me, Jay," Margi cried. "I'm so terrified of the anesthesia. They're going to put a mask over my face. I can hardly bear to think about it."

"You can do this, my dear," Jay promised. "You are in charge. You can tell your parts that they must stay behind and let you take care of this. Tell them you are going to do it. Your core will need to stay up front."

"What if I can't?" Margi questioned. "Tester could be a problem."

Tester was a part whose job it was to warn Margi about anyone and everything that might be a trick. Tester didn't trust anybody, and she held all the pessimism and suspicion. She came out front frequently and always brought a lot of negativity with her.

"I've been watching you do this for years," Jay replied. "This time the situation is a bit more serious, but the process is still the same. You're the boss, Margi . . . you're even the boss of Tester. You are the core. You've got this."

There was a moment of silence as they both considered the journey they had taken together over the past several years. Just the sound of Jay's voice gave Margi the resolve and courage to move forward. "You're some kind of wonderful," Jay said.

. . .

"How are you feeling about things, Margi?" the doctor asked. He seemed gentle, professional, and perceptive. He was personally speaking with Margi in pre-op and helping her feel at ease.

"I'm really nervous," Margi replied. She looked over at Dennis, who was in the room with her.

"That's to be expected," the doctor said. "I'm going to take good care of you."

Margi's eyes widened.

"Margi, I know about your history. I've talked more to Dennis and Megan. I know that I'm a man—but I can't really help that, can I?" The doctor smiled. "But you are safe, and you're going to be okay. I'm going to make sure of that, and I won't leave your side during surgery."

Tester was screaming inside. Margi closed her eyes and focused as the core. She wanted to trust this doctor. Dennis and Megan had both promised he was a good man.

"Okay," was all Margi could mumble.

"The nurse who works with me in surgery is the best in the business. He's also a man, but I've worked with him for many years, and I trust him. Margi, it's your call. I'll get another nurse to assist in surgery if you need a woman."

Margi noticed her hands were trembling. She wondered if the doctor noticed. She clasped her fingers together and looked at the doctor.

"If you trust him, then I'm okay," Margi said.

The nurse entered the room shortly after the doctor left. He was positive and sensitive to Margi.

"The doctor has told me so much about you, Margi," the nurse said. "He's the best. We're going to take good care of you and make

294

sure you get home to those grandkids real soon."

As the nurse busied himself checking vitals and making the necessary preparations for surgery, Margi started talking and laughing about all the silly things little kids say and do. The nurse shared some personal information about himself and slowly gained her trust. Margi was beginning to feel okay about this.

There was a tap on the door, and a man's face peeked through.

"Hello, are you Margi?" he asked.

"Yes, that's me."

"Hi; I'm the anesthesiologist who is going to be helping you in surgery today. I'm the guy who makes sure you have a good, long nap."

"Oh, dear," Margi said. She took a deep breath to steady her nerves.

"Your doctor has talked to me, and I'm very aware of what happened to you in the past and of your fear of drugs," he said. "I would imagine that you're mostly scared of that fuzzy space between receiving the drug and when everything goes dark. Am I right?"

"Oh, yes. I don't want to feel that. Even if it's just ten seconds!"

"I understand, and I have a plan." Standing by her bedside, the anesthesiologist described a step-by-step process he could do so Margi would never even feel that ten-second space. She'd be out as quickly as turning off a light switch.

Margi smiled. "Thank you so much. I'm so grateful."

. . .

Dennis shook his head. He was overwhelmed with the compassion that everyone on this medical team had shown Margi. They really cared, and they had lessened her fears. It was wonderful to witness.

It was time for Margi to be wheeled to the operating room. Dennis looked at his wife. He knew how hard this must be for her, and he was so proud of her. He squeezed her hand as a loving gesture.

"You're gonna rock this, Margi," Dennis whispered.

. . .

"Is this Dennis?" The cell phone startled Dennis when it rang. He was in the surgical waiting room.

Dennis quickly sat up straight. He recognized the voice of the surgical nurse.

"Margi is doing well and she's still in surgery. The doctor wants me to let you know that one of her ovaries is definitely diseased. He wants to remove both ovaries and send them out for further testing. He'll know what Margi is dealing with after he gets those biopsy results."

Dennis leaned forward and rubbed his forehead trying to absorb the news.

"Whatever you think is best," Dennis replied. "Thank you for the update." He tried to keep his voice from shaking. "Please let me know when Margi wakes up."

. . .

Margi squinted her eyes. Dennis knew she would still be a bit numb and sleepy from the surgery.

"You did great, Margi," Dennis said. "The doctor said the surgery was successful. He saw some problems with your ovaries and removed them. You're going to be okay now."

Dennis silently worried about what the discovered disease meant. They would tackle that issue when they knew more. His mind raced back to his daughter's insistence that Margi find answers despite her fears.

"It was a miracle, Margi," Dennis whispered. "An absolute miracle."

Margi smiled softly then closed her eyes and fell back to sleep. Dennis watched her and wondered if the nightmares would leave her alone in this medicated sleep. He hoped so.

Dennis prayed that Margi could simply rest peacefully.

. . .

The days were long and nights even longer during the days following the surgery. Margi's body was sore during her recovery, but the emotional wait for the biopsy results was the worst. The following Monday, Margi's daughter Megan came over to the house for moral support and to help with household tasks. The unanswered questions were looming on everyone's mind.

"Any word yet?" Megan asked.

"Nothing," Margi replied. "I'm going to call their office just in case the results came in this morning."

Margi dialed the doctor's office phone number. She told the receptionist her name and her reason for calling.

"Just a minute, Margi. Let me see if we have received anything."

"Hello, Margi."

The lower voice startled Margi. It was the doctor.

"Margi, the results just came back from the biopsy and, unfortunately, the results came back positive."

Margi knew how much he cared about his patients and imagined it was difficult for him to deliver unsettling news.

"You have ovarian cancer," the doctor said. He paused for a moment, probably waiting for the news to sink in before continuing. As he did, his tone was kind and gentle but serious.

"This is really aggressive, Margi, so we also need to be aggressive in our treatment. There's about a six-month window here, and you've been having symptoms for at least three months," the doctor explained. "You're going to need to see an oncologist immediately for more surgery and potentially some chemotherapy. I know a woman who is the best oncologist in the business. I'm putting in a referral right now. You need to call her today, Margi."

Margi hung up the phone and looked over at Megan, who was crying. Megan had heard bits of conversation, pulled it together along with the look on her mother's face, and felt the reality of the news.

"I'm going to be okay," Margi said. "It's okay." Tears rolled down her face as she tried to console her daughter.

And herself.

Chapter 58

Tensions were high as Margi and Dennis sat in the oncologist's office. They listened as she reviewed the results of the second surgery. They were hoping for good news but were prepared for the worst.

The oncologist explained in detail all the procedures that had been performed and the biopsies that were required afterward. Margi felt the knot beginning in her stomach and sensed her present reality slowly fading from her as she listened. Finally, the doctor stood up from her chair. With a warm smile on her face, she walked over to Margi and gave her a big hug.

"After reviewing all of the imaging and test results, I feel confident we caught this early and the chance of it returning is less than 10 percent."

Margi looked directly at her doctor who seemed elated to share this incredibly good news. The words took a moment to sink in. Margi turned and locked eyes with Dennis. There was a sigh of relief and tears of joy.

But there was still one final step.

. . .

Margi opened her closet and grabbed a comfortable pair of sweats and a cozy shirt. She slipped on the clothes and walked into her bathroom. She caught sight of herself as she walked past the mirror. Margi stopped and took a good hard look at her reflection. She was going to change. The doctor said there was no question: she would lose her hair. All of it.

Chemo. How will I do this?

Margi ran a brush through her hair, wondering when it would fall out. Perhaps she would keep her hair until after the last treatment. Hair was the least of her worries. Having people flood drugs into her veins was the real issue.

A long conversation with Jay had given Margi some confidence. He always knew exactly what to say, and she could never have done this without him. What a blessing he was in her life. Now it was up to her. She needed to put years of experience with Jay to practice. Nothing like the first day of chemo to provide a real-life test!

Margi returned to her bedroom and took a seat. It was time to have an internal conversation with her parts. This time it would save her life.

I need to be the adult. I'm going to be okay, and there are good people who are going to take care of us. They're not going to put hallucinogenic drugs in us. They are not psychoactive drugs. This is what I need. This is what I—the core—want.

Margi continued. She was focused, strong, and assertive.

This is what I want from you. I really need you. You have been so helpful throughout my life. Today I still need you, but today I'm going to be the adult. I need you all to work on the farm in the Safe Place. You can read books or do whatever you want. You can come with me if you want, but you must stay behind me. You are probably better off in the Safe Place.

I'll be okay by myself.

. . .

Margi arrived early at the chemo center for a consultation. She and Dennis were escorted into a small room; a kind, smiling woman entered and sat down across the desk. The oncologist's eyes were filled with compassion as she walked Margi and Dennis through the treatment plan. Her voice was soft and positive.

"This treatment plan is just what I'm calling it. *A plan.* We are planning on the cancer never returning. You'll have a life full of time with your family. I understand your kids are joining you today for your first treatment."

Margi nodded her head. They were all going to be there. This was a family affair designed to make sure Margi could do this. They were there to keep Margi optimistic. Focused. And, above all, present.

Margi was escorted down the hall to the treatment center. As she walked through the doorway, she saw a row of chairs lined up with IV poles nestled next to each one. It could have been a scene from one of her nightmares—dental chairs, drugs, and an enormous dose of fear. *Oh, I shouldn't have agreed to this. What have I done?*

Just then all the kids entered the room.

"Hey, Mom. Heard there was a party in here today."

It brought Margi back to the present. How she loved her family. Here they all were in an effort to love her through this. Margi had tried to explain to her children the fear of sitting in a chair to receive intravenous drugs. They were empathetic but more concerned about the risks of refusing the chemo treatments. Her children promised their full support if she would make the brave commitment. They all understood that their mother was alone during the most horrific time of her life as a child. They knew this was frightening for her, but they vowed she would not be alone this time. Margi looked up at her children and forced a nervous smile.

A sweet nurse gently guided Margi over to a chair and told her to take a seat. She explained that she would need to insert a needle so Margi could receive the medication for the treatment. Margi briefly explained her fear of the process and some abuse she'd had as a child in hospitals. The nurse spoke softly and promised she would take care of Margi and not allow anything like that to happen.

Don't believe her. They're trying to trick you. Tester was sounding off warnings.

"Besides, I see you have a real fan club here to help you," the nurse said, smiling.

The nurse explained that the first medication would be a form of Benadryl that might make her a bit dizzy. It was all too familiar. *Oh, no! How do I trust you? What if it takes my mind and I can't come back? What if I go to that drug place and never come back?*

Her daughter Emily grabbed her hand and held it tight. "You're

301

okay, Mom. You're okay." Margi focused on the feel of her daughter's hand clasped tightly around hers.

The other two kids joined in with Dennis and started cracking jokes to lighten the mood. It brought Margi back to the present. She focused on her beautiful family. She was doing this for them. Margi closed her eyes and found a sliver of strength.

Margi suddenly felt surrounded by more than her family. A warm sensation enveloped her heart, and she knew God was aware of her in this terrifying place. She was sure angels surrounded her chair and were helping her through this wall of fear. Margi relaxed in the chair and released it all to Him. Over and over she repeated in her mind the thought, *God led me to it—He'll lead me through it.* Margi's next thought was clear and direct. *You're not going to die from this.* It was the first time Margi had really believed that. Margi considered everything that had come with this experience: Megan's insistence on finding answers. Compassionate doctors and tender nurses who gave Margi reason to trust. And a family who loved her deeply through it all. Margi's heart burned with a comforting warmth. *God led me to it—He'll lead me through it.*

Margi knew it as truth.

. . .

Margi had noticed the clumps of hair in the shower, in the sink, and on her pillow. She knew this was going to happen, but to see it was startling. The loss of her long, brown hair was both a physical and emotional benchmark on this journey of healing.

Megan stood behind her mother with a pair of scissors in her hand.

"Let's do this," Margi announced. "Cut it short."

Megan forced a smile and tenderly combed a section up to grasp with her other fingers for the first cut. Margi winced; her scalp was tender, and it was uncomfortable to have her hair cut. Sections of hair continued to fall out while Megan carefully worked with her mother's remaining hair.

Megan blinked back the tears. She must be strong for her mother. Over and over Megan's heart broke as pieces of her mother's hair fell without effort into her hands. How many haircuts had she done for people in her salon over the years? Hundreds, maybe thousands. Usually it was a good thing and made people happy. But of all the haircuts, this is the only one that broke her heart.

"Okay, Mom. All done," Megan said. Another forced smile. "It's a new you! You look so cute with short hair."

· · ·

Margi looked in the mirror and tears rolled down her cheeks. Her daughter had worked hard to make the best of it. Margi brushed the tears aside and looked up at Megan. Her children were with her during every single step. How could she have done this without them?

· · ·

Megan was determined to put up a strong front for her sweet mom, but her emotions were raw and on the brink of collapse. Long pieces of beautiful brown hair puddled at her feet. The wall holding back tears was starting to crack. Quickly she created an excuse and retreated to a bathroom down the hall.

Silently and privately, Megan wept.

· · ·

"I want a turn," Margi's oldest grandchild declared.

It had been only a few days since Margi's initial short haircut. Sections of hair were now falling out so fast that she decided to shave her whole head. Dennis and the kids wanted to make an event of it. They had all come together under one roof, vowing to shave it as a family.

Even the older grandkids wanted to take a turn. They each buzzed a small section. It was a loving effort of support and solidarity. And it was the unity of all hearts coming together. For one.

. . .

Margi smiled as she walked across the room and over to the wall. It was a momentous occasion. Everyone waited breathlessly as she grabbed the small rope and jerked it to life.

The bell rang loudly and filled the silence in the treatment room. There was a roar of celebration from her family, the nurses, and the other patients. There were hugs and cheers for Margi, who was the center of attention that day. This wasn't just any day. It was her last chemo treatment, and ringing the bell was the ceremonial ending.

Margi reached up and adjusted the cap on her head. Her beautiful brown hair was completely gone. Even her eyebrows and eyelashes had fallen out. It was an expected side effect of the chemo drugs. But the hair was insignificant to the long-term result. Her hair would grow back—and hopefully the cancer would not.

Once again, Margi had conquered a seemingly insurmountable climb. This mountain had been so steep, but she had been able to armor up and fight every battle on this treacherous trail of cancer. Margi had surprised even herself.

She really was a survivor. Again.

Chapter 59

Looking in the bathroom mirror, Margi barely recognized herself. The brown hair that had fallen out during chemo was growing in gray. It made her look old. Feel old.

Even worse was the visual reminder that she had been sick. Every reflection in household mirrors and grocery store windows spoke of it. Even a simple glance into the rearview mirror of her car before backing out of the driveway revealed the memory. *I was sick. I had cancer.*

Margi had pushed the cancer so far down during the experience that she resented the constant jarring thoughts. She wanted to move forward and forget. Margi decided she would color her hair. A soft brown shade would work. It would help her not feel quite so old. *I'm not ready to be old.*

Old and gray like my scary mother.

. . .

The nineties are tough—it is often the age when the body breaks down, and even the strongest mind and most powerful determination can't stop it. Such was the case with Margi's mother. Though her body was quickly deteriorating, she was every bit as ornery and stubborn as she had been while younger. She had recently reached the age of ninety-eight.

To help with the preparation of food and other household and personal needs, Reen had hired a health aid, Anna, to come to her home for a few hours each week. Her service enabled Reen to stay in her home and gave peace of mind to the family to know that someone was frequently there to check on Reen.

The family had met Anna many times and appreciated her care.

Margi had divulged that her relationship with her mother was strained. She explained that she had been raised in a very dysfunctional family and that her mother held a number of secrets from Margi's youth. Anna explained that she had seen evidence of a proud, stubborn woman and that she wasn't surprised, especially after hearing Margi refer to her mother as *Reen* instead of *Mom*.

One day, Margi's phone rang. She recognized Anna's number.

"Hello, Anna," Margi said. "Is everything all right?"

"Your mother is feeling very low," Anna explained. "She's very tired and losing patience with life and her struggles."

"What do you need me to do?" Margi asked.

"I think you should come over right now," Anna suggested. "She's starting to divulge some information. She just said 'something bad happened to Margi as a child and it troubles me. I know what's wrong but won't admit it.'"

"Really? She said that?"

"Yes, just one minute ago. I left the room to give you a call. I thought you'd want to know."

"Thank you, Anna! I'll be right over."

Margi arrived at her mother's house within minutes and found her mother resting in her bedroom. Margi asked her mother about her day and then decided to be direct and get straight to the point.

"Anna told me that something bad happened to me when I was little and you're upset by that," Margi said. "Is there something you can tell me? Anything?"

Margi's mother avoided her daughter's penetrating gaze. Margi could see the wall going up.

"I don't remember," Reen said.

"Don't remember what? I'm right here. Talk to me."

"I don't remember anything," Reen said with a scowl on her face. "I don't know why I would say anything else."

It was a convenient excuse. A detour away from the truth.

"See you later, Reen," Margi said on her way out. She touched Anna on the arm and thanked her for the phone call.

That woman is going to her grave with secrets.

. . .

It was Anna again. This time she sounded alarmed.

"Margi, your mother has fallen. They're taking her to the hospital right now."

Margi hung up the phone and grabbed her car keys. She would talk to her head in the car on the way. It was something she had to do every time she saw her mother.

At the hospital, she found the attending physician in the emergency room. He updated Margi on her mother's condition.

"It appears she's broken her hip," he said. "A fall at ninety-eight years of age is never a good thing. We don't believe we can operate and repair the hip at her age. I've already called a hospice center. I'm afraid she won't be able to return home. She's going to need round-the-clock care because she won't be able to get out of bed. I'm really sorry."

Margi sat by her mom's bed for a few hours, but her mother was so medicated with painkillers that she never knew Margi was there. Margi decided to go home and make some phone calls to family members and Anna. Margi recognized the irony of the situation: she was in charge and was caring for her mother. *She was never there for me.* Margi considered that perhaps there was a lesson to be learned.

Margi would rise above the unfairness of it all and serve her mother for the short time her mother had left.

. . .

Margi really didn't want her mother to go this way; she was going to be in pain until she died. The hospice center made sure she slept most of the time, day and night, by administering a heavy dose of pain meds. Margi talked to her head and went to see her mother several times a week.

Reen was declining rapidly, and her body was beginning to shut down.

Margi's emotions were all over the place. She wondered how she was going to react to the death. Her children parts still needed their mother. They would never stop wishing for her to fill that role. Despite the emotional difficulty, Margi continued to show up at her mother's bedside. One day her mother opened her eyes.

"Hi, Mom. It's me, Margi. I'm right here. What are you thinking about?"

"I just want to go home. Not to our old house."

Margi believed there was good in everybody, even if you had to look deep to find it. In her belief, she knew that God wanted all His children to come home. Surely, there was a place in heaven for everybody where all could continue to learn and grow. Margi looked at her mother's face and trusted that God had a heavenly home prepared.

Reen closed her eyes again. Margi contacted the family. Those out of town needed to make their travel plans. The end was near.

.   .   .

Margi pulled up a chair and sat by her mother's side. It was the last few minutes of her mother's life. Jennifer had flown in and was there to support Margi; she stood close by along with Barbara and another niece, Kristie. Women had come together to support one another during this somber time. Margi held her mother's hand.

The children parts were restless. Margi fought for control. There were moments when she looked up at her mother and was consumed by thoughts of confusion and bewilderment. *Who is this woman? I think I lived with her. She can't be my mom, because I wasn't parented.*

Margi closed her eyes and reminded herself to stay present. *My core is strong and out front.* This was not the right time for the others to join her. She squeezed her mother's hand and spoke directly to her.

"I love you, Mom," Margi whispered. "You were a hard mom. Maybe one day we'll figure this out."

Margi watched as her mother let out one final breath. Her face relaxed and her body lay motionless. Tears poured down Margi's cheeks—desperate tears for a mother whose nurturing love was never given. Guilty tears for a belief that somehow, she had never been a good enough daughter. And disappointed tears for wicked secrets that would die with her mother.

Margi leaned over and whispered final words in her mother's ear. "Go home."

Chapter 60

For as long as she could remember, Margi felt a frightening and compulsive connection to her mother. It was something she often talked about to Dennis and later with both Jay and Jennifer. Margi struggled to find words that could adequately describe the dark bond that held her captive to her mother. She referred to it as *invisible cords*.

Those invisible cords linked Margi to her mother whether she was at elementary school, in the Children's Psychiatric Hospital, or living her own adult life. The cords somehow tied Margi and her mother together both physically and mentally. Margi had spent her life trying to break those cords. She had never been successful.

The day Margi's mother died was different. Margi felt it immediately. The invisible cords had been cut.

"Something has changed," Margi told Jennifer. "They're gone! All those cords of darkness! I feel they've been taken. She took them with her."

Margi had talked about the invisible cords for years. Those cords supported the suspicion that her mother had not just been absent but had certainly played some sort of role in physical or ritual abuse. They would never know the details now. The specifics would go to the grave with Margi's mother, but the release Margi felt was a great blessing.

With that release of cords came a surge of happiness and relief. It was a paradox of grieving her mother's loss and embracing some peace. Nothing could erase the trauma of the past, but the load Margi would carry into her future was now a little lighter.

. . .

Family members gathered to discuss funeral and burial decisions. Distant relatives and friends offered assistance with so many details. The list of things needing attention was long and overwhelming. Financial matters, legal matters, household matters, and dozens of other items left behind after the death needed to be handled. Family members questioned how and who would step up to take the task.

"I'll handle it," Margi volunteered. "I need to do this."

"Are you sure? That's a lot of work, Margi."

"I'm sure. I'll go through her house one box and one drawer at a time. Don't worry about me."

Margi made her mother's house a mission. Every day she entered with the goal of rummaging through reams of paperwork and belongings. Unfortunately, her search for understanding brought even more confusion. She found a receipt for an earlier bankruptcy and a number of large loans. It appeared her parents used to owe money to everybody. Margi shook her head. At that time, her mother didn't own the house or a car. She wondered where all the money they borrowed had gone. It was just one more mystery added to the pile.

Margi found more of her father's uniforms from the Korean War in a box along with some other things that had belonged to him. There were piles of clothing and more paperwork from the past that had belonged to both parents. Margi looked through every single item she encountered. No other family members wanted anything. Margi filled garbage bags and boxes with the unwanted items. Destination? A dumpster. She certainly didn't want her parents' belongings in her own house.

As Margi's hands held the clothing and the items in the house, a part of her felt a wave of sadness. It tugged on her heart. But the process gave her power. For the first time in her life, she had control over something to do with her parents. Little by little as she began to manage the belongings in the house, the house itself became less menacing.

For as long as she had lived, Margi felt like an outsider in her parents' home. She never really felt as if she belonged to anyone or anything. The house and everything in it, including the furniture, felt to her as if they had absorbed the oppressive gloom of its occupants. Oddly, the darkness attached to it moved with them from house to house as if they couldn't be separated. All of this made up the dark box they lived in. Items were never removed. They just lingered inside because they were all connected as one.

As Margi went from room to room sorting through a lifetime of memories, she became empowered for the first time in her life. Margi was now dismantling her past. The menacing, old house became weak and fragile as each bag of its worldly goods went to the dumpster. Margi knew God was with her during this intimidating and daunting task of managing her parents' estate, but she also knew this was how it was meant to be.

. . .

"My nightmares have lessened," Margi told Jay. "They're still there, but they're not as horrific and dark as before. They've come down a level."

"That's good. Why do you suppose that's happened?"

"Well, I think it has to do with the release of those invisible cords. Until I get all my memories, I think I'll still have nightmares, but they've slowed down."

"Good for you," Jay said. "Catalytic events like the death of a parent can be big trouble for multiples. You've charged through this with amazing strength. The funeral, your mother's house, the paperwork—it's impressive."

"You know, there's something else," Margi continued. "You remember that obsessive compulsion I had to drive north every Sunday? I had done that for years, but I haven't felt that since my mother died. Now I don't have to go."

"Yes, you used to say they were waiting for you," Jay reminded. "Clear evidence of some mind control and programming. You've never known who *they* were."

Margi considered that.

"Nope. I don't have that memory yet, but *they* must have had something to do with *her*."

. . .

"Mom, I'm going over to the cemetery today to put flowers on Grandma's grave. You want to come with me?"

Margi's youngest daughter, Emily, had called earlier in the day. Margi agreed, and they planned to go together. Margi had not shed many tears since her mother died months earlier, and she was feeling a little guilty. She kept waiting for more tears, but they never came. Perhaps she had shed enough tears over a lifetime, and now there were no more left.

Her kids had cried at the funeral. It was the end of an era. They had some fond memories of their grandmother in younger days, but as revelations emerged about how she had treated Margi, they felt resentment. Because of that, their grief was complicated and compartmentalized.

Margi and her daughter walked up to the gravestone to pay their respects. They stood together quietly, each with her own internal thoughts. The sight of the gravestone brought about a strange, distant reaction from Margi. It shouldn't have surprised her—it matched her relationship with her mother.

Is my mother up in heaven scowling at me because I have no tears? Because I'm not falling apart? Mother was always mad at me. Why wouldn't she be now?

Margi wondered if her mother was with her father now. Together, on some level, they were united in her abuse here on earth. Did her mother want to join her husband once again? Were they together in some dark, twisted place far removed from joy, or were they kneeling in regret and working toward forgiveness?

Margi tipped her head back and noticed a bright, blue sky with beautiful cloud formations and birds soaring in the distance. She felt a light breeze on the back of her neck. As she stood with her shadow over the gravestone, a merciful release filled her soul. She would hand it over. She would give all the judgment and eternal possibilities to God. He would work something out. She could be free to move forward. That was difficult enough.

Margi closed her eyes, took a deep breath, and embraced the warm sunshine. She smiled softly and felt the light on her face.

Chapter 61

Dennis turned the radio up, opened the windows, and let his mind disappear. Through the windshield he saw grassy fields, rolling hills, and occasional wildlife. He was headed to Wyoming.

It was just Dennis, his camera, and a much-needed getaway to God's beautiful country. Time behind the lens of a camera wasn't only his career, it was a visual escape. It had been quite a year with the death of Margi's mother and the consuming stress that came from it. Emotions had been high, low, and everyplace in between. Sometimes Dennis needed to get away and save himself.

Who knew that lucky break at a television station in his thirties would steer his career on a path in the film and publishing industry? Latter-day Saint Church history had always been fascinating to Dennis, and his love for it had landed him on several large projects thanks to a number of acquaintances and friends who shared that fervor.

Dennis recognized that his love of learning history coupled with his career were incredible gifts. The timing of good people and events put directly in his path were not coincidental. They were blessings from God, and Dennis knew it.

His marriage certainly had its good and bad times. Much of the pressure came as a result of traumatic events from the past, things that weren't the fault of Dennis or Margi. But the effects from the past haunted their lives every single day.

Dennis's thoughts switched from the open plains back to Margi at home. He had been with her since they were kids in high school. He'd been there during the early days in their marriage when things in Margi's mind didn't make sense, and he'd been there in the later years when the memories came crashing through. It was a life he could never have predicted. Now with Jay's help, they could both make some sense out of everything.

Margi had come so far, but life was still challenging. The things that were done to her were unspeakable. Wicked people had attempted to steal her soul, but Margi had risen above. He still had to reassure her that she wasn't crazy—she was harmed. And he still had to tell her often that he wasn't going anywhere. He was here to stay.

Dennis wasn't afraid of praying. If he needed help in low times, he asked for it. He often felt guilty; Margi was really the one in need. She was going through so much. But Dennis suffered on a different level. He was hurting too.

Because of all of it, this road trip felt necessary. Dennis's heart needed a bit of healing. He wondered if God was aware of him. His foot punched the gas pedal as he raced up the highway heading east.

. . .

The open fields in Wyoming were breathtaking. Dennis's eyes caught sight of antelope miles away in far-off fields. If he even hit the brakes, they were gone—so easily spooked. He still needed several photos for a big Church history book project, so Dennis turned off the highway toward Chimney Rock, Nebraska.

Maybe he could get lucky and capture a cool shot out on the prairie with some antelope in the distance. He had a long zoom lens with him. He thought about the ultimate picture. *Boy, wouldn't that be cool to photograph a big old buck.*

Dennis started at Chimney Rock and took still shots as his car meandered over the road toward Independence Rock. There was no wildlife in sight, but he had seen them hanging out on previous trips over by Devil's Gate. *I've got that zoom lens in my bag.* Dennis pulled over and took some long shots in the distance where the antelope could barely be seen.

Dennis climbed back in the car and drove down the pothole-riddled frontage road that paralleled the actual pioneer trail. He got about a mile down the road and took a couple of shots of Martin's Cove, which was on the other side of the road. If he looked closely, he could see the trail, which was thirty feet off the road. There might be a fun shot of antelope in the distance with the trail going down the road through the sagebrush. Dennis grabbed his camera and walked toward it.

Suddenly, Dennis looked up, and there it was. Twenty feet in front of him stood a big, beautiful buck, all alone. It was the most majestic antelope he had ever seen.

"You're kidding," Dennis said out loud.

He slowly positioned the camera and took the picture. The buck didn't move—just stood his ground looking straight at Dennis. Again and again the camera clicked while Dennis zoomed in and took dozens of magnificent shots.

Dennis pulled the camera away from his face, and the two just looked at each other. Time stood still for a moment.

"Thank you," Dennis said to the antelope.

The antelope turned and slowly walked away, and Dennis started down the trail. Dennis turned to take one more look at the beautiful animal. *Where did you come from?* It was like he had been dropped from the sky.

Dennis looked up with tear-filled eyes. *Thank you, Jesus.*

The photograph would be perfect in the book. People would marvel at the amazing close-up of a shy animal. But they would never know the meaning behind it. It was so much more than a great shot. It was a miracle. A tender mercy.

He was not alone. God was aware of him. Dennis knew that without a doubt. His struggles would not be taken away today, but God was aware. It was a glimmer of hope.

It was enough.

Dennis pulled the camera away from his face, and the two just looked at each other.
Time stood still for a moment.

Chapter 62

Margi drove the few blocks to church with one foot on the brake. There were parts of her who fought the desire to attend each Sunday— parts who were frightened and hated anything connected to religion. Margi understood but pushed through each week to attend.

There were still expressions of despair and doubt, because there was nothing casual about attending church. It was a conscious effort for Margi to prepare herself for the experience and to keep that commitment against all the negativity that stood in her way.

"I'm going to give up," she often said.

"No, you're not," Dennis always replied.

"I'm never going to church again."

"Yes, you will," Dennis always said. He recognized that Margi had undying faith that never stopped looking for light, but he also knew there were parts of her that abhorred any kind of worship. The reasons were becoming more and more obvious as ritualistic memories came forward.

Some days at church were more difficult than others. Days when other members testified about answered prayers and miraculous healings were both inspiring and challenging. Margi knew it was unlikely she would ever stand and declare that God had healed her mind. She intentionally skipped church on Mother's Day and Father's Day; it was too much to hear others honor their amazing parents. But like a faithful, obedient child, Margi still found her way to church most Sundays.

Margi's earnest prayers asking for the strength to attend always began on Saturday night. *Help me to go to church tomorrow and feel your Spirit. Help me know I'm at the right place. Let me feel one thing that helps me know you love me.* Each week she received something. Each week she experienced a moment of peace that was enough to get her through the following week.

Quiet time during the administration of the sacrament was most important to Margi. It was a precious time each week to renew her commitment and join with Christ. The bread and water were symbolic of Christ's gift to Margi. She in turn reverently spoke the words in her heart as she partook. *This is my gift to you and our relationship. I want to stay present and honor you.*

It was a time to sit by herself and take advantage of the opportunity to try again tomorrow. *Don't let me give up. I love my faith. Please help me hold on to it.*

Margi bowed her head and closed her eyes once more, this time to offer a different prayer. She opened her eyes briefly and looked around the chapel. Men, women, and children filled the pews. Margi's heart was soft as she silently began her request. *And please bless all these beautiful people. I'm sure they have losses and struggles too. We all desire the amazing comfort that comes with our faith. Help them feel loved.*

Margi understood that prayers had saved her life since she was a little girl. She also believed that maybe her prayers could save others as well.

.   .   .

Margi opened her eyes. The golden light from the morning sunrise was peeking through the bedroom window. Margi had survived yet another night and knew she must begin a new battle of preparing for another day. During the darkest of times, she so often heard a voice—*just wait.* That light was enough to help her focus on blessings in her life.

So often, Margi would tell her kids that good things came to those who waited, and that God knew what they needed to be happy. Margi had always noticed the simple things in life—things others seemed to miss. Gratitude filled her heart as she considered all the gifts from God in her life.

Margi pondered the flowers that grew tall and healthy from a simple seed. She noticed the tiny veins in the petals and the individual colors that made each one unique. She loved the beauty of trees as they reached their leafy arms toward the heavens. The clouds created beauty in the sky and appeared in all kinds of inspiring shapes and sizes.

Margi loved being surrounded by mountains. The blue sky and the sunshine accessorized the mountaintops in such a way that Margi often broke into tears of gratitude. *Thank you, Heavenly Father, for these beautiful mountains and clouds. You have made the day beautiful, and I am so grateful you have created all this for me.*

Margi thought about her gratitude for food. The sight of delicious red apples lined up in the produce section always made her cry. She was grateful to those who planted and harvested and brought the food to her store. She felt blessed to have funds in the bank so she could purchase food for her family. The food brought health and a gathering around the table where her family members could love and laugh together.

Margi's thoughts turned to her family. She was grateful for her husband, a best friend who had stuck by her since she was fifteen. He was loyal and steadfast in a world that seemed broken. How she loved him! She had told God she was afraid to have children, but He gave three miracles to her anyway. Then He taught her how to love them, because she had never learned from her own mother. When they were all together, Margi would stand back, marvel at her children, and silently wipe her thankful tears. And her grandchildren—little people with ringlets and infectious smiles—loved unconditionally and made her laugh. They brought light and joy into the darkest of days by simply bouncing into a room.

She was so thankful for her home, a place to gather in safety. Her clean house and lovely yard demonstrated her gratitude for such a gift. Margi worked hard creating a space where friends and family could feel at peace—a place so very different from the dark box of her youth.

Finally, she was so grateful for laughter. She loved giggling for hours with Dennis over nothing and laughing so hard with kids around the dinner table that tears of hilarity rolled down all their cheeks. It was a simple emotion she deeply treasured because for much of her life she had never known it.

When Margi considered all these simple gifts, she knew Christ had His hand in her life. Finding gratitude in simple blessings provided comfort in a complex and complicated world. And gratitude got Margi out of bed every morning. *Thank you, Heavenly Father, for all these gifts.*

Margi's heart was humbled at the recognition of simple joy and beauty in her life.

Chapter 63

Margi placed her scriptures in her lap. She had only a thimble-sized amount of spiritual knowledge, but within that thimble were undeniable truths. She pondered a favorite scripture she had read just moments ago:

And the light which shineth, which giveth you light, is through him who enlighteneth your eyes, which is the same light that quickeneth your understandings.[1]

Margi understood that divine *light* had guided her in reaching for people, learning, and wisdom. That *light* came directly from God and lit her path when darkness surrounded her. Margi knew she had done the hard work, but also recognized that God had placed both people and clarifying insight in her dark path for her own enlightenment.

If only all her parts could have the same understanding. Margi's greatest desire was for all her parts to be happy and safe in the present. She continued to remind them of the truth she recognized: *There's nothing to fear now. These are good people. There's joy and laughter. Come join me.*

On difficult mornings and evenings when God seemed very far away, Margi knelt by her bedside and pictured Christ kneeling with her. She imagined Him putting His healing hands on her so she could feel and know He was there. That visual encouraged Margi to open her heart in tender communication with Him.

Margi believed Christ wept with her. Surely, He wept over her situation and her suffering with great love and mercy. Certainly, Christ knew Margi's heart and soul and the strength she desperately desired from Him. After all, God had given Margi the gift of a mind that had protected her. As she imagined God kneeling beside her, Margi was confident that He knew each of her beautiful parts as well.

Margi spoke from deep inside her heart. *I just want you to be proud of me.* Margi encouraged her children parts to pray and listen with her. *Bless the children that they'll find peace. Help them come out of their dark place. Help them see that there is light.*

Margi still chose not to end her prayers with the usual "amen." That would mean she was finishing her communication with God. Margi didn't want that to end. She needed Him right beside her all day. If she said "amen," she was afraid He might go somewhere else. *I'll just put you on hold . . .*

Please stay close.

. . .

Margi walked out to her back porch and began to whistle. Nothing. She stood patiently for a few minutes, then whistled again.

Suddenly Margi heard a response and saw a flash of blue as two birds soared into the backyard and landed on the grass in front of her. Margi smiled. She loved this little family so much.

"Well, hello, Mr. and Mrs.," Margi exclaimed. "I have a treat for you today."

Mr. and Mrs. were the blue jay parents to five recently hatched babies. Margi had always loved birds, but she had a special bond with this little family. They seemed to adore her as well.

Margi bent down slowly and placed a peanut in front of each bird. They were so cute with their two little legs trying to manage life. She pondered the idea of having no arms. They used what God gave them and found a way to survive—a metaphor for her own life.

"Okay, you come back. I have more for the babies," Margi said cheerfully.

The birds looked at Margi as if they understood fully. This little family had learned that Margi was kind and gentle. It was safe to dance around the yard while Margi sat smiling on the porch. Often a brave blue jay would come close to the kitchen window when Margi was inside, peering through the window into the kitchen to solicit its trusted friend. If Margi left the door open, Mrs. Blue Jay occasionally hopped inside as a welcome guest.

.   .   .

Dennis walked in from a busy day behind the camera. He noticed Margi out back when he walked past the kitchen window. Dennis shook his head. She was feeding the birds again. He had warned her that peanuts also attract rats, but Margi wouldn't even consider stopping. Her little bird family was depending on her.

Dennis stood for a moment and watched his dear Margi through the window. He smiled at her happiness. He could see on her face the joy that a simple love of birds could bring. The Light of Christ in his wife was unbelievable. She had been brought to the breaking point so many times, but she always managed to climb out of the dark abyss and take the high road. His love and admiration for her was deep and sure. *Margi . . . she always rises above.*

Dennis stood quietly with his own thoughts. He wanted to protect her. He didn't know why God couldn't make this disappear, but Dennis could listen, and he could love. Their love story was, perhaps, more irregular than most, with plenty of winding trails and tough uphill battles. But it was their story—the story of Dennis and Margi. And so he watched her smiling on the back porch.

A beautiful love story was still unfolding before his eyes.

.   .   .

Hope.

It was a simple word with a powerful meaning. Margi had heard the word tossed back and forth in church and in scripture. She understood

327

that hope was an eternal concept, and she clung to that comforting belief, but Margi also knew that her idea of hope was different from that of most.

At the age of seven, Margi *hoped* to live through the night. For as long as she could remember, she *hoped* to get through the day as a whole person. And through the darkest periods later in life, Margi *hoped* she would not take her life that day.

Fortunately, Margi knew that faith and hope were closely linked. While members of her family had failed her when she was a child, Margi's faith had not. A combination of faith and hope had enough force to get her from terrifying mornings to nine at night when the cycle began all over again. Hope gave Margi a reason to start again—every single day.

She had reason not to trust God. Why should she? Why would she believe Him? Too many times she had felt abandoned. Forgotten. But beneath all the layers of unspeakable offense and hurt, she felt a connection to Christ. A child-like, unshakable faith that He existed and a powerful belief that He really did know her.

On her own unique journey in this life, Margi embraced her own definition of hope as well as the eternal definition of hope. Her heart clung to a quiet thought that gave perspective and comfort: *At some point, this won't matter.* That strong spirit of hers was divinely linked to a larger, beautiful plan in heaven. Trials lived through on earth would be swallowed up in lessons learned through enduring it well. Margi knew she had a higher purpose.

Many times—even in the darkness of betrayal—Margi had still heard tender, heavenly words of encouragement giving her the strength to whisper through tears, *I will stay here. I will finish my mission.*

They were words of faith. Words of love.

Words of hope.

AFTERWORD

We all have stories. Each one is vitally important in its own unique way. We *live* our stories in this journey called life, and we look for relief, understanding, and strength. Something inside each of us yearns to grow and develop into something better. It's not enough to simply survive. We want to thrive.

Sometimes someone else's story can have a profound impact on us. Change us for the better. Such has been the case with Margi's story. Throughout the interview process and writing of this book, I wept many times. Those tears taught me empathy and compassion. There were other times I rejoiced. Those feelings of joy taught me perspective and promise. It has been a journey with a wide range of emotion and lessons throughout. In short, I have been edified, enlightened, and changed—for the better.

Margi taught me to trust my core. Each of us has a divine spirit and identity that has goodness within. That divinity inside is a direct link to God. Despite how many times we get mud on our face, mess up our lives, or find ourselves in bad circumstances, our link to God will never be severed. God doesn't love our future self any more than our present self. He loves us right where we are. That love is unconditional and everlasting.

Margi's abusers attempted to break her body, her mind, and her will. But in all her brokenness, they couldn't break her spirit. That unbreakable goodness may get covered up, but deep down we all have a strength that defines our value and worth.

Margi taught me to anchor in hope. When we are anchored, nothing moves us. We are sure and steadfast. We can be buffeted by the waves of life—waves filled with delays, disappointments, and unanswered prayers. But if we stay anchored, we won't drift away from faith.

Sometimes circumstances cause us to pull up our anchor, and we begin to drift. Drifting leads to discouragement, negative thoughts, doubts, and apathy. It can happen to the best of us. The scriptures wouldn't use the word *anchor* unless there was danger of drifting. Our anchor should never be placed in circumstances or people or things. If you're not anchored to the right thing, you'll drift and risk anchoring yourself to bitterness or fear. Our anchor of hope should be solidly placed in the Lord.

Margi's anchor of hope not only allowed her to survive during her abuse and its immediate aftermath, but it feeds the good cheer and kindness that so many love about her now. She is turning her sunset into a sunrise. With her anchor in place, she carries her own cross in happiness. What happened to Margi is dark, but *she* is light.

Margi taught me persistence. Most of us are great starters but poor finishers of everything we set out to accomplish. Most are willing to do something once; many will do it twice; some will do it ten times; and a few will do it hundreds or thousands of times. The will to succeed expresses itself only through relentless perseverance.[1]

The call to discipleship is really a call to continue. We must carry on, persist, endure, and finish. The Lord wants us to make the commitment and then walk the road—no matter how difficult or challenging—to the very end.[2]

I think of Margi as a little child begging the Lord, *Please take this pain away. Please stop this.* At that time, the Lord didn't change her circumstance. He didn't change the abuse being inflicted on her or remove the abusers. Instead, the Lord gave her that beautiful mind to dissociate. He gave her an ability to survive, so He could one day answer those prayers in a different way.

Years later, the Lord placed people in Margi's life to love, support, and guide her. Those heartfelt prayers took a very, very long time to be answered, yet Margi continues to pray—every single day. After all she's been through and after all the unanswered prayers from her childhood, she still turns to Him. Margi is the definition of persistence.

Perhaps some of Margi's blessings are generational. Sometimes through great persistence and patience we struggle to see our own divine sanction. How our own life is blessed. Maybe we are the sole sowers of seeds for the next generation. Maybe our own sacrifice and faith become *their* blessings. These are called *generational blessings*.

Margi was the first to begin a legacy of faith and hope. She has a level of endurance and persistence that can end a cycle of abuse and can begin a cycle of gratitude, faith, hope, and enduring to the bitter end. Her spirit is strong enough to change patterns from the past and influence a better destiny and path for others to follow. Margi's future generation is better because of her.

At the close of my writing, I think back to an early conversation I had with Margi. It captured the hesitation we all feel about our own stories. The doubt that we are enough.

"I'm not sure I have a story worth anything," Margi said. "And I don't have an ending. How can you write a story with no ending?"

I am certain that Margi has a story. And her ending?

Her ending is relentless, unwavering, faith-inspired hope.

"Do not be dismayed by the brokenness of the world.
All things break. And all things can be mended.
Not with time, as they say, but with intention.
So go. Love intentionally, extravagantly, unconditionally.
The broken world waits in darkness
for the light that is you."

— L. R. Knost

PSALM 91

WORDS OF COMFORT TO SURVIVORS

1 He that dwelleth in the secret place of the most High shall abide under the shadow of the Almighty.

2 I will say of the, *He is* my refuge and my fortress: my God; in him will I trust.

3 Surely he shall deliver thee from the snare of the fowler, *and* from the noisome pestilence.

4 He shall cover thee with his feathers, and under his wings shalt thou trust: his truth *shall be thy* shield and buckler.

5 Thou shalt not be afraid for the terror by night; *nor* for the arrow *that* flieth by day;

6 *Nor* for the pestilence *that* walketh in darkness; *nor* for the destruction *that* wasteth at noonday.

7 A thousand shall fall at thy side, and ten thousand at thy right hand; *but* it shall not come nigh thee.

8 Only with thine eyes shalt thou behold and see the reward of the wicked.

9 Because thou hast made the, *which is* my refuge, *even* the most High, thy habitation;

10 There shall no evil befall thee, neither shall any plague come nigh thy dwelling.

11 For he shall give his angels charge over thee, to keep thee in all thy ways.

12 They shall bear thee up in *their* hands, lest thou dash thy foot against a stone.

13 Thou shalt tread upon the lion and adder: the young lion and the dragon shalt thou trample under feet.

14 Because he hath set his love upon me, therefore will I deliver him: I will set him on high, because he hath known my name.

15 He shall call upon me, and I will answer him: I *will be* with him in trouble; I will deliver him, and honour him.

16 With long life will I satisfy him, and shew him my salvation.

NOTES

Chapter 9
 1. Ether 12:6.

Chapter 14
 1. Helaman 5:12.

Chapter 19
 1. Alma 34:41.

Chapter 23
 1. Jacob 3:1.

Chapter 24
 1. Samuel Medley, "I Know That My Redeemer Lives," in *Hymns of the Church of Jesus Christ of Latter-day Saints* (Salt Lake City: The Church of Jesus Christ of Latter-day Saints, 1985), 136.

Chapter 25
 1. Bessel van der Kolk, *The Body Keeps the Score: Brain, Mind, and Body in the Healing of Trauma* (New York: Penguin Books, 2015), 135.
 2. International Society for the Study of Trauma and Dissociation, www.isst-d.org/resources/dissociation-faqs.

Chapter 28
 1. Bessel van der Kolk, M.D., *The Body Keeps the Score: Brain, Mind, and Body in the Healing of Trauma* (New York: Penguin Books, 2015), 43.
 2. van der Kolk, 89–90.
 3. van der Kolk, 70.
 4. van der Kolk, 73.
 5. van der Kolk, 68.

Chapter 30
 1. Lynn Mary Karjala, *Understanding Trauma and Dissociation: A Guide for Therapists, Patients and Loved Ones* (Atlanta: Thomas Max Publishing, 2007), *1, 5.*
 2. Karjala, 8, 24.
 3. Karjala, 25.
 4. Karjala, 26.
 5. Karjala, 27.

6. Herschel Walker, *Breaking Free: My Life with Dissociative Identity Disorder* (New York: Touchstone and Howard Books, 2008), 16.
7. Karjala, 29.
8. Bessel van der Kolk, *The Body Keeps the Score: Brain, Mind, and Body in the Healing of Trauma* (New York: Penguin Books, 2015), 312–313.
9. Karjala, 28.
10. Karjala, 28–29.
11. Karjala, 45–46.
12. Karjala, 50–51.

Chapter 40
1. Lynn Mary Karjala, *Understanding Trauma and Dissociation: A Guide for Therapists, Patients and Loved Ones* (Atlanta: Thomas Max Publishing, 2007), 57.
2. Karjala, 58.
3. Karjala, 58–62.
4. Karjala, 59.
5. Karjala, 63.
6. Karjala, 66.

Chapter 45
1. Bessel van der Kolk, *The Body Keeps the Score: Brain, Mind, and Body in the Healing of Trauma* (New York: Penguin Books, 2015), 221.

Chapter 54
1. Doctrine and Covenants 88:49–50.
2. Doctrine and Covenants 61:36.

Chapter 63
1. Doctrine and Covenants 88:11.

Afterword
1. Roderick L. Cameron, "Grant Oratorical Contest," December 1, 1964, *BYU Speeches of the Year* (Provo, UT: Brigham Young University Press, 1964), 4.
2. Robert L. Millet, *An Eye Single to the Glory of God: Reflections on the Cost of Discipleship* (Salt Lake City: Deseret Book Co., 1991), 80.

SOURCES CITED

Cameron, Roderick L. "Grant Oratorical Contest." *BYU Speeches of the Year*. Provo, UT: Brigham Young University Press, 1964.

International Society for the Study of Trauma and Dissociation. www. isst-d.org/resources/dissociation-faqs.

Karjala, Lynn Mary. *Understanding Trauma and Dissociation: A Guide for Therapists, Patients and Loved Ones*. Atlanta: Thomas Max Publishing, 2007.

Lennon, John, and McCartney, Paul. "Two of Us," *Let It Be*. London: Apple Studio. Phil Spector. 1970.

Medley, Samuel. "I Know That My Redeemer Lives." *Hymns of the Church of Jesus Christ of Latter-day Saints*. Salt Lake City: The Church of Jesus Christ of Latter-Day Saints, 1985.

Millet, Robert L. *An Eye Single to the Glory of God: Reflections on the Cost of Discipleship*. Salt Lake City: Deseret Book Co., 1991.

Van der Kolk, Bessel. *The Body Keeps the Score: Brain, Mind, and Body in the Healing of Trauma*. New York: Penguin Books, 2015.

Walker, Herschel. *Breaking Free: My Life with Dissociative Identity Disorder*. New York: Touchstone and Howard Books. 2008.

ABOUT THE AUTHOR

Heidi Tucker won a Book of the Year Finalist Award and Best Inspirational Book for her first and second books, *Finding Hope in the Journey* and *Servie's Song*. Her passion for writing and speaking about light and hope has inspired thousands. Heidi is known as a great storyteller who motivates others to rise up and find new strength. Through her writing and speaking, she teaches how to find hope in your own journey and how to make a difference.

When Heidi isn't writing her next book or speaking at a conference, you'll find her spending time outdoors with her husband, four grown children, and ten grandchildren. She loves sunflowers, hiking, and ice cream . . . not necessarily in that order.

FIND OUT MORE ABOUT HEIDI AND HER BOOKS AT:

HeidiTucker.com

ALSO BY HEIDI TUCKER

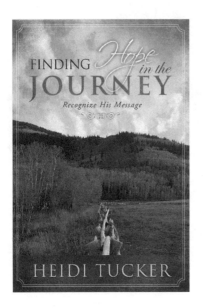

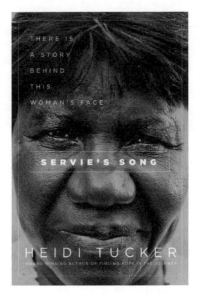

2019 BOOK OF THE YEAR FINALIST 2017 BEST INSPIRATIONAL

2019 OUTSTANDING COVER 2018 BEST INSPIRATIONAL

There are glimpses of hope all around that are unique and divinely meant just for you, and you will find them by watching, listening, and tuning all your senses. Heidi's inspiring words will help you learn to position your heart, mind, and soul to recognize quiet messages of hope from God.

One woman's emotional journey from tragedy and heartbreak to an inspiring path of hope and triumph. This true, inspiring story will motivate you to grab onto your faith and move forward— even in the midst of struggle—trusting that you are never alone.

AVAILABLE AT:

HeidiTucker.com | Amazon | Deseret Book | Barnes & Noble